The Food of Campanile

Mark Peel

Nancy Silverton

In collaboration with Ian Smith
Photographs by Steven Rothfeld

Villard New York

The Food of Campanile

The Library of Congress has cataloged the hardcover edition as follows:

Peel, Mark.
The food of Campanile / Mark Peel and Nancy Silverton.
p.   cm.
Includes index.
ISBN 978-0-812-99203-8
1. Cookery.   2. Campanile (Restaurant)   I. Silverton, Nancy.
II. Title.
TX714.P439   1997
641.5'09794'94—dc21   96-36962

DESIGNED BY BARBARA MARKS

144915995

To everyone—cooks, waitstaff, dishwashers, purveyors, customers, critics—who has contributed to the life and food of Campanile

Acknowledgments

To our editor, Peter Gethers, who, after buying the book, trusted his associate, Amy Scheibe, to make sure that it happened.

To Ian Smith, who spent so many hours with us, making sure that even a beginner cook could follow these recipes and learn something about food in the process.

To Judy Gethers, who tested the recipes and translated them so you could make them at home.

To Steven Rothfeld, our official photographer, who has the eye of an artist and the patience of Buddha.

To Manfred Krankl, our partner, who is a man of many specialties: winemaker, general manager, team leader, and sunburn doctor.

To our chefs, Suzanne Tracht, Tina Wilson, Suzanne Goin, Corrina Weibel, and Ann Sprecher, who have run the kitchen, planned the menu, and always made sure that the food of Campanile remained true to our vision. And to our pastry chefs, Brendt Rogers, John Davis, Kim Sklar, and Gerry Moss, who assured that there would be a sweet spot in every meal.

To our cooks Govin Armstrong, Brad Winnaman, George Erasmus, Mark Boucher, Mary Kay Halston, Chrissa Kaufman, Jeff McMann, Robert Herrera, Michelle Biting, Margaret Fishlein, Jose Mejia, Emilio Vasquez, Edgar Lopez, Rogelio Garcia, and Annie Miller, and our prep cooks Eloy Mondez and Rigo Mendoza, and everyone who has worked so hard on the line (even those who quit two or three times).

To our maître d'/restaurant manager extraordinaire Claudio Blotta, who remains amazingly organized and usually serene, even during Saturday night rush, and always manages a few minutes for a chat. (And thank you to Frank Harris for filling in in Claudio's absence.)

To our friends Paul Schrade and Jack Stumpf, who volunteer their time every Wednesday morning to push the cart, pay the vendors, and load the truck at the farmer's market. Without them we'd be buying sprouted onions and bitter garlic.

To all our purveyors and farmers who for many years have given us marvelous products and great inspiration.

To Teri Neville, who faxed recipes all over the place.

To German Alarcon, who is still fixing our broken-down equipment.

To Jonathan Gold, who is not only a continuing source of enthusiasm and support but one of our favorite eaters at Campanile (all our customers should be such adventurous eaters).

To Brad Springer, who besides all his hard work and dedication was also our Olly's first good friend.

To our waitstaff, especially Ron Brooks and Salvador Gualito, who have been here since day one.

To Nick Vinyaratn, our bartender, also an original staff member, who is patient and thoughtful and makes the best martinis in Los Angeles.

To Harvard Gordon, for whom there will always be a place setting at our bar (sometimes next to Margy).

To our agents for the past thirteen years, Eric and Maureen Lasher.

To our production editor, Benjamin Dreyer, who with some pretzels, chocolate cookies, and a Campanile cap could be placated until the finished copy came in.

To our designer, Barbara Marks, who made this book look as good as the last one.

To our adorable and loving best friends, Margy Rochlin and Wendi Matthews: When both of us were too busy to leave the restaurant, you were always willing to bring us news of the outside world.

And, of course, to our children, Vanessa, Benjamin, and Oliver. We love you too much to put into words.

Contents

The Food of Campanile

Cooking and Eating

Chapter 1

COOKING—and the communality of eating—is an important part of the glue that binds society together. A person *eats* to satisfy hunger, to survive, but a person *cooks* to please the senses, to make food more palatable and digestible. We do this not only because we have to but because we like to.

Almost everyone takes pleasure in eating; it is an experience common to every society and culture. People around the world smile much the same way when they bite into a perfectly ripened tomato, picked from the vine and still warm from the sun. Eating ensures survival; eating well provides the opportunity to slow down and enjoy life for a few hours out of the day.

The purpose of this book is not to document the latest fashion in food, or to dazzle people with food based on a school of architecture, but to illustrate that everyone, with a little concentration and passion, can prepare flavorful and deeply satisfying food. We wanted to write a book about the food that is important in our lives, meals made from only the best ingredients, and the techniques of cooking we use to enhance and combine these ingredients.

The common qualities in the food of Campanile cannot be traced back to a defined region or to a specific era. We prepare the food that we want to eat. Because California is blessed with a climate similar to that of the Mediterranean coast, much of our food is influenced by the cuisine of that region. Our cooking philosophy has very little to do with intricate plate arrangements, but is simply: Does it taste wonderful and look beautiful? For the recipes in this book we have tasted and tested and cooked and cooked again, until we can state that this is a book of food that pleases our senses.

COOKING, TASTING, AND KNOWING YOUR INGREDIENTS

If the chef at your favorite restaurant isn't actually tasting the food, something is sadly lacking. You want that chef to dip a spoon in the sauce from time to time, to sample a leaf of arugula drizzled with vinaigrette, to sneak a crumble of browned veal sausage as it goes from the sauté pan to the plate. If the chef isn't always tasting the food, it probably isn't at the level it could be. He or she

NANCY AT THE FARMER'S MARKET: "WE WANTED TO WRITE
A BOOK ABOUT THE FOOD THAT IS IMPORTANT IN OUR LIVES,
MEALS MADE ONLY FROM THE BEST INGREDIENTS."

should be bursting with curiosity: Does that sauce obliterate the subtle flavor of the meat? How much is too much? Is the crushed black pepper a little too pungent on that pasta? Is the flavor of the fish too strong for the delicate flavor of the broth?

In our restaurant, we try to ensure that every dish is tasted before service, so that the flavors are genuine, the contrast of textures is balanced, and the realization of the dish is true to the concept. Throughout the evening, the chef should occasionally steal a little bite to taste the dish, in order to make sure its integrity is maintained. The same principles apply to the home cook as well. Blindly following recipes will help you learn to cook at first, but it will eventually hinder you as your confidence and knowledge develop. Most of the trouble with less-than-satisfying home cooking is from lack of self-confidence and attention. If you don't pay close attention to the flavors of what you cook, you won't develop the knowledge you need to be able to taste a dish and know exactly what it's lacking.

You need some knowledge of flavor and the courage to trust your perceptions. Taste what you make; if it seems a little flat to you, try salting it a little more or adding a squeeze of lemon juice or some chopped herbs, just to push the flavor in what you think is the right direction. The knowledge to be adventurous in cooking will come with some time and practice, but if you care about what you're doing and pay attention, most of the mistakes you make along the way will not be disastrous. Make notes on the recipe so that the next time you will remember the changes you made. Use a pencil so you can change your mind.

If you hurry through a dish and don't taste it until it is on the table, it's too late—there's nothing you can do. Think about what you're tasting, what the various ingredients contibute to the whole, and what effect the cooking technique has on those ingredients.

If a steak needs to be well browned for flavor, for example, brown it well; don't back off or pull the heat down. Pay attention: Don't burn it, but give it a good browning; there is a lot of flavor in that color. Even a prime, well-aged ribeye steak doesn't look good if it's cooked to a pale gray, and it doesn't taste like much, either. The more familiar you become with the food you cook, the better you will be able to know when the flavors are perfect.

You might push too far sometimes and ruin something. Just try not to do it when you've got a dozen well-cocktailed guests seated in the dining room expecting the Meal of all Meals. At least some of the meal should be based on dishes you feel comfortable making. On the other hand, the greatest advances sometimes occur when working under intense pressure, and that can be a wonderful surprise—not only for your guests, but for yourself as well.

CHARACTERISTICS OF INGREDIENTS AND COOKING TECHNIQUES

Different foods have different characteristics: flavor, texture, size, shape, fat content, moisture content, chemical composition, and so forth. Therefore it makes sense that certain foods respond better to some cooking techniques than others. A tender, well-marbled steak should not stew on the back of the stove all day long. Not coincidentally, if you quickly grill a steak-size portion of Select-grade beef brisket, you might be chewing all day long. Hamburgers exist because there is meat on a steer that *needs* to be ground, or at least cooked a very long time, to be palatable. At Campanile, we try to match our cooking techniques and our raw ingredients. We try to cook harmoniously with the food, not against it. Fresh fava beans need only the slightest cooking to brighten their flavor. Potatoes, however, need to be cooked through completely to be enjoyed. To reduce that cooking time, one could grate the potatoes into hash browns, much like hamburger, and sauté them, or slice them in quarters and roast them with high heat until they're well browned and crispy. The characteristics of the food itself are the best guide in determining the optimum ways of preparation.

BAKING

Whereas grilling and roasting can be seen as arts, baking is surely more of a science. In reality, baking and roasting are essentially the same method of cooking, but when we refer to *baking* we generally mean the making of breads and pastries—a common element being that most of these foods are leavened in some way. A leavened product is one that uses gas (air, water vapor, or carbon dioxide) to rise. The baking heat then sets the risen shape before the gas has escaped, resulting in the basic texture of bread or cake. One small exception to this is pies, which do not really rise, but still require precise measuring of ingredients and even heat to bake properly.

In other methods of cooking there are usually many paths to a good end product, but in baking there are only a few. There are endless ways to produce a leaden loaf of bread or tough, flavorless cookies, but only by doing every step properly will you end up with perfect results. In baking there is far less margin of tolerable error in the measuring of ingredients, the way in which they are combined, and the precision of the heat in the oven, than is allowed for roasting. And of course in this light a baked potato should be called a roasted potato, but common usage prevails.

BLANCHING

Blanching is primarily a method of partially precooking food, usually in boiling water. In restaurants it is used primarily to reduce the time necessary to cook the food during the service rush. Blanching is especially useful if you intend to grill vegetables. The high heat of the grill is such that many raw vegetables will burn on the outside before they are cooked all the way through. If they are blanched first, they need be on the grill only long enough to finish cooking and absorb a smokey flavor. Additionally, blanching will reduce the bitterness in many greens such as kale, mustard greens, and collard greens.

To blanch vegetables properly, it is important that you have a generous amount of well-salted boiling water and a ready container of ice water into which the blanched vegetables must be plunged to stop the cooking process at the right moment. The vegetables should be in the ice water only long enough to chill them—just a few minutes; any longer and they will start to lose flavor.

BRAISING AND BROWNING

Braising is the technique used to tenderize and bring out flavor in tough or fibrous foods. Braising is a moist cooking method halfway between roasting and poaching. The food is cooked partially covered in liquid, usually vegetable broth, meat stock, or olive oil. The liquid conducts heat efficiently and evenly, without drying out the food.

In almost all foods there is a trade-off between tenderness and flavor. Excluding fish, the foods that are the most tender usually have the least flavor. Stewing chickens have much more flavor than fryers, but it takes a few hours in the cooking pot to make them tender. Tough cuts of meat, the parts of the animal that do the most work, usually have a much more robust flavor than the more widely preferred tender portions. It is these tough yet flavorful foods that are well suited to braising.

With many foods, it greatly adds to the flavor of the dish to brown them before they are braised. Browning doesn't seal in any juices, but it does provide better flavor and color to both the food and the cooking liquid.

The brown-and-braise method isn't just for meats; it can infuse superb flavor into vegetables as well. While good browning is simply a matter of temperature and technique, good braising requires flavorful stock or broth. The intent is to enhance the flavor of the food, not to leach it out with a bland braising liquid.

DEGLAZING

Deglazing is the process of adding liquid to a hot pan in which a protein food such as meat, poultry, or fish has been sautéed or roasted. The intent is to loosen the browned particles that have adhered to, or *glazed,* the pan during cooking. There is a great deal of desirable flavor and color in the glaze, unless it has burned. A burned glaze will produce a bitter sauce.

Deglazing liquid is usually wine or stock rather than water, because water dilutes the flavor instead of enhancing it. Often, all that is necessary for a simple, flavorful sauce is a quick deglazing of the pan, a touch of butter, salt, and pepper, and a pass through a fine mesh strainer.

GRILLING

Grilling, second to roasting, is about as venerable a cooking method as one can find. It is slightly more efficient than roasting because the metal grill collects heat and conducts it directly to the food. Grilling is called for with hearty food, when you want blackened edges and smokey flavors and aroma.

Food that is to be grilled should be inherently tender, flavorful, and small enough to cook through quickly. Items that are too large will be burned on the outside by the violent heat of the fire before they are cooked through to the center. Foods should not be so tender that they will be impossible to turn, however. Many varieties of fish, such as halibut and plaice, are too delicate for the grill. Beyond these few limitations, the grill is very versatile. Meats, poultry, fish, shellfish, many kinds of vegetables, and sometimes even bread are suited to the grill.

The most important part of grilling is understanding the level of heat under the grill. As very few people are blessed with a true wood-burning indoor grill, the following recommendations pertain to outdoor grilling.

• Use hardwood lump charcoal. It burns hotter than standard briquettes, which are made of compressed sawdust, and it is ready to use sooner and provides more even heat than actual hardwood. At Campanile, we use mesquite lump charcoal, but your decision as to what sort of hardwood charcoal to use should primarily be based on availability.

• Don't be overly frugal with the charcoal. The price of a couple of steaks is far higher than the cost of a few extra pieces of charcoal. Once the meat is on the grill, it is too late to add charcoal. If you do add it the heat will decrease while the new charcoal is igniting. It will take at least 15 minutes to come up to the proper temperature. It is far easier to remove a few hot coals than to add fuel and wait for it to come up to temperature.

• For grilling, a fire should not exhibit any real flames, and the coals should be evenly coated with gray ash. For the average outdoor grill, it takes about 30 to 40 minutes to reach the appropriate stage for cooking. The level of heat from your fire should be intense. A good measure of an all-around hot fire is to hold your hand about 4 inches from the grill and count off the seconds before you are forced to withdraw your hand. A proper temperature should allow you to count off 2 or 3 seconds. If you can hold your hand there any longer, the fire simply isn't hot enough for grilling, and a moderate amount of additional fuel should be added and allowed to ignite completely.

• When the fire is ready, you need to redistribute the charcoal to provide for both a high-temperature portion of the grill and a moderate temperature section. The lack of precision in grilling necessitates having a moderate-temperature section to which food that is cooking too quickly can be moved. Also, usually there are a few different foods on the grill, and different foods need different temperatures. If you've ever had a piece of chicken that was burned on the outside but still raw on the inside, the importance of having a variety of heat levels should be clear.

• Experience is the key for consistent grilling. But even experienced chefs don't hesitate to poke the tip of a knife into the food to check the degree to which it is cooked. The times listed in all the recipes are guidelines only; the variables in cooking over fire are so great that it is impossible to provide exact instructions.

• Have the proper equipment. Use long, heavy-duty, spring-loaded tongs, as described in the section on equipment. Make sure you have more than one pair of tongs handy at all times, as they tend to hide when you need them the most. Most scissors tongs are too short and awkward, and the long, one-piece type that comes as part of the grill tool set is flimsy and cumbersome. If you intend to grill using short or poorly designed tongs, you may as well just throw your food in the coals and intentionally burn your hands.

Kitchen towels, the kind you can get really dirty without causing household disruption, are a necessity as well. They are handy for cleaning up, grabbing hot things, wiping oil on the grill—all sorts of uses.

A long-handled, heavy-duty grill brush is necessary to keep the grill clean. A clean grill will help prevent food from sticking and will improve the appearance of the cooked food, as there won't be any small blackened bits from previous use left on the grill. As is true of tongs, the small, poorly made brush that came with the barbeque set is not adequate for serious use. The short handle inevitably leads you to burn your hands and scrape your knuckles across the hot grill.

Roasting

Roasting is a dry heat method of cooking, relying on air for the transfer of heat. About as simple as cooking gets, roasting is based on exposing food to the hot air produced by a fire. Actual roasting—on a spit over an open flame— has been replaced for the most part by grilling and oven roasting. The relatively small portions of food we cook today are more easily handled on a grill or in an oven, rather than skewered and turned over a roaring fire. To regain some of that flavor lost in the transition from spit roast to oven roast, a lot of the roasted food at Campanile is browned on a mesquite grill prior to going in the oven.

Roasting in a conventional oven is really very similar to baking. Up to about 400 degrees, call it baking; hotter than that, and it is roasting—unless of course the food is bread or a dessert item, in which case you're baking again, regardless of temperature or surface effect. At La Brea Bakery we bake our bread at up to 475 degrees, and we get a nicely browned crust, but we still call it baking.

We like to make the distinction between roasting and baking based on the intended outcome of the food, and perhaps a little on the oven temperature. If the food is going to get a lot of deep color, it's roasted; if it is more mildly browned, it is baked. Baked fish or baked lasagna call for low temperatures, and the food doesn't get a dark browning. A dish like roast shoulder of pork or a roasted whole chicken is well browned with high heat, and roasted to a crisp-skinned finish. The high-heat process imparts great color to the food and alters the texture and flavor of the surface.

Meat suitable for roasting should be high quality and tender, either whole (in the case of small game or poultry) or a large section (in the case of beef, pork, or lamb). The bone should be left in because it preserves the wholeness of the piece of meat. The bone conducts heat to the inside of the meat and seems to help in terms of flavor as well. The less cutting you do, the less surface area there will be, and the less moisture you will lose.

True roasting originated with whole animals on a spit, and the method seems to work the best with meat that is as close as possible to its whole state, with the bones left in. For good color all around, roasted items should be turned a few times to brown evenly during cooking. Beef and lamb should be inherently tender and well marbled. Pork is usually brined. Poultry for roasting is best whole, and stuffed with a layer of herbs and some form of fat under the skin. Fish for roasting should be whole, skin on, firmly fleshed, and rich in flavor.

Meats and poultry should be roasted on a rack in a roasting pan. The rack elevates the meat from the surface of the pan and prevents it from burning on the bottom. Another option is to roast on a bed of vegetables, such as carrots, onions, and celery. The vegetables protect the meat from the hot roasting pan and add some flavor to the pan juices. The amount of vegetables required depends on the size of the item to be roasted. All that is necessary is to support the meat so it doesn't touch the pan; usually three or four carrots and the same number of celery stalks are sufficient for an average-sized roast or chicken. If some care is taken to prevent them from burning, the roasted vegetables can be chopped and served along with the meal.

Roasting is not the first method that comes to mind when you think of cooking vegetables, but many vegetables—especially root vegetables—are appropriate for roasting. Roasting vegetables caramelizes them and concentrates their flavor. When properly roasted with meat, the vegetables absorb some of the meat juices, adding a complex, flavorful element. They can then be served as they are, or some of them can be pureed and included in the pan juice sauce.

Many smaller items should be browned first in a pan or on the grill before roasting, as they will cook so quickly in the oven that a good, deep color can't be achieved on the surface without overcooking the interior. If you are roasting multiple small items like game birds, roast them in a shallow pan and allow a few inches between the items; this will ensure proper air circulation.

REDUCTION

Reduction is the process of boiling down a sauce or stock to concentrate its flavor and color. Stock should be reduced at a gentle boil so the fat will rise to the top to be skimmed off. If boiled too vigorously, the fat will be emulsified into the stock rather than separated from it. Sauces, which should be relatively free from fat, can be reduced more quickly, before the butter is added and the sauce is finished.

RENDERING

Rendering is the term given to the method of slowly cooking meat, usually bacon or some other fatty meat, with the intent of melting and removing (rendering) the fat from the meat. *Rendering* is a term also used for the process of clarifying animal fats by boiling them with a large quantity of water. As fat floats on water, any meat particles or foreign matter will sink to the bottom of the pot, and the pure fat can be skimmed off for use in terrines, confit, and such.

SAUTÉING

Sautéing is versatile, quick, and effective. It is the method of cooking that is most easy to control, and it is easy to judge when something is done. Almost anything can be sautéed properly. Delicate vegetables can be lightly sautéed, just to bring out the flavor. A thick Porterhouse can be sautéed over high heat for a crisp, well-browned crust and a bloody rare center. Chicken can be cooked gently for a subtle dish, or really well browned for bolder flavor.

A high-quality sauté pan should be efficient in conducting heat to the food and heavy enough to distribute heat evenly. Most of the sautéing at Campanile is done over a medium-high flame, in a cast-iron skillet or heavy sauté pan that has been swirled with a little vegetable oil.

Many people are reluctant to sauté because of the similarity to frying, and the perceived level of fat. Actually, the amount of oil used in sautéing is generally quite small, only about 1 or 2 tablespoons. The oil prevents the food from sticking to the hot pan, greatly improves the transfer of heat from the pan, and therefore provides complete browning without burned spots.

We use canola, safflower, almond oil, or butter for almost all our sautéing. Vegetable oils have a smoke point of about 450 degrees and are almost flavorless; unclarified butter has a smoke point of about 250 degrees, and a lot of flavor. Using pure vegetable oil ensures high cooking temperatures, resulting in thorough browning of the exterior surfaces without overly drying the interior of the food. However, if you want the flavor of butter it is possible to sauté in clarified butter or some combination of butter and vegetable oil. This will have a lower smoke point than pure vegetable oil, so more care must be taken.

Clarified butter is pure butterfat, with almost all of the milk solids and water removed. Regular unsalted (sweet) butter can be clarified by melting at least one pound of butter over low heat without allowing it to simmer or boil. The heating will cause the milk solids and water to separate from the butter fat. Skim off the foam that collects on top of the clarified butter. Pour the clarified butter into a small bowl, taking care to separate the butter from any water that may have collected in the bottom of the pan. Clarified butter will keep in the refrigerator for much longer than regular butter.

SCALDING

Scalding is usually only applied to milk or cream that is to be used in making a dough or batter of some sort. To scald milk or cream, bring it almost to a boil over high heat, removing the pan from the heat before it foams and boils over. The process alters the dairy protein structure in such a way that the milk or cream is better able to blend with the proteins in flour, producing a strong dough. It also binds with egg yolks better to produce a smoother ice cream and it resists curdling when acids such as lemon juice, wine, or tart fruits or vegetables are used.

Equipment

Chapter 2

THE array of cooking utensils available to today's consumer is truly incredible. There are pots and pans of all sizes and materials, ranging in price from modest to astronomical. There are more specialized tools and clever motorized devices than one would think possible. But all the variety obscures the truth that what is needed are some basic versatile items of quality. A special asparagus steamer is not necessary to properly steam asparagus, nor is a decorative terra cotta dish required for roasting garlic.

This list is roughly prioritized in order of basic general necessity. Good pans and knives are simply far more useful than an ice cream maker. Of course some items are always more necessary than others, and we assume you have a stove.

KNIVES

Good knives are as essential as good pots and pans. Poor-quality knives will frustrate you, waste your time, and possibly even injure you. This doesn't mean you need to buy extremely expensive European knives with forged steel blades. There are modestly priced, stamped steel–bladed knives that are of comparable quality. In fact, the forged steel–bladed knives are more difficult to sharpen properly. A decent sharp knife is much better than an excellent dull knife. Most manufacturers have a secondary line, with stamped blades, and they usually represent the best value.

We have a number of Japanese carbon-steel knives that are wonderful because they are easy to sharpen and they hold an edge well. However, they require more maintenance because the steel isn't stainless, and thus it will rust and discolor. Fruits and vegetables with high acidity, such as lemons or artichokes, will blacken when cut with carbon-steel knives.

The quality of your knives is important, but proper sharpening will make an even greater difference in how your knives work. A sharpening stone, a good steel, and practice will help keep your knives in fine working shape. Restoring a proper edge can take quite a long time if the knife has been allowed to become very dull. The industry standard for knife edges is 22 degrees, or approximately one quarter of the way from flat to vertical. The easiest option is to have your knives sharpened by a professional. It isn't expensive, and it will probably be done correctly.

If you wish to do it yourself, use a stone with a fine grit abrasive surface. A coarse stone will produce an edge more quickly, but it will be ragged and short lived. Japanese water stones make a very good edge, because the abrasive is quite fine.

There are really only four knives you need; they are absolutely essential if you are to work efficiently in the kitchen.

8- to 10-inch chef's knife

This is the single most versatile knife to own. It is suitable for chopping, slicing, carving, or mincing. Find one that is well balanced and comfortable for your hand.

5- to 6-inch boning knife

Thinly bladed, this is the perfect tool for cutting meat, boning chickens, or filleting fish.

3- to 4-inch paring knife

This is the knife to use for small jobs like removing the core from apples, thinly slicing garlic, or trimming shallots.

10- to 12-inch serrated bread knife

For slicing bread, no other knife will perform like a true bread knife. You will be able to cut thin, uniform slices with relative ease. A good serrated knife is also great for slicing tomatoes.

ADDITIONAL KNIVES

Beyond the minimum requirements, there are some other knives that are sometimes useful.

12-inch chef's knife

An extra-large knife makes mincing herbs easier, and on those rare occasions when you serve a large roast it is a tremendous help in producing uniform slices.

Salmon-slicing knife

When slicing smoked salmon or gravlax, this knife is the best way to make long, thin, translucent slices. A salmon slicing knife is usually about 12 inches long, thin and narrow, and very sharp. The knife blade is designed to produce the least friction with the fish in order to reduce the tendency of the flesh to tear.

Sharpening steel

The name is misleading because a steel shouldn't be used to sharpen knives, but only to straighten the cutting edge. A good steel should be about 14 inches long, and smooth. We have found that the diamond-coated or coarsely grooved models will damage your knives because they are too abrasive and remove metal from the cutting edge, rather than just straightening the edge. The steel that we use is a butcher's steel made by Henckels. It is stainless steel and has no grooves at all.

Pans

If you can get a peek in the kitchen of a quality restaurant, you will find that although there may be an overwhelming number of pots and pans, the majority of them are either sauté or sauce pans, and there simply isn't the variety of configurations one might expect.

You need only a few basic pans, but they should be of superior durability, because they will be in constant use. It is worthwhile to make the commitment and buy pans and utensils that will last and continue to perform well. The initial purchase price may seem steep, but after a few months of using superior cookware, you will wonder how you ever managed without it. Unless an item is lost, stolen, or given away, you should never have to replace it.

It is important to determine what you really need and buy only those items. Rather than buying the prepackaged set that may contain six pans of limited utility, get three pans of boundless utility. A 2-quart saucepan at three quarters the price of a 4-quart pan is not a bargain. In general, it is better to have a pan that is too large, rather than too small, for any given task. There is really no reason, other than storage concerns perhaps, to have a 2-quart saucepan when you could have a 4-quart pan.

For stockpots, 8 quarts isn't enough; you really need at least 10 to 12 quarts of capacity. An 8-inch sauté pan is handy now and then for individual portions, but it actually has less than half the capacity of a 12-inch sauté pan. A good 12-inch sauté pan, about 3 inches deep, can be used for most cooking tasks, as long as it's ovenproof.

The very best pans are the heavy French copper pans. They used to be lined with tin, but that was impractical because they needed to be recoated somewhat frequently. The technology has improved to the point that nickel or stainless steel can now be bonded to copper to produce a much more durable pan. A lighter and less expensive alternative is a thick aluminum pan lined on the interior with stainless steel. Stainless steel on its own is a poor conductor of heat and it warps easily, but bonded to aluminum or copper it results in a pan with good heat conductivity, ease of cleaning, and durability. It should have a thick, heavy bottom for even heat distribution, and a reasonably tight-fitting, ovenproof lid. Thin steel pans are to be avoided because the distribution of heat is poor. Be sure not to buy any pan that has a plastic handle or even a plastic knob on the lid. It should have strong cast-metal handles well riveted through the pan. Some professional cookware have shaped sheet-metal handles that are spot-welded to the pan, and these are quite acceptable, as long as there are plenty of welds.

All-Clad makes superior cookware that seems to be virtually indestructible. There are other manufacturers that produce quality products as well, however, and as this will be a significant investment, it is important to compare a number of different options before deciding on a purchase.

Large sauté pans

Ideally you should have one 10-inch and one 12-inch sauté pan. Each should be about 3 inches deep, with a lid, and a heavy bottom for even heat distribution.

Large stockpot

You really need only one of these. It should be at least 10 to 12 quarts in capacity, with a lid, and a heavy bottom for even heat distribution.

Saucepans

You should have two 3- or 4-quart and one 5- or 6-quart saucepans. They should all have lids, and heavy bottoms for even heat distribution.

Roasting pan

A roasting pan should be large enough to comfortably hold a 20-pound turkey. It should be thick and sturdy, and about 2 to 3 inches deep. It should have strong handles well riveted through the pan. Although the really expensive copper- and tin-lined French pans are beautiful, stainless steel and thick aluminum are probably the most sensible materials. For roasting smaller things you want a pan that has low sides to prevent a steam envelope from forming within the sides. Large or small, you should get a pan you can put over high heat on the stovetop to deglaze without it warping like a pretzel.

Double boiler

Sometimes referred to as a *bain marie,* a double boiler is simply a set of two saucepans that nest together snugly. It is ideal for keeping sauces, syrups, or purees warm without the risk of burning. Just about any delicate preparation can be easily kept warm over simmering water. An inexpensive alternative is to use a stainless-steel mixing bowl over a saucepan of simmering water.

Baking pan

Baking pans have sides, somewhere between ½ inch and 2 inches high. Short-sided versions are sometimes referred to as jelly-roll pans. The best value is the large, heavy-duty nonstick variety. Cheap models usually warp at high temperatures.

Baking sheet

Baking sheets are similar to baking pans, except that they are flat, with sides no more than ½ inch high. They are also referred to as cookie sheets. As with baking pans, the best value is the large, heavy-duty nonstick variety.

Nonstick individual pie molds

These molds are wonderful for individual pies or potato galettes. They are about 4 inches in diameter, 1 inch deep, and coated with Teflon or a similar nonstick surface.

Cast-iron skillets

A large, cast-iron skillet is the best value, in terms of versatility and quality. A 10- to 12-inch cast-iron skillet is usually about one fifth of the price of a high-quality sauté pan, and it will perform most tasks as well, and some a little better. Steaks, pancakes, fried chicken—they always end up in the cast-iron skillet. Cast-iron cookware is ovenproof, and it has great heat distribution.

A small 8-inch skillet is good for small galettes and other personal-portion types of dishes. Of course, you can never have too many cast-iron skillets.

Newly purchased cast-iron cookware must be washed, and then lightly coated inside with vegetable oil and heated in a moderate oven (350 degrees) for 30 minutes. This is called "seasoning" a pan. The downside of cast-iron cookware is the heavy weight, the lack of a tight-fitting lid, and the care needed to avoid rust. Cast-iron cookware must be thoroughly dried and lightly oiled after every washing to prevent rust. This makes storage a little messy. Once a cast-iron skillet is properly seasoned, it has much less propensity to cause food to stick than most other uncoated pans. In addition to cookware retailers, sporting goods stores and hardware stores usually carry cast-iron cookware.

"EACH TOOL HAS SPECIFIC FUNCTIONS THAT IT CAN PERFORM
BETTER THAN OTHER TOOLS."

Nonstick omelet pan

These come in handy for sautéing with very little oil, or for making omelets and crepes. These pans usually aren't thick enough for good heat distribution, and they won't last a lifetime, but there certainly will be times when you will be glad you have one.

ADDITIONAL KITCHEN EQUIPMENT

In many of the recipes in this book, at least some of the items listed below will be required. Not every tool is essential, and at first some of them may seem to duplicate another in function. But in actuality, each tool has specific functions that it can perform better than other tools. A food mill and a food processor can both puree tomatoes, but only the food mill can separate the puree from the seeds and the skin, whereas a food processor can puree raw spinach, and a mill cannot.

Colander

There are bad colanders out there. It seems hard to believe, but a device as simple as a colander can be poorly designed. The plastic models are out of the question; they always melt, and usually at the worst possible moment. Thin aluminum ones eventually fall apart, and even some stainless-steel models don't have enough holes. Look for a sturdy aluminum, enameled, or stainless-steel version, with a diameter of about 12 inches and as many holes as possible. The holes should be about ⅛ of an inch in diameter. Handles are an essential feature, as is a stable circular base. The models that perch precariously on three or four spindly legs are disasters waiting to happen.

Stainless-steel mixing bowls

Stainless-steel mixing bowls are better than glass for most tasks. They are less expensive, unbreakable, and lighter. It is good to have at least four or five of various sizes. Almost every time I work in the kitchen I need a stainless-steel mixing bowl. When mixing, it's always better to have too big a bowl rather than too small.

Large, coarse-mesh stainless-steel strainer

The coarse-mesh strainer should fit inside your large saucepan, and be about 4 or 5 inches deep. By blanching the vegetables in the strainer, you don't have to dump the boiling water; you simply remove the strainer, and you're ready to blanch something else. It saves so much time when blanching vegetables or cooking pasta that you will soon find the strainer invaluable.

Small, fine-mesh stainless-steel strainer

This differs from the coarse-mesh model in that it is conical. It is most useful for straining sauces and stocks. Stainless is the material of choice; it provides the best durability.

Bamboo steamer

For placing over a saucepan containing an inch of simmering water, it should fit snugly over your large saucepan. Asian markets usually carry steamers of all shapes and sizes, and they are generally inexpensive and work quite well.

Utensils

3 wooden spoons and 2 stainless-steel spoons
Wooden spoons of all sizes are useful, and so are stainless steel spoons, both solid and perforated.

Stainless-steel spatula
A wide, flexible, stainless-steel spatula is invaluable when sautéing or grilling delicate things.

Stainless-steel tongs
It is essential to have a pair of long, stainless-steel tongs for turning chops, steaks, chicken, or vegetables. The scissors type are more difficult to use. The best tong is the spring-loaded type, hinged at the end of the handle section.

Ladles

A couple of good stainless-steel ladles, one 2-ounce and one of at least 4 to 6 ounces capacity, are almost indispensable.

Brushes

A 2-inch-wide, natural-bristle paintbrush will be useful for brushing oil on toast rounds and various other things, or basting turkeys. Don't use the same brush for pastry and garlic marinades, as it is difficult to remove strong flavors from the brush.

Stainless-steel whisks

A couple of stainless-steel whisks with wooden handles are essential in a well-equipped kitchen. A large one and a small one will be the best combination. They are particularly useful for making vinaigrettes and mayonnaise.

Zester

A zester is needed for removing the zest from lemons and other citrus fruits.

Vegetable peeler

A good, sharp vegetable peeler is essential for every kitchen. It should be inexpensive enough that it can be quickly replaced as soon as it becomes dull, as sharpening fees are generally equal to purchase prices.

Rubber spatulas

Rubber spatulas are essential tools in the kitchen. For scraping down the sides of a mixing bowl or when you need to get that last tablespoon of vinaigrette out of the bowl, there are no suitable alternatives.

Food mill

A food mill looks a little like a colander with a crank handle. It has interchangeable sieves with different hole sizes. The food is forced through the sieve by turning the handle; anything larger than the hole size, such as skins or seeds, is separated out.

Many contemporary cooking publications specify the use of food processors, rather than food mills, in most recipes. This is based on the assumption that more home cooks have processors than mills. Although this is true, it fails to account for the fact that the two machines do not perform the same operations. Both machines are useful, but if we had to choose between the two, we would buy the food mill. A high-quality food mill should be sturdy enough to last a long time, because you will come to depend on it.

Mandolin

A cutting utensil similar in use to a carpenter's plane, a mandolin is very helpful for slicing vegetables extremely thinly, or julienne. We recommend the inexpensive plastic-bodied models from Japan rather than the pricey French stainless-steel ones, because the plastic mandolins have stainless steel blades that are just as sharp, come with a number of interchangeable blades to provide just as many slicing options, and generally cost about 75 percent less than the French models.

Mortar and pestle

A good mortar and pestle is a luxury, but it is exceptionally useful. Using a mortar and pestle is the only way to make a true pesto. It will produce textured emulsions that cannot be duplicated with an electric device. It is great for grinding spices or making preparations like anchoide or rouille. Unlike a food processor, a mortar and pestle does not generate heat or incorporate air into the mixture. The best models we have found come from England. They are made of thick, unglazed porcelain, and the pestle has a sturdy wooden handle. The mortar, or bowl, being made of porcelain, is breakable, but if treated with reasonable care, the set can last a lifetime.

Cutting board

A good cutting board should be as large as possible for use in your kitchen. Eighteen by 24 inches is an ideal size if you can fit it on your countertop. Butcher-block countertops look great, but the damage that regular use will cause will soon have you using a replaceable cutting board.

Pasta machine

The Atlas pasta machine from Italy is the standard. It is affordably priced and reasonably well made. It looks a bit like a miniature old-fashioned wringer washer. Some tasks are better accomplished without electrically powered mechanical aid: Rolling out fresh pasta is one of them. The machine we use at the restaurant is a larger, more durable version of this machine. This machine simply rolls out a thin sheet of pasta. It is hand-cranked, easy to control, adjustable, and simple in design. A pasta machine will produce thinner and more consistent sheets of pasta than is possible with a rolling pin.

Food processor

This is the familiar old standby found in most kitchens across America. It has multiple attachments and a myriad of uses. However, it really isn't as useful as the manufacturers would like us to believe. It has all sorts of hard-to-clean corners and seams, and the attachments are easily lost or misplaced. All too often, a food processor is used for tasks that could be accomplished better with a good, sharp knife. The task at which a food processor excells is pureeing, which is also its main fault; it purees everything, making a mousse out of anything it touches. At home we got one to make baby food.

Blender

Blenders are much like food processors; they puree and whip the food, often more than is desired. At home you can use a blender for processing smaller amounts than would be practical in a food processor. At Campanile, 95 percent of the work done by blenders is done in the bar. If you need one, get a good, sturdy model made of glass with a heavy metal bottom. The number of speeds or settings is irrelevant, as long as the machine has low and high.

Spice grinder

This is the fairly inexpensive coffee grinder with the single rotating blade. For superior coffee you might want an adjustable mill, but for spices this sort of crude pulverizing machine is quite suitable. Just don't ever grind coffee with it after you've ground spices. There are people with a taste for spiced coffee; we are not among them. However, if that is your desire, you should add the chosen spices to your coffee rather than settle for whatever may have accumulated in the spice grinder.

Electric mixer

Kitchen Aid makes the best countertop machines available for the consumer. They come with whisk, paddle, and dough hook attachments. The machines are very well made and have a coupling that allows the attachment of various other devices such as a meat grinder.

Kitchen scale

An inexpensive scale that measures in ounces and grams is essential for a large number of baking recipes, and can be helpful in portioning foods. Weight is more accurate than volume as a means of measurement.

Cheesecloth

Cheesecloth is a cheap, loosely woven cotton fabric that is useful for straining stocks and sauces, enclosing herbs for a bouquet garni, or for wrapping galantines or whole fish for poaching.

Ice cream machine

Ice-and-rock-salt-model machines, whether hand cranked or electrically powered, work quite well, are affordable, and are readily available at most hardware stores. White Mountain is a good brand.

Appetizers

Chapter 3

AN appetizer is usually the first food impression a customer will have in a restaurant. It sets the tone for the whole meal to follow. Each appetizer should be considered a whole meal in microcosm, with every bite yielding multiple flavors and textures. It should be intriguing, enticing, and flavorful, but only up to the point of provoking a desire.

The first course should tease one's senses, perhaps with a little more intrigue and more vibrancy of flavor than would be prudent in a large main course. As appetizers are generally smaller than main courses, they can be more concentrated, richer, or more intensely flavored. The logic is that the more intensely flavored a dish is, the less of it there should be. Something like anchovy or sheep's cheese is not usually consumed by the plateful.

There is always a need for balance between the appetizer and main-course dishes. The relationship between the two is a vaguely defined yin and yang situation. There should be a little overlap of flavor or texture sensations and some elements in common, but there should be clear differences, or contrasts, as well. Panfried scallops, for instance, could be a great appetizer for a lighter main course such as a pasta gnocchette with beans. A lighter appetizer such as prosciutto with figs would be a great starter for soft-shell crabs, because the season is right for both of them. The rich prosciutto and the soft fig prime the palate for the delicately flavored crab in the crispy tempuralike coating. Lamb stew, a hearty, filling main course, would be well preceded by something crisp, like a refreshing Greek salad.

Soups can be great appetizers, although the form is so different they require a sort of mental shift. You have to ensure that a bowl of soup isn't one long, mundane endurance of uniformity, but a soothing blanket that envelops little surprises and taste sensations, such as croutons, pasta, or chopped vegetables. Simple chicken stock, if kept in 1-quart containers in the refrigerator or freezer, can be quickly made into an easy and incredibly refreshing soup with the addition of some tart greens, garlic, and a little pasta. Most people think of soups as a winter or fall sort of dish, but perfect gazpacho can only be made in the summer, and making fresh tomato soup from tomatoes right off the vine is a wonderful way to use up extra produce from your garden.

In Italy, pasta is not served as a first course. Rather, an *antipasto* (translated "before pasta") is served first. However, in the United States, it can be an appetizer course, a second course, a side dish to an entrée, or a simple, full meal. Everyone likes it in some form, and it is generally inexpensive. Most of the pastas at Campanile can be eaten as an appetizer or a full dinner portion, and the same can be done at home. A recipe that serves four as a main course can usually accommodate six or eight as an appetizer.

Figs and Prosciutto

Serves 4

Figs and Prosciutto is a classic Italian dish, but we never understood it properly until we had the combination of perfect figs and the best-quality prosciutto de Parma. With less than perfect ingredients this dish is mundane and unsatisfying. Perfectly ripe figs, from late summer or fall, need only to be split and arranged with the prosciutto around a plate on a bed of lightly dressed arugula. Black mission figs are the best choice; the flesh is juicy, deeply red, and concentrated in flavor.

12 black mission figs
1 bunch arugula
Extra-virgin olive oil
Fresh lemon juice
Kosher salt
8 ounces prosciutto, in 8 thin slices
Freshly cracked black pepper

Split the figs vertically into halves. Remove the stems from the leaves of arugula. In a large mixing bowl, drizzle a tablespoon of olive oil over the arugula. Add ½ teaspoon of fresh lemon juice and ¼ teaspoon of kosher salt, and toss very lightly.

To serve, divide the arugula equally among 4 large plates, arrange the figs around the edges of the plates, and place 2 full slices of prosciutto (2 ounces) over each serving of figs. Add a drizzle of olive oil and a pinch of freshly cracked black pepper, and serve immediately.

Note: If your figs are slightly underripe, split the figs vertically and put them cut side up on a baking sheet. Pour about 1 teaspoon of good port into each fig, and put them into a 350-degree oven for about 5 minutes or under the broiler for 3 minutes. They should be warm all the way through, but not really cooked. Remove them from the oven, allow them to cool, and chill them in the refrigerator for 1 hour or so.

Cold Steamed Mussels with Marjoram Pesto

Serves 4

THIS is a great pass-around appetizer. The chilled mussels are subtly rich, and flavored with hints of shallot and garlic. The mussels are beautifully shiny, and the marjoram pesto adds a deep green accent. When we serve these on New Year's Eve at Campanile, they disappear faster than we can replenish the platters. Present them on a bed of crushed ice.

2 pounds fresh mussels, Prince Edward Island
    variety preferred
¼ stick (1 ounce) unsalted butter
2 large garlic cloves, peeled and minced
    (2 teaspoons)
4 large shallots, peeled, trimmed, and minced
    (¼ cup)
½ cup dry white wine
½ cup Chicken Stock (see page 187)
½ cup Marjoram Pesto (see page 214)

Have ready

The Chicken Stock, warm, in a small saucepan
    over low heat
The Marjoram Pesto

SCRUB the mussels well under cold running water, and then remove the beard found on the side of the mussel. Do not use any mussels that have broken or opened shells. Melt the butter in a large sauté pan over medium heat. Sauté the garlic and shallots until translucent, about 4 to 5 minutes.

Add the mussels, and gently toss to coat with the garlic and shallots, about 1 minute. Add the wine and stock, increase the heat, and bring to a boil; cover and steam until the shells open, about 3 minutes. After the majority of the mussels have opened, use a slotted spoon to remove the opened ones to large, warmed soup bowls. Continue to cook any unopened mussels for 1 additional minute to determine if any more will open. Remove any opened mussels to the soup bowls, and discard any unopened mussels. Continue to simmer the broth over medium heat.

When all the mussels have been removed, and have cooled sufficiently to allow easy handling, remove and discard the half of the shell that is not connected to the mussel; then detach, but do not remove, each mussel from the remaining shell. Place the half-shelled mussels on a platter and refrigerate to chill, about 1 hour. Boil the broth until it reduces by two-thirds, about 15 minutes. Remove the pan from the heat and allow the broth to settle about 10 minutes.

Using a fine-mesh, stainless-steel strainer lined with 3 layers of cheesecloth, strain the broth into a medium mixing bowl. Discard the garlic and shallots. Allow the broth to cool about 10 minutes, and then refrigerate it for at least 45 minutes.

To serve, remove the platter of mussels and the reduced broth from the refrigerator. Add the broth to the Marjoram Pesto and mix well. Spoon about 1 teaspoon pesto over each of the cold mussels, and serve immediately with some good rye or country bread.

Fava Bean Puree

Serves 4 to 6

FAVA Bean Puree can be an appetizer when used as a simple spread for crostini, or it can be part of a main course when used as a filling for vegetarian ravioli. If Fava Bean Puree is to be used as a ravioli filling, it should be chilled.

1 pound fresh fava beans, removed from pods
    (4 pounds in the pods)
½ cup extra-virgin olive oil
Kosher salt
Fresh lemon juice

IN a large stockpot, bring approximately 2 quarts of water to a boil and add 2 tablespoons of kosher salt. Fill a large mixing bowl with ice water.

Blanch the shelled fava beans in a fine-mesh, stainless-steel strainer in the boiling water for about 30 seconds. Remove the strainer of blanched fava beans from the stockpot and plunge it into the ice water for about 30 seconds; allow to drain. Using your fingers, remove the peel of the fava beans by pinching off one end of the skin and gently squeezing the bean out of the skin. Reserve the shelled and peeled fava beans in a medium saucepan.

Add the olive oil and about 1 teaspoon of kosher salt. Over high heat, bring to a gentle boil. Remove the pan from the heat, and allow to cool for about 10 minutes.

Using a rubber spatula, scrape the beans and oil into a food processor fitted with a steel blade. Process only until the beans achieve a creamy consistency. Take care not to over-process. Correct the seasoning to taste with kosher salt and fresh lemon juice. Serve immediately, or allow to sit for up to 4 hours at room temperature.

Gravlax

GRAVLAX is a Swedish version of cured salmon, originally intended as a way to preserve the fish without refrigeration. At Campanile we make it with a softer cure using much less salt, and the Aquavit adds a slight scent of caraway.

The subtle balance between flavor and texture is lost if it is served in thick slabs. The trick to properly slicing Gravlax is to have a smoked salmon knife, a long, very thin, very sharp knife. The Gravlax will keep, refrigerated, for about a week.

2 cups packed coarsely chopped fresh dill
    (½ pound)
½ cup kosher salt
½ cup freshly cracked black pepper
¼ cup granulated sugar
One salmon fillet, 4½ pounds, skin retained on
    one side
1 ounce Aquavit (optional)
Dill Cream (see page 209)
1 loaf rye or pumpernickel bread
Caviar for garnish (optional)

IN a large mixing bowl, combine the chopped dill, kosher salt, black pepper, and sugar, and mix well. Using about one quarter of the dill mixture, spread out a ¼-inch-thick layer in a baking pan. The dill mixture layer should be slightly larger than the salmon. A lot of juice will be drawn out of the salmon by the salt and sugar, so don't use a sideless baking sheet.

Place the salmon, skin side down, on the bed of dill. Pack the remaining dill mixture over the entire surface of the salmon, with a little bit extra on the thicker sections of the salmon.

Cover the baking pan with plastic wrap and place a second baking pan on top of the plastic. Weight the baking pan with 4 or 5 large cans or bricks (at least 16 ounces each) evenly arranged along the length of the top pan. The pressure of the weight will help force the moisture out of the salmon. This is an important part of the curing process. Refrigerate for 2 days. The salmon will darken in color and become much firmer to the touch.

Remove the cans, the top pan, and the plastic wrap. Gently scrape away the dill mixture. It isn't important to remove every last bit of it. The odd bit here and there will add texture to the Gravlax. The salmon should be drizzled with Aquavit at this point, if desired, then wrapped in fresh plastic, placed on a clean baking pan, and refrigerated for 1 more day.

On the day you intend to serve the Gravlax, prepare the Dill Cream and reserve.

Using a long, very thin, very sharp knife

CURING SALMON WITH FRESH DILL: "IN SUMMER, GRAVLAX CAN BE LIGHT AND REFRESHING; IN WINTER, IT HAS A RICH, WARMING QUALITY."

(a knife designed for smoked salmon is ideal for this), beginning about 6 inches from the tail (narrow end), cut toward the tail, making long slices about 1/16 inch thick. The blade of the knife should be at a shallow angle to the cutting board, about 25 degrees. Continue to slice the salmon, progressing toward the head with each slice. The first slice off the tail should be discarded; it will be too tough and salty. The technique will take some practice to perfect.

To serve, place each slice of Gravlax on a piece of thinly sliced toasted rye or pumpernickel bread. Drizzle a little Dill Cream over it,

and spoon some caviar in the center, if desired, and serve immediately. (Use good caviar: sevruga, osetra, or beluga—even golden caviar is fine. Lumpfish caviar is awful. One teaspoon per portion is enough.) Two slices make a sufficient portion as an appetizer.

Gravlax can also be served on the Potato Galette (see page 234). Prepare the galette and arrange slices of Gravlax on the top.

Swiss Chard Stuffed with Grilled Pecorino, Eggplant, and Red Bell Pepper

Serves 6

THIS appetizer is a neatly wrapped little taste of the Mediterranean summer. It is important that a young pecorino Romano is used, for one that is too aged will be difficult to slice properly and may be too salty. The Swiss chard leaves must be large enough to enclose the filling entirely. It is possible to overlap two smaller leaves if necessary. This appetizer can be cooked under the broiler, but the grill will produce far superior flavor. The Swiss chard bundles can be prepared early in the day and refrigerated until needed.

8 to 12 (depending on size) large Swiss chard
    leaves
¾ cup olive oil
2 red bell peppers (1 pound)
6 slices eggplant (6 ounces), ¼ inch thick, 3½
    inches square
6 ounces pecorino Romano, cut into six
    ⅛-inch-thick slices, 3½ inches square
Freshly cracked black pepper
1 cup regular balsamic vinegar, or 1 ounce
    premium balsamic vinegar
1 head radicchio, thinly sliced (2 cups)

IN a large stockpot, bring approximately 4 quarts of water to a boil and add 2 tablespoons of salt. Fill a large mixing bowl with ice water.

Blanch the Swiss chard in a fine-mesh, stainless-steel strainer in the boiling water until just softened, about 30 seconds. Remove the strainer of greens from the stockpot and plunge it into the ice water for about 30 seconds; allow it to drain. Pat dry with a kitchen towel.

Start a fire in the grill and allow it to burn to medium temperature.

Rub a little olive oil all over the red peppers, eggplant slices, and cheese slices. Season the eggplant and cheese with black pepper.

Roast the peppers on the grill, or under a broiler, turning as necessary, until the skin blisters and blackens on all sides.

Grill the eggplant on each side until tender, about 2 minutes. Remove the eggplant from the grill and set aside to cool.

Grill the cheese about 30 seconds, until the cheese begins to color and just soften. Remove the cheese from the grill and set aside to cool.

Place the peppers in a paper bag to soften the skin as they cool, about 15 minutes. When the peppers are cool, peel away the charred skin, and remove the cores and seeds. Cut each pepper into 3 equal pieces and trim each piece to approximately 3½ inches square, and set aside.

Spread each Swiss chard leaf on a flat surface so that the center rib projects up. Using a sharp knife held parallel to the cutting surface, shave away most of the thick part of the rib. The intent is to shave away the tough part of the rib but to preserve the shape of the whole leaf. This operation, plus the blanching, leaves the chard very pliable so the bundles hold together by themselves.

To assemble the bundles, spread out 1 large Swiss chard leaf, or 2 small leaves overlapping, and rub the Swiss chard with a little olive oil. Place a slice of cheese in the middle of the Swiss chard, then a slice of red pepper, then a slice of eggplant. Fold up the edges toward the center to form a completely enclosed package. Rub the entire bundle lightly with olive oil and place on a large platter. Repeat the procedure with the remaining leaves, cheese, peppers, and eggplant. Refrigerate, covered, until needed.

If you're using regular balsamic vinegar, in a small saucepan, over medium heat, reduce the vinegar by half. (You don't want to reduce premium vinegar.) Drizzle a little vinegar and then olive oil on 6 plates. Scatter some radicchio on each plate and season with black pepper.

Grill the Swiss chard packages until lightly browned, and the cheese is soft and melted, about 2 to 3 minutes on each side. The packages will hold together if turned gently with stainless-steel tongs.

To serve, using a very sharp knife, cut each bundle in half diagonally, forming 2 triangles, and arrange atop the radicchio on each plate. Serve immediately.

Lamb Carpaccio with Arugula

Serves 6

IT seems these days that almost every restaurant has a carpaccio on the menu. In most cases, the beef tenderloin that is used has very little flavor or texture. We use lamb loin because it has a wonderfully mild flavor and a firm texture. The loin comes from half a saddle of lamb, completely boned and trimmed of all connective tissue. You will not find this at the supermarket, but a good service butcher will be able to provide it.

12 ounces boned lamb loin
¼ cup extra-virgin olive oil
½ small onion, peeled and very thinly sliced
4 artichokes
Juice of 1 medium lemon
Kosher salt
Freshly cracked black pepper
2 cups arugula leaves
2 ounces Parmesan cheese, in 1 piece

TRIM the lamb meat to remove any fat, sinew, or membrane, and cut, across the grain, into 1-ounce portions, or ask the service butcher to do it for you.

Spread out a 1- by 2-foot piece of plastic wrap on a cutting board. Brush a little olive oil around the center of the plastic wrap, to about 2 inches from the edges. Put 2 pieces of lamb, end grain facing up, on the oiled half of the plastic wrap about 6 inches apart. Brush a little oil on top of the lamb. Fold the plastic over the lamb and, using the flat of a meat mallet, pound the meat very thin, to a thickness of between ¹⁄₁₆ and ¹⁄₃₂ inch. Leave the meat in the plastic wrap to prevent discoloration and drying.

Repeat the procedure with the remaining lamb meat, reserving 2 tablespoons of oil. Put the wrapped, flattened meat in the refrigerator.

In a medium mixing bowl, soak the sliced onion in water for about 10 minutes. Drain and dry the onion slices, and return them to the mixing bowl.

Trim away and discard all the leaves of the artichokes. Cut away and discard the fuzzy choke from the heart. Peel off the tough skin on the stem, removing about ⅛ inch all around the stem. Using a mandolin, or a very sharp, thin-bladed knife, slice the artichoke hearts vertically as thinly as possible.

Add the sliced raw artichoke, about half the lemon juice, the reserved 2 tablespoons of olive oil, 1 teaspoon of kosher salt, 1 teaspoon of black pepper, and the arugula to the sliced onions, and toss gently.

To serve, divide the salad evenly among 6 large plates. Remove the wrapped lamb from the refrigerator. Gently unwrap it, and place 2 pieces on each portion of salad. Drizzle a teaspoon of extra-virgin olive oil over each portion, and sprinkle lightly with kosher salt and black pepper. Using a vegetable peeler, add 5 or 6 thin shavings of Parmesan cheese and a few drops of fresh lemon juice to the top of each portion, and serve immediately.

Panfried Scallops with Grilled Romaine and Fava Bean Vinaigrette

FOR this dish we use Cape Cod Bay scallops, lightly coated in cornmeal and panfried to create a crunchy texture. Fresh scallops should be firm, translucent, and have the distinct scent of the sea. If the scallops are parchment-white, flabby, and lacking any scent, they have been soaked in a chemical bath, which adds to their weight and shelf life but not to their quality.

Vinaigrette

4 ounces fresh fava beans, removed from pods
    (1 pound in the pods)
Zest of ½ medium lemon
2 tablespoons champagne vinegar
1 large shallot, peeled, trimmed and minced
    (1 tablespoon)
1 teaspoon fresh lemon juice
2 tablespoons extra-virgin olive oil
2 tablespoons Lemon Oil (see page 219)
½ small red bell pepper (3 ounces), cut into
    ¼-inch dice
½ small yellow bell pepper (3 ounces), cut into
    ¼-inch dice
1 tablespoon chopped fresh parsley
1 tablespoon chopped fresh basil

Scallops and Romaine

1 small heart of romaine
1 medium head radicchio
¼ cup vegetable oil
Kosher salt
Freshly cracked black pepper
12 ounces small Bay scallops, preferably
    Cape Cod
1 cup fine-ground cornmeal

Have ready

The Lemon Oil

TO prepare the vinaigrette: In a large stockpot, bring approximately 1 quart of water to a boil and add 2 teaspoons of salt. Fill a large mixing bowl with ice water.

Blanch the shelled fava beans in a fine-mesh, stainless-steel strainer in the boiling water for about 30 seconds. Remove the strainer of blanched fava beans from the stockpot and plunge it into the ice water for about 30 seconds; allow it to drain.

Remove the peels of the fava beans by pinching off one end of the skin with your thumbnail, and then gently squeezing the bean out of the skin. Reserve the shelled and peeled fava beans in a small bowl.

In a medium mixing bowl, combine the lemon zest, vinegar, shallot, lemon juice, olive oil, and Lemon Oil and whisk briefly; reserve. Add the fava beans, peppers, and herbs just before serving.

To prepare the scallops and romaine: Start a fire in the grill and allow it to burn to medium temperature, or preheat a large sauté pan over medium-high heat.

Cut the heart of romaine in half lengthwise. Cut the radicchio into quarters, through the core. Do not remove the core of either the romaine or the radicchio. Rub a little of the vegetable oil over the leaves and season lightly with kosher salt and black pepper. Grill or sauté the greens, flat sides down, until lightly browned but still crisp, about 2 to 3 minutes. Remove the greens from the heat and allow them to cool. When cool, trim out the cores, separate the leaves, and scatter them equally on 4 large salad plates.

In a medium mixing bowl, lightly season the scallops with kosher salt and black pepper. Add the cornmeal to the scallops and toss gently but thoroughly. Remove the scallops from the cornmeal, shaking off any excess. In a large sauté pan, over high heat, preheat the remaining vegetable oil. Sauté the scallops until lightly browned, about 1½ minutes on each side.

To serve, divide the scallops evenly among the salad plates, placing the scallops on top of the grilled greens. Add the fava beans, bell peppers, and herbs to the vinaigrette, and toss gently but thoroughly. Drizzle equal amounts of the vinaigrette over the scallops and the greens, and serve immediately.

Shrimp and Crab Cakes

Serves 6 as an appetizer,
4 as a main course

THIS recipe is a little different from what you might encounter on the docks of Maryland. We add shiitake mushrooms, green beans, and some sweet red bell pepper. When buying fresh green beans, you should look for the small (6-inch), firm ones, not the large and tough-skinned ones.

You can make these cakes with crab and shrimp, crab and cod, just shrimp, or simply crab. Using cod instead of shrimp will make the cakes a little flakier and less expensive as well. If you use cod, steam the fish over Court Bouillon (see page 197) and then flake it apart with a fork.

⅓ cup vegetable oil
3 ounces fresh shiitake mushrooms, stemmed
　　and cut into thin slices (about 1 cup)
4 ounces fresh green beans
¾ pound uncooked shrimp, peeled and cut into
　　¼-inch dice, or cod
2 large garlic cloves, peeled and minced
　　(2 teaspoons)
1 tablespoon dry sherry
¾ pound cooked lump crabmeat, Dungeness
　　or Eastern Blue
1 extra-large egg, beaten
1 medium red bell pepper (8 ounces), cored,
　　seeded, and cut into ¼-inch dice
1 bunch scallions, trimmed and thinly sliced
　　(⅓ cup)

1¾ cups moist white bread crumbs
¼ cup unbleached all-purpose flour, plus
　　additional for dusting
Kosher salt
Freshly cracked black pepper
½ teaspoon ground red chile pepper
Celery Root Slaw (see page 56)
Roasted Garlic Tartar Sauce (see page 208)

Have ready

The cooked crabmeat
The Celery Root Slaw
The Roasted Garlic Tartar Sauce

IN a large sauté pan, over medium-high heat, preheat 1 tablespoon of vegetable oil. Sauté the mushrooms until just wilted, about 1 to 2 minutes. Remove them from the heat and transfer them to a large mixing bowl. Wipe the sauté pan clean.

In a large stockpot, bring approximately 4 quarts of water to a boil and add 2 tablespoons of salt. Fill a large mixing bowl with ice water.

Blanch the green beans by placing them in a fine-mesh, stainless-steel strainer in the boiling water for about 4 minutes. Remove the strainer of blanched beans from the stockpot and plunge it into the ice water for about 30 seconds; allow it to drain.

Trim the beans on both ends, and cut them into thin, diagonal slices. Add the beans to the large mixing bowl with the mushrooms.

In a large sauté pan, over medium-high heat, preheat 1 tablespoon of vegetable oil. Sauté the shrimp until just colored, about 1 to 2 minutes. Stir in the garlic and deglaze the pan with the sherry, about 2 minutes. Remove the pan from the heat, allow the contents to cool for 10 minutes, then add it to the large mixing bowl. Wipe the sauté pan clean.

Add the cooked crab, egg, red bell pepper, scallions, bread crumbs, flour, 1½ teaspoons kosher salt, ½ teaspoon black pepper, and ground chile pepper to the large mixing bowl. Toss gently but thoroughly. Adjust the seasoning to taste with additional salt and pepper as necessary.

Divide the mixture into 12 even portions and form cakes about 2½ inches across. Be sure to press them into patties, but don't compress them too tightly. Dust a plate with a small amount of flour. Gently press each side of the crab cakes into the flour to lightly coat. (At this point, the cakes can be refrigerated, covered, until needed, for about a day.)

In 2 large sauté pans, over medium-high heat, preheat the remaining vegetable oil. Sauté the cakes until browned, about 3 to 4 minutes on each side. Using a steel spatula, remove the crab cakes from the pans and drain them on absorbent paper.

To serve, mound ¼ to ½ cup of Celery Root Slaw in a small haystack on the middle of each warm plate. Place 2 or 3 cakes next to each haystack, and dab a teaspoon of Roasted Garlic Tartar Sauce on each cake. Serve immediately.

Steamed Mussels with Scallion Pumpernickel Toast

Serves 4

THE old guideline of eating mussels and oysters only during months with an *R* holds true for the most part, but now there are good mussels available into the early part of June. We recommend using only small black mussels; the Prince Edward Island variety are usually quite good. Stay away from the green-lipped mussels; they are tough and flavorless compared to the black ones.

Mussels must be purchased live. Any that are open and don't close up when you poke at them are dead; don't buy them. You want to select live mussels as if you were picking fruit, choosing the consistent-looking individuals that are heavy for their size and shiny, avoiding any that are broken.

This dish is a very quick appetizer, but it can be easily increased into a hearty main course. Simply add 1 extra pound of mussels and, at the end, 1 cup of cooked cannellini beans to the broth with the tomatoes, and heat it through a little longer.

30 scallions (about 3 bunches), trimmed
¾ cup extra-virgin olive oil
4 slices good pumpernickel bread, ¼ inch thick
3 pounds small black mussels
1 tablespoon vegetable oil
2 large garlic cloves, peeled and minced (2 teaspoons)
1 large shallot, peeled, trimmed, and minced (1 tablespoon)
½ cup dry white wine
1 cup Fish Stock or Chicken Stock (see page 194 or 187)
2 medium tomatoes, cored, seeded, and chopped (1 cup)
¼ stick (1 ounce) unsalted butter
1 tablespoon chopped fresh parsley
1 tablespoon chopped fresh basil
1 tablespoon chopped fresh mint
1 teaspoon chopped lemon zest
Juice of ½ medium lemon
Kosher salt
Freshly cracked black pepper

Have ready

The Fish Stock or Chicken Stock, warm, in a small saucepan over low heat

Coarsely chop the scallions. Pour the olive oil into a blender, add the chopped scallions, and process until combined. Using a pastry brush, brush the scallion oil over the slices of bread and toast them under the broiler just until the edges begin to brown. Cut each slice in half; arrange 2 halves in each of 4 large soup bowls and set aside.

Scrub the mussels well under cold running water and then remove the beard found on the side of each mussel. Do not use any mussels that have broken or opened shells. In a large sauté pan, over medium heat, preheat the vegetable oil. Sauté the garlic and shallot about 1 minute. Add the mussels and gently toss to coat with the garlic and shallots, about 1 minute. Add the wine and stock. Bring to a boil, cover, and steam until the shells open, about 3 to 5 minutes. After the majority of the mussels have opened, remove the opened ones to the soup bowls, placing them on top of the toast. Continue to cook any unopened mussels for 1 additional minute to determine if any more will open. Remove any opened mussels to the soup bowls, and discard any unopened mussels. When all the mussels have been removed, add the chopped tomatoes and butter to the sauté pan and cook just until the butter melts, about 1 minute. Remove the pan from the heat. Stir in the chopped herbs and lemon zest, and season to taste with the lemon juice, kosher salt, and black pepper.

Splash the broth equally over the mussels and toast in the bowls, ensuring that the herbs and tomatoes are distributed evenly. Serve immediately.

Tuna Tartare

Serves 4

THIS makes a great first course before a dinner of Grilled Portobello Mushrooms with Spinach and Polenta (see page 254), or it can stand in as a lunch entrée, preceded perhaps by Tuscan Minestrone soup (see page 90).

The importance of buying only the very best possible tuna, for reasons of both taste and safety, cannot be overemphasized. Be sure to use only sashimi-grade tuna from a well-trusted fish supplier. If you cannot find Japanese cucumber, hothouse cucumber will do.

Vinaigrette

2 tablespoons fresh lemon juice
2 tablespoons champagne vinegar
2 teaspoons kosher salt
1 teaspoon freshly cracked black pepper
1 teaspoon lemon zest
⅓ cup extra-virgin olive oil

Tuna

¾ pound fresh tuna, bluefin, or yellow fin cut into ⅜-inch dice
1 small sweet white onion (4 ounces), peeled, trimmed, and cut into ¼-inch dice
4 ounces Japanese cucumber, peeled, split, seeded, and cut into thin slices
½ cup fresh basil leaves, cut into julienne
Kosher salt
Freshly cracked black pepper
1 cup mâche leaves or lamb's lettuce

TO prepare the vinaigrette: In a medium mixing bowl, whisk together the lemon juice, vinegar, kosher salt, black pepper, lemon zest, and olive oil.

To prepare the tuna: When ready to serve, combine the diced tuna, diced onion, all but 12 perfect slices of the sliced cucumber, and the julienne of basil in a second medium mixing bowl. Add most of the vinaigrette to the tuna mixture and gently toss to combine. Correct the seasoning to taste with kosher salt and black pepper.

Divide the tuna mixture and mound an equal amount in the center of each of 4 chilled plates. Arrange the mâche leaves and remaining cucumber slices around each of the mounds. Drizzle the remaining vinaigrette over all, and serve immediately.

Salads

Chapter 4

Arugula and Belgian Endive Salad with Concord Grapes and Cabrales Cheese

Serves 4

CHOOSING to include fruit in salads is risky; it seems a little out of place, or incongruous, but in this case the Cabrales cheese and the grapes go quite well together. Cabrales is a Spanish blue cheese somewhat similar to Roquefort. It is quite formidable in flavor, almost a little acidic, and is contrasted well by the musky sweetness of the grapes.

The salad can be prepared in advance except for the slicing of the arugula and endive; they must be sliced just before serving so they do not brown and wilt.

Vinaigrette

2 tablespoons sherry wine vinegar
1 large shallot, peeled, trimmed, and minced
　(1 tablespoon)
2 teaspoons fresh lemon juice
1 teaspoon kosher salt
½ teaspoon freshly cracked black pepper
3 tablespoons hazelnut oil
3 tablespoons almond oil

Salad

1 ounce (about 12 whole) hazelnuts
4 ounces (3 cups) arugula leaves
2 heads (10 ounces) Belgian endive
2 ounces Cabrales cheese, broken into small
　pieces (¼ cup)
6 ounces Concord grapes, cut in half and pitted
　(1 cup)

PREHEAT the oven to 325 degrees.

To prepare the vinaigrette: In a medium mixing bowl, whisk together the vinegar, minced shallot, lemon juice, kosher salt, and black pepper. Slowly whisk in the hazelnut oil and the almond oil until well combined, and reserve.

To prepare the salad: Put the hazelnuts on a small baking pan and toast in the oven about 10 minutes, turning after 5 or 6 minutes. Cool slightly and remove as much of the skin as possible by enclosing the nuts in a clean towel and rubbing gently. Chop the toasted hazelnuts finely and reserve.

Trim the stems from the arugula. Slice the heads of the endive on the bias into ½-inch-thick pieces.

Gently toss together the arugula, sliced endive, and about ⅔ of the crumbled Cabrales cheese in a large mixing bowl. Add the grapes and the vinaigrette and toss to combine well. Divide the salad equally among 4 large plates. Sprinkle the chopped hazelnuts over each portion, top with the remaining cheese, and serve immediately.

Baked Radicchio with Gorgonzola and Red Pears

Serves 4

BECAUSE this is a warm salad, only a young, sweet Gorgonzola should be used; avoid older, pungent cheeses. To counter the flavor of the Gorgonzola, the pears should be ripe and sweet, but still firm. The radicchio can be stuffed and baked in advance, and then simply warmed in the oven when ready to be served.

Apple Cider Vinaigrette

¼ cup almond oil
2 tablespoons apple cider vinegar
1 tablespoon walnut oil
1 small shallot, trimmed, peeled, and chopped
     (1½ teaspoons)
Kosher salt
Freshly cracked black pepper

Salad

1 head (12 ounces) radicchio
3 tablespoons extra-virgin olive oil
1 teaspoon chopped fresh rosemary
1 teaspoon chopped fresh thyme
1 small garlic clove, peeled, and finely minced
     (½ teaspoon)
Kosher salt
Freshly cracked black pepper
½ cup fresh walnut bread crumbs, or bread
     crumbs of your choice
4 ounces Gorgonzola cheese, finely crumbled
     (½ cup)
2 bosc or bartlett pears (¾ pound), unpeeled

PREHEAT the oven to 450 degrees.

To prepare the vinaigrette: In a medium mixing bowl, whisk together the almond oil, cider vinegar, walnut oil, and chopped shallot. Adjust the seasoning to taste with kosher salt and black pepper, and reserve until needed.

To prepare the salad: Cut the radicchio head into quarters through the core, but don't remove the core. Place the radicchio pieces in a baking pan that is large enough to hold them in one layer. Pour the olive oil into a small mixing bowl and whisk in the rosemary, thyme, and garlic. Season the mixture lightly with kosher salt and black pepper, and pour it over the radicchio, tossing to coat all sides. Place the baking pan in the oven and bake, just until the leaves begin to brown and separate, about 5 to 7 minutes. Remove the pan from the oven and set it aside, leaving the radicchio in the baking pan to cool.

Combine ¼ cup of the bread crumbs and the crumbled Gorgonzola in a small mixing bowl and mix well. When the radicchio is cool enough to handle, carefully separate but do not detach the leaves. Stuff the Gorgonzola mixture between the leaves. Gently re-form the radicchio quarters to their original shape. At this point, the radicchio can be refrigerated until needed. Remove from the refrigerator about 15 minutes before baking to allow it to warm to room temperature.

Cut each pear in half vertically and remove the core and seeds. Cut the pear halves into long, thin slices and toss them lightly with some of the reserved vinaigrette.

Put the baking pan with the radicchio back in the oven and bake just until the cheese melts, about 4 to 5 minutes.

Arrange a warm radicchio quarter on each of 4 salad plates. Place a few pear slices around the radicchio, sprinkle the remaining bread crumbs over, and drizzle about 1 tablespoon of the vinaigrette over the radicchio and pears. Serve immediately.

Celery Root Slaw

Serves 6 to 8

THIS quick, refreshing take on classic American coleslaw isn't just for a nostalgic summer picnic, although it is great when you fire up the backyard grill for the hot links. We serve Celery Root Slaw with Shrimp and Crab Cakes (see page 46), Soft-shell Crabs with Beer Batter (see page 148), and grilled sausages.

1½ pounds celery root, after peeling and
  trimming, all dark spots cut away
Kosher salt
½ head (8 ounces) radicchio
1 medium red bell pepper (8 ounces), seeded
  and cut into julienne
½ cup celery leaves
2 celery stalks, trimmed, peeled, and cut into
  very thin slices
¼ pound sugar snap peas, trimmed and cut into
  very thin slices
¾ cup Roasted Garlic Tartar Sauce
  (see page 208)
Juice of ½ medium lemon
Kosher salt
Freshly cracked black pepper

Have ready
The Roasted Garlic Tartar Sauce

WITH a mandolin or a thin, sharp knife, cut the celery root into ⅛-inch-thin slices and then using a sharp 8-inch chef's knife into ⅛-inch julienne. Transfer to a colander. Place the colander in a large mixing bowl and sprinkle the celery root with 3 tablespoons of kosher salt. Toss and allow to wilt, about 15 minutes. About ½ cup of water from the celery root should collect in the mixing bowl. Using the colander, rinse the celery root well under cold running water. Drain the celery root, and dry it thoroughly in a clean kitchen towel. Return the celery root to a clean large mixing bowl.

Cut the radicchio in half vertically, remove the core, and cut the leaves into thin strips. Add the radicchio to the celery root mixture. Add the red bell pepper, celery leaves, sliced celery, and snap peas and toss gently but thoroughly to combine. Refrigerate, covered, until needed.

Just before serving, add the Roasted Garlic Tartar Sauce and the lemon juice and toss again. Correct the seasoning to taste with kosher salt and black pepper, if necessary.

Chicken Salad with Belgian Endive, Apples, and Walnuts

Serves 6 to 8

IN this distant cousin of Waldorf salad, the sweet apple works as a flavor contrast to the tartness of the mustard vinaigrette. The toasted walnuts have a tannic flavor that is complimented by the mildly bitter undertones of the Belgian endive. The recipe can be easily increased as desired for picnics or summer evening potlucks with the neighborhood watch committee.

1¼ cups walnut halves
1 medium red onion, peeled and cut into
    ¼-inch dice (1½ cups)
3 cups cooked, shredded chicken, chilled
    (3½-pound chicken)
2 celery stalks, peeled and thinly sliced
    diagonally (1 cup)
6 heads Belgian endive, thinly sliced (3 cups)
2 small Golden Delicious or Fuji apples
Kosher salt
Freshly cracked black pepper
1¼ cups Mustard Vinaigrette (see page 225)
½ cup chopped Italian parsley

Have ready

The Mustard Vinaigrette

PREHEAT the oven to 325 degrees.

Place the walnut halves on a baking pan and toast in the oven about 8 to 10 minutes, stirring with a spatula halfway through. Take care not to brown the walnuts, as it will produce a bitter flavor. Remove the baking pan from the oven, remove the walnuts from the baking pan, and allow them to cool.

Put the diced onion in a strainer and rinse with cold water. Allow to drain; transfer it to a large mixing bowl.

Add the shredded chicken, sliced celery, and Belgian endive to the diced onion. Coarsely chop the toasted walnuts and add them to the mixing bowl. Peel and quarter the apples. Remove the cores and cut each quarter into 3 chunks. Thinly slice each of the 24 apple pieces, add them to the mixing bowl, and toss briefly to combine. Add about 1 teaspoon of kosher salt and ½ teaspoon of black pepper, and mix well.

To serve, add the Mustard Vinaigrette and the chopped parsley, and mix gently but thoroughly. Correct the seasoning to taste with kosher salt and black pepper.

Chopped Salad

Serves 4

Nancy woke up one morning with a fixation on chopped salad. Not just some health-food-store-leftovers sort of chopped salad, but an authentic La Scala old Hollywood–style chopped salad. Through a little local research, Nancy found that old Hollywood is mostly a memory, certainly in terms of chopped salad.

We set out to polish the faded luster, just a little, and went to work on our own chopped salad. We tried variation after variation to find the right balance. There can't be one dominant flavor; the salad has to be a smooth blending of all the ingredients, and it has to go just right with a dry martini. There are no large, unwieldy pieces in a chopped salad, which might impede languid conversation and delightful repartee. Chopped salad, when done right, is a delicious combination, a sum greater than its parts. When done wrong it resembles a compost heap.

Vinaigrette

¼ cup red wine vinegar
Juice of 1 medium lemon (¼ cup)
2 teaspoons kosher salt
1 teaspoon freshly cracked black pepper
1 teaspoon dried oregano
1 large garlic clove, peeled and minced
    (1 teaspoon)
¾ cup extra-virgin olive oil

Salad

¼ head iceberg lettuce, chopped in ½-inch
    pieces (2 cups)
1 medium tomato, cored, seeded, and cut into
    ¼-inch dice
4 ounces Italian provolone cheese, cut into
    ⅛-inch julienne (¾ cup)
4 ounces salami, cut into ⅛-inch julienne
    (¾ cup)
4 ounces dried garbanzo beans, cooked and
    chilled (1 cup after cooking) (for cooking
    instructions, see Marinated Bean Salad,
    page 65)
¼ red onion, minced (½ cup)
1 bunch fresh basil, cut into julienne (½ cup)
Kosher salt
Freshly cracked black pepper
Fresh lemon juice
About 20 Niçoise olives

To prepare the vinaigrette: In a medium mixing bowl, whisk together the vinegar, lemon juice, kosher salt, black pepper, oregano, and garlic. Whisk in the olive oil until well blended, and reserve.

To prepare the salad: In a large mixing bowl, combine the chopped lettuce, chopped tomato, provolone cheese, salami, garbanzo beans, and the minced onion.

Pour enough of the vinaigrette over the salad to moisten it moderately and mix gently, but thoroughly, adding vinaigrette as necessary to ensure that the whole salad is moist, but not drenched or dripping. The vinaigrette should not run off the salad or pool on the plate; there should be just enough to coat, but not overwhelm, each little chopped ingredient. Correct the seasoning to taste with kosher salt, black pepper, and fresh lemon juice.

To serve, divide the salad equally among 4 large salad plates. Sprinkle the julienne of basil on top and scatter the olives around the perimeter of each plate.

Couscous Salad

Serves 4

COUSCOUS is a northern African dish, but it works well with many other Mediterranean flavors. This couscous dish is perfect as part of an antipasto platter or all by itself as a hearty luncheon salad.

There are a number of different brands of ricotta salata cheese available. Some of them are overly salty; select one that is not by asking for samples at your cheese store.

Lemon Vinaigrette

Juice of 1 medium lemon (¼ cup)
1 teaspoon champagne vinegar
1 large shallot, peeled, trimmed, and minced (1 tablespoon)
2 teaspoons kosher salt
⅓ cup olive or vegetable oil
2 tablespoons chopped fresh mint

Salad

1 cup dry couscous
2 tablespoons olive or vegetable oil
1 medium carrot, peeled and diced (¼ cup)
1 medium parsnip, peeled and diced (¼ cup)
2 scallions, trimmed and cut on the diagonal into thin slices
½ head radicchio
2 ounces diced ricotta salata cheese (¼ cup)
½ bunch fresh Italian parsley, leaves only, chopped fine (½ cup)
Kosher salt
Freshly cracked black pepper
12 small, perfect mint leaves for garnish

To prepare the vinaigrette: In a small mixing bowl, whisk together the lemon juice, vinegar, shallot, and kosher salt. Slowly whisk in the oil and then the chopped mint leaves.

To prepare the salad: In a medium

saucepan, over high heat, bring approximately 1 cup of water to a boil. Put the couscous into a large mixing bowl and pour ½ cup of boiling water over it and then fluff with a fork. Add the other ½ cup, then fluff with a fork again. Cover tightly with plastic wrap and refrigerate to stop the cooking process.

In a small sauté pan, over medium-high heat, preheat 1 tablespoon of oil. Sauté the carrot and parsnip until lightly browned, about 10 minutes. Remove from the heat, allow to cool, and then toss gently with the couscous. Add the sliced scallions.

Cut the half radicchio head into two pieces, vertically. Brush the flat sides lightly with oil. In a large sauté pan, over medium-high heat, preheat another tablespoon of oil. When the oil is almost smoking, put the radicchio quarters in the pan flat side down, and sear until the edges begin to brown, about 5 minutes. Turn the radicchio over and sear the other side until browned, about 5 minutes. Remove the radicchio from the heat and allow to cool, about 10 minutes. Remove and discard the core of the radicchio quarters, then julienne the leaves and add to the couscous. Add the ricotta salata and the parsley, and gently toss to combine.

Pour the vinaigrette over the couscous and toss gently but thoroughly. Correct the seasoning to taste with kosher salt and black pepper.

Divide the salad equally among 4 large salad plates, add the whole mint leaves to the top of each salad, and serve immediately.

Grilled Eggplant Salad

Serves 2 to 3

THIS summery outdoor salad should be served at room temperature or, if you're serving it with leftover lamb, just lightly warmed. This dish will benefit from spending the night well covered in the refrigerator, because the garlic will exude a little more flavor, the olive oil will infuse the eggplant with extra richness, and the seasonings will mingle throughout the salad, adding full flavor and sharp accents.

6 Japanese eggplants (¾ pound)
½ cup extra-virgin olive oil
Kosher salt
Freshly cracked black pepper
2 large garlic cloves, peeled and minced
   (2 teaspoons)
1½ cups Onion Compote (see page 242)
2 tablespoons fresh lemon juice
Large pinch cayenne pepper
2 bunches (½ cup, about 20) small fresh basil
   leaves

Have ready

The Onion Compote

START a fire in the grill and allow it to burn to medium temperature.

Cut the eggplants in half lengthwise. Brush each side lightly with a little olive oil and season lightly with kosher salt and black pepper. Grill the eggplants, cut side down, to brown and show grill marks, about 10 minutes. Turn the eggplant halves over and continue to grill until tender, 6 to 8 minutes longer. Remove the eggplants from the heat and allow them to cool to room temperature.

When the pieces of eggplant are cool, trim the ends of each piece and cut each in half, down the center, to make quarter sections. Then cut them in half again, crosswise on the diagonal. Transfer the eggplant pieces to a large mixing bowl and add the garlic, the remaining olive oil, ¼ teaspoon of kosher salt, ⅛ teaspoon of black pepper, the Onion Compote, lemon juice, and the cayenne pepper. Toss gently to combine, and marinate at least 15 minutes. At this point the salad can be refrigerated, well covered, up to 1 day. When ready to serve, add the basil, toss again, and correct the seasoning to taste with kosher salt and black pepper.

Greek Salad

Serves 4 to 6

The heart of this salad is the tomatoes. It is not worth making if the tomatoes aren't at their peak. Flavorless, pink, winter tomatoes are not up to the challenge of the tart and salty feta cheese. When Nancy was 20 years old she spent a summer in Athens, living on little but Greek salad and tepid Coca-Cola. Of the two, the salad left a better impression. She has long wanted to re-create the memory of the flavors of a Greek salad.

Here we use hothouse cucumbers because they are larger and juicier than Japanese cucumbers, but either will do fine. If you can only get regular cucumbers, they should be peeled and seeded.

For lunch this could be served by itself; at dinner it could precede a simple grilled fish course. It will serve three as a luncheon entrée, or four to six as an appetizer.

Cucumber Marinade

1 large hothouse cucumber (1 pound)
½ medium red onion (4 ounces), trimmed
¼ cup extra-virgin olive oil
¾ teaspoon dried Greek oregano
Kosher salt
Freshly cracked black pepper

Tomato Marinade

1 large red tomato (1 pound)
1 large yellow tomato (1 pound)
¼ cup extra-virgin olive oil
2 bunches fresh basil leaves (½ cup)
¼ cup fresh Italian parsley leaves
1 large garlic clove, peeled and minced
    (1 teaspoon)
Kosher salt
Freshly cracked black pepper

Salad

½ pound feta cheese (Bulgarian, if possible)
2 tablespoons extra-virgin olive oil
Freshly cracked black pepper
16 to 20 whole Niçoise olives
1 cup Garlic Croutons (see page 226)
Dried Greek oregano

Have ready

The Garlic Croutons

To prepare the cucumber marinade: Trim the cucumber and cut into quarters lengthwise. Slice the quarters thinly, and transfer to a large mixing bowl. Slice the onion thinly, and add it to the bowl. Add the olive oil, oregano, ½ teaspoon kosher salt, and ¼ teaspoon black pepper. Toss to combine and marinate about 15 minutes.

To prepare the tomato marinade: Core the tomatoes, then cut them into 4 to 6 wedges. Transfer the tomatoes to a medium mixing bowl and add the olive oil, basil, parsley, garlic, 1 teaspoon kosher salt, and ¼ teaspoon black pepper. Toss to combine and marinate about 15 minutes.

To prepare the salad: Break up the feta cheese into bite-size pieces and put it in a small mixing bowl. Add the olive oil and ½ teaspoon black pepper, and toss lightly just to coat the cheese with the oil.

The ingredients can marinate for up to 1 hour before being combined. The cucumber will have exuded a lot of moisture in the marinade. It should be strained and the liquid discarded before adding it to the other ingredients. When ready to serve, divide the tomatoes with the marinade equally among the plates. Top with the cucumbers and onion. Then finish by scattering the feta, olives, and croutons with a little crumbled oregano over the top. Serve immediately.

Grilled Porcini Mushrooms with Parsley and Tomato Salad

Serves 4

FRESH porcinis are available in the fall, September through November, and good tomatoes can still be found at that time as well. We roast the mushrooms in the oven before grilling them because it reduces the chance of burning on the grill, and it softens them to make it easier to skewer them without breaking them.

Soak the wooden skewers in water for 30 minutes before skewering the mushrooms to prevent the skewers from burning on the grill. The mushrooms can be readied in advance and left to marinate until just before grilling.

Mushroom Marinade

1 pound fresh porcini mushrooms
¼ cup extra-virgin olive oil
1 teaspoon chopped fresh mint
1 teaspoon chopped fresh thyme
1 large garlic clove, peeled and minced
    (1 teaspoon)
Freshly cracked black pepper

Salad

½ pound fresh Italian parsley
2 medium tomatoes
Kosher salt
3 tablespoons extra-virgin olive oil, plus
    additional as needed
1 tablespoon fresh lemon juice

4-ounce piece Parmesan Reggiano cheese
Freshly cracked black pepper

To prepare the mushroom marinade: Gently wipe the mushrooms with a damp kitchen towel to clean them. Slice off the dried end of the stem, and then slice the mushrooms in half vertically. Place the mushrooms in a medium mixing bowl, drizzle with the ¼ cup of olive oil, and season with the herbs, garlic, and 1 teaspoon black pepper. Toss gently to combine. Marinate for 1 hour.

Preheat the oven to 350 degrees.

Distribute the mushrooms in a single layer on a baking sheet, and roast in the oven for 15 minutes. Remove the mushrooms and allow them to cool. Using 10-inch wooden skewers, skewer 4 or 5 mushroom halves through the stem, cut side down, on each skewer. If this is done early in the day, refrigerate the mushrooms, covered, until needed.

Start a fire in the grill and allow it to burn to medium temperature.

To prepare the salad: Wash the parsley and dry it thoroughly in a kitchen towel. Remove and discard the stems from the parsley. Cut the tomatoes in half and remove the core, pulp, and seeds of the tomatoes, leaving the outer flesh and skin. Using a sharp knife, cut the tomatoes into thick julienne. Combine the parsley and tomatoes in a small mixing bowl, and reserve.

Season the mushrooms with kosher salt and black pepper. Grill until tender, about 5 to 7 minutes, turning with stainless-steel tongs after 4 minutes. Take care not to char the mushrooms.

Remove the mushrooms from the skewers and add them to the parsley and tomatoes. Dress with 3 tablespoons of extra-virgin olive oil and 1 tablespoon of fresh lemon juice, season to taste with kosher salt and black pepper, and toss gently but thoroughly. Divide the salad into equal portions and pile in the center of 4 large salad plates. Drizzle each salad lightly with a little more extra-virgin olive oil, and using a vegetable peeler, shave 4 or 5 thin pieces of Parmesan cheese over the top of each salad. Serve immediately.

Marinated Bean Salad

Serves 8

THIS is that American summer classic, three-bean salad from the days of drive-in movies and chicken à la king, pulled into the present with a modest makeover. We use all sorts of dried beans—scarlet runners, appaloosas, borlotti, Christmas limas, and so on. The different sizes, shapes, and colors make this salad very eye catching, with all sorts of little bursts of color.

At Campanile we make this in large quantities, so for more variety, we combine five or six different kinds of beans. However, for a small salad, using just three kinds of beans will keep things simple. Many of these beans can be found at various ethnic markets, but others— the unusual and beautiful ones—can be ordered by mail.

¾ pound assorted dry beans (Christmas limas, cannellini, scarlet runners, black runners, appaloosas, borlotti)
Kosher salt
1 head radicchio (½ pound)
3 tablespoons vegetable oil
6 scallions, trimmed
3 medium shallots, peeled, trimmed, and minced (3 tablespoons)
¼ cup extra-virgin olive oil
3 tablespoons balsamic vinegar
Freshly cracked black pepper
1 cup mizuna, arugula, or Italian parsley sprigs

PUT each variety of bean in a separate medium saucepan, cover with water, and add 1 teaspoon of kosher salt to each saucepan. Over medium heat, bring each to a gentle simmer. Reduce the heat to low and cook until the beans are tender, about 45 minutes to 1½ hours. The beans should still hold their shape, retain their skins, and be completely cooked without being mushy. Allow the beans to cool in the cooking liquid. When the beans are cool, drain and rinse them. Allow the rinse water to drain for about 10 minutes, then transfer them all to a large mixing bowl.

Cut the radicchio head in quarters vertically. Brush the flat sides lightly with vegetable oil. In a large sauté pan, over medium-high heat, preheat 1 additional tablespoon of vegetable oil. When the oil is almost smoking, put the radicchio quarters in the pan, flat side down, and sear until the edges begin to brown, about 5 minutes. Turn the radicchio over and sear the other side until browned, about 5 minutes. Remove the radicchio from the heat and allow to cool, about 10 minutes. Cut the radicchio quarters into julienne and add to the beans.

Cut the scallions on the bias into very thin slices. Add the scallions and the minced shallots to the mixing bowl. Add the olive oil and the vinegar and toss gently, but thoroughly, to combine. Season to taste with kosher salt and black pepper. Refrigerate for 1 hour and add a little more olive oil if necessary.

To serve, mound the beans in a large salad bowl or on a platter and surround with the greens or parsley sprigs.

Fennel, Pear, and Arugula Salad

Serves 4

THIS salad is particularly good in the fall, when the fennel, arugula, and pears are all at their peak. The mild licorice flavor of fennel and the peppery sharpness of the arugula complement the sweetness of the pear. The walnuts add a tannic counterpoint to the pear and complete the impression of fall.

½ cup whole walnut halves, shelled
1 fennel bulb, trimmed (¾ pound),
    ¼ cup fronds reserved whole
1 bosc pear, unpeeled
2 cups arugula leaves, whole
2 tablespoons chopped fennel fronds
Lemon Oil Vinaigrette (see page 220)
Kosher salt
Freshly cracked black pepper

PREHEAT the oven to 325 degrees.

Spread the walnut halves on a baking pan and toast in the oven about 8 to 10 minutes, stirring with a spatula halfway through. Take care not to brown the walnuts, as it will produce a bitter flavor. Remove the walnuts from the oven and set aside.

Cut the fennel bulb in half, through the core, and then into very thin slices, using a thin, sharp knife or a mandolin. Reserve ¼ cup of the most tender, pale green fronds. Transfer the slices to a large mixing bowl.

Cut the pear in half vertically and remove the core, seeds, and stem. Cut the pear halves into long, thin slices. Add the pear slices and the arugula to the fennel in the large mixing bowl.

Add ¼ cup of the Lemon Oil Vinaigrette to the salad and toss gently but thoroughly. Taste, and add more vinaigrette, if necessary. Correct the seasoning to taste with kosher salt and black pepper. Add the toasted walnut halves and the chopped fennel fronds, and toss gently but thoroughly.

Divide the salad equally among 4 large salad plates, top with the reserved whole fennel fronds, and serve immediately.

Haricots Verts Salad with Prosciutto, Walnuts, and Mustard Vinaigrette

Serves 4

LITTLE green beans are so very French, especially mixed with walnuts and a Dijon vinaigrette. The prosciutto could be replaced with *jambon de pays* for a truly authentic French experience. This would be a perfect salad to lead into a dinner of roasted chicken, or it could be ideal for lunch with a lightly chilled rosé.

"LITTLE GREEN BEANS ARE SO VERY FRENCH."

1 pound haricots verts
1 cup walnut halves
3 large shallots, peeled, trimmed, and thinly
    sliced (3 tablespoons)
½ cup Mustard Vinaigrette (see page 225)
Kosher salt
Freshly cracked black pepper
8 to 12 very thin slices prosciutto (4 ounces)

Have ready

The Mustard Vinaigrette

PREHEAT the oven to 350 degrees.

Trim the haricots verts at the stem end
only, retaining the finely pointed tips. In a large
stockpot, bring approximately 4 quarts of water
to a boil and add 2 tablespoons of kosher salt.
Fill a large mixing bowl with ice water.

Blanch the trimmed haricots verts in a fine-
mesh, stainless-steel strainer in the boiling
water for 8 to 10 minutes. They should be
cooked through, but still firm. Remove the
strainer of blanched haricots verts from the
stockpot and plunge it into the ice water for
about 2 minutes; allow it to drain, and pat the
beans dry with a clean kitchen towel.

Spread the walnut halves on a baking pan
and toast in the oven about 5 minutes, stirring
with a spatula halfway through. Take care not to
brown the walnuts, as it will produce a bitter
flavor. Remove the walnuts from the oven and
set aside.

Combine the cooked green beans, toasted
walnuts, and the sliced shallots in a large mixing
bowl. Add the Mustard Vinaigrette and toss
gently but thoroughly. Correct the seasoning to
taste with kosher salt and black pepper.

Divide the salad equally among 4 large
salad plates. Arrange 2 or 3 slices of prosciutto
around the beans and serve immediately.

Roasted Beet Salad with Horseradish Vinaigrette

Serves 6

I never liked beets until we made this salad; it was something about the color that put me off. In this recipe, the beets are roasted to bring out a sweet, earthy, and concentrated flavor. It was the flavor that overcame my resistance to beets. We serve this when the horseradish and beets are in their prime, as part of an antipasto platter, or as a fall salad all by itself. This salad is a perfect first course before a roasted meat dinner.

Sometimes fresh horseradish root from the supermarket is not strong enough in flavor. If that is the case, add a little of the bottled horseradish to fortify the vinaigrette. If horseradish root is not available, increase the amount of bottled horseradish by ¼ cup. Try to find a good bottled horseradish, one made with only horseradish and vinegar. Regardless of the type of horseradish used, the greens should have real presence of flavor, to complement the strong horseradish.

Salad

2 pounds (2 bunches) red beets
1 teaspoon kosher salt
⅛ teaspoon freshly cracked black pepper
5 sprigs fresh thyme, whole leaves only
    (2 teaspoons)
¼ cup extra-virgin olive oil
½ large red onion (6 ounces), cut into very thin
    slices
¼ cup chopped fresh Italian parsley
½ cup arugula leaves, watercress, or other
    greens, for garnish

Horseradish Vinaigrette

About 6 ounces horseradish root
½ cup vegetable oil
¼ cup apple cider vinegar
3 tablespoons chopped fresh Italian parsley
½ teaspoon freshly cracked black pepper
2 to 4 tablespoons prepared white horseradish
    (optional)

PREHEAT the oven to 400 degrees.

To make the salad: Wash the beets and trim the ends. Place the beets in a large mixing bowl and toss with kosher salt, black pepper, thyme, and extra-virgin olive oil, coating all the beets well. Place the beets on a large baking pan in 1 layer, cover the pan with aluminum foil, and roast for about 1 hour. Uncover and roast about 10 minutes longer, or until the beets are tender. Remove them from the oven and allow to cool to room temperature. When the beets are cool, the skins will slip off easily by hand. After you have done this, cut them into 4 to 6 wedges and transfer to a large mixing bowl.

To make the vinaigrette: While the beets are roasting, wash the horseradish. Using a vegetable peeler, peel the horseradish. Remove any discolored portions, and then, using a grater, shred the horseradish to yield about ½ cup. In a medium mixing bowl, combine the fresh horseradish, vegetable oil, vinegar, parsley, and black pepper, adding prepared horseradish to taste if desired. Mix the vinaigrette well and reserve.

Toss the vinaigrette, red onion, and the beets, and correct the seasoning to taste with kosher salt and black pepper.

Mound the beets in the center of a large platter. Sprinkle them with the chopped parsley and surround them with the leaves of arugula, or greens of your choice, and serve immediately.

Roasted Chanterelle Salad

CHANTERELLES pop up after the spring rains along the Pacific Coast, so April, May, and June are the best times to prepare this salad. Chanterelles are more substantial and meaty in texture than shiitake mushrooms, but more delicate in flavor. If walnut bread is not available, use another dense, whole-grain, hearth-baked bread.

Balsamic-Lemon Vinaigrette

¼ cup plus 1 tablespoon vegetable oil
1 tablespoon plus 1 teaspoon balsamic vinegar
2 shallots, peeled, trimmed, and minced
    (2 tablespoons)
Juice of 1 medium lemon
Kosher salt
Freshly cracked black pepper

Salad

8 ounces chanterelle mushrooms, wiped clean
    and torn into halves or quarters
Kosher salt
Freshly cracked black pepper
3 tablespoons vegetable oil, plus additional for
    frying parsnips
2 thick slices walnut bread, crusts removed
    (4 ounces)
1 medium parsnip
1 bunch fresh Italian parsley leaves (1½ cups)
2 ounces (2 cups) frisée
1 teaspoon truffle oil (optional)

To prepare the vinaigrette: In a small mixing bowl, whisk together the vegetable oil, balsamic vinegar, minced shallots, and lemon juice. Adjust the seasoning to taste with kosher salt and black pepper. Reserve at room temperature for as long as 1 hour, and whisk just before using.

To prepare the salad: Preheat the oven to 375 degrees.

Put the mushrooms pieces on a baking pan, season lightly with kosher salt and black pepper, and spoon 2 tablespoons of vegetable oil over, tossing to combine. Roast in the oven until evenly browned, stirring often, about 15 to 20 minutes. The mushrooms should be crisp and well colored, but not burned.

Tear the bread into small pieces (they do not have to be of a uniform size). Spoon 1 tablespoon of vegetable oil over the pieces, season lightly with kosher salt and black pepper, and toss to combine. Toast in the oven until crisp, about 10 minutes.

Fill a medium mixing bowl with cold water. Using a vegetable peeler, remove (and discard) the skin of the parsnip. Then peel off long strips. Try to get 12 to 16 strips. Keep the peeled strips in the medium mixing bowl of cold water to prevent them from turning brown. Dry the strips of parsnip with a clean kichen towel.

In a large sauté pan, over medium-high heat, preheat until almost smoking enough vegetable oil to cover the bottom of the pan to a depth of ⅜ of an inch. Put the strips of parsnip a few at a time into the preheated oil and fry until very lightly brown and crisp, about ½ minute. Using a slotted spoon, remove the parsnip strips and drain on absorbent paper. Season the crisped parsnips with kosher salt.

In a large bowl, toss the toasted bread in the vinaigrette. Add the roasted mushrooms, parsley leaves, and frisée and toss to combine thoroughly. Season with kosher salt and black pepper to taste. If desired, finish with a little truffle oil. Divide the salad among 4 large plates, garnish the top of each portion with some crisped parsnip, and serve immediately.

Grilled Rare Tuna Salad

Serves 4 to 6

THIS antipasto salad, frequently served at the restaurant with crostini, is also a wonderful main-course lunch. Deep red, sashimi-grade tuna, as fresh as possible, is the only tuna that should be used for this salad. The tuna salad can be prepared up to several hours in advance, omitting the vinaigrette, and refrigerated, covered, until needed.

Marinated tuna

¼ cup extra-virgin olive oil
1 teaspoon chopped fresh thyme
½ teaspoon freshly cracked black pepper
1 pound very fresh, sashimi-grade,
    blue or yellow fin center-cut tuna steak,
    1 to 2 inches thick

Vinaigrette

⅓ cup extra-virgin olive oil
2 tablespoon white wine vinegar
1 tablespoon fresh lemon juice

Salad

1 medium ripe tomato, cored, cut in half,
    seeded, and cut into ¼-inch dice
⅔ cup cooked cannellini or navy beans
    (see Marinated Bean Salad, page 65)
    (4 ounces), cooled and rinsed
1 small red bell pepper, cored, seeded, and cut
    into ¼-inch dice
1 small yellow bell pepper, cored, seeded, and
    cut into ¼-inch dice
¼ cup thinly sliced, oil-cured olives
    (1½ ounces)
12 large fresh basil leaves, cut into julienne
6 scallions, trimmed and thinly sliced
Kosher salt
Freshly cracked black pepper
2 heads chicory or 2 cups baby greens, washed
    and well dried
2 tablespoons chopped fresh chives (1 bunch)

To prepare the marinated tuna: In a medium mixing bowl, combine the extra-virgin olive oil, thyme, and black pepper and mix well. Add the tuna, turning to coat all sides, and marinate at least 30 minutes, refrigerated.

    To prepare the vinaigrette: In a small mixing bowl, whisk together the extra-virgin olive oil, white wine vinegar, and fresh lemon juice. Reserve.

To prepare the salad: Start a fire in the grill, and allow it to burn to high temperature; or, in a cast-iron skillet, over high heat, preheat 1 tablespoon of vegetable oil. Using a paper towel, pat dry the marinated tuna. Grill or sear the tuna 1 minute (rare) to 2 minutes (medium rare) on each side, taking great care not to over-cook the tuna. It should be deep red on the inside. Remove the tuna from the heat, allow it to cool, and refrigerate it, covered, until thoroughly cold, about 1 hour.

Using a very sharp knife, cut the tuna into ½-inch dice and transfer it to a large mixing bowl. Add the diced tomato, beans, diced red and yellow peppers, olives, basil, scallions, ¼ teaspoon kosher salt, and ½ teaspoon black pepper, and gently toss to combine.

Pour half the vinaigrette over the salad and again gently toss to combine. Adjust the season-ing to taste with kosher salt and black pepper.

Remove and discard the tough green outer leaves of the chicory, reserving only the tender, pale yellow hearts. Wash the hearts of chicory and dry them thoroughly with a clean kitchen towel. Using a sharp knife, slice the chicory hearts in 1-inch pieces, discarding the core.

Toss the sliced chicory hearts with some of the remaining vinaigrette, just to coat, and arrange on salad plates. Divide the tuna salad evenly and mound it in the center of each por-tion of chicory, with a hint of the greens show-ing around the edges. Garnish with a sprinkle of chopped chives, and serve immediately.

Roasted Shiitake Mushroom, Mizuna, and Italian Parsley Salad

Serves 4

MIZUNA is a subtle and softly flavored green with a very crunchy texture. It resembles a dandelion leaf. Italian parsley has a strong, clear flavor that doesn't waver; it's always consistent and focused. The roasted shiitake mushrooms add concentrated earthy flavor and a satisfying chewy texture. This makes a wonderful first course, or it can accompany a main course as a side dish.

8 ounces fresh shiitake mushrooms, stems removed, and quartered (2 cups)
¼ cup extra-virgin olive oil
1 teaspoon chopped fresh rosemary
2 large shallots, peeled, trimmed, and thinly sliced (2 tablespoons)
2 bunches Italian parsley leaves (1½ cups)
1½ cups mizuna leaves
Kosher salt
Freshly cracked black pepper
1 tablespoon fresh lemon juice

PREHEAT the oven to 400 degrees.

In a large mixing bowl, toss the quartered mushrooms with 2 tablespoons of the olive oil and the chopped rosemary. Spread the mushrooms out evenly in a medium roasting pan and roast for 15 to 20 minutes, until the gills are lightly browned but still firm. Stir the shiitake mushrooms about every 10 minutes to ensure that they do not burn. Remove the mushrooms from the oven, allow them to cool, and reserve.

Rinse the sliced shallots in a medium mixing bowl filled with water. Drain the shallots and dry them thoroughly in a kitchen towel.

In a large mixing bowl, combine the roasted shiitakes, the shallots, parsley, mizuna, the remaining 2 tablespoons of olive oil, 1 teaspoon of kosher salt, ½ teaspoon of black pepper, and the lemon juice. Toss gently but thoroughly. Correct the seasoning to taste with kosher salt, black pepper, and fresh lemon juice. Divide equally among 4 salad plates and serve immediately.

Soups

Chapter 5

Exceptional soup is rarely based on anything other than excellent stock. In making soup, starting with canned broth is faulty economy, as every additional ingredient will be constrained by the quality of the stock to achieve less than its natural potential. The Campanile Chicken Stock recipe is, with the addition of some noodles and a few greens, a definitive simple broth soup: clear, clean of flavor, warming, and savory. The reduced essence of its ingredients is invigorating and inspiring in a pure and uncomplicated fashion.

If you make chicken stock on a Sunday afternoon and turn most of that into two or three quarts of simple soup, it can eliminate the need for hours of cooking time over the course of the next three or four days. If a quart of stock is left over, the skeletal structure for an entire week's worth of meals is in place.

While the preparation time required for superior soup is long, the actual amount of work is modest. The bulk of the time involved in making soup is invested in the making of the stock. Once the stock is made, the soup should come together quickly—especially if you use your leftovers wisely. Additionally, soup, like stock, freezes well and thus can be made in large quantities. A pot of soup with some good bread and a salad is a delicious meal for a relatively small amount of money. Taking into account its versatility, soup can be perceived as very good eating that is compatible with a brisk pace in life.

Eloy Mondez's Albondigas Soup

Serves up to 10

Eloy Mondez works in the kitchen at Campanile and often cooks this albondigas soup for the staff meal. It is a hearty soup of meatballs and spicy tomatillo broth. The jalapeños don't make it hot, but it is strongly flavored with garlic and fresh cilantro. The soup was so popular with the staff that it ended up on the menu when we opened for lunch.

Soup

2 pounds fresh tomatillos, husks removed
1 medium onion (8 ounces), peeled and
    coarsely chopped
7 large garlic cloves, peeled
2 small jalapeño peppers, split and seeded
½ teaspoon freshly ground cumin
1 tablespoon kosher salt
1 teaspoon freshly cracked black pepper
5 cups Chicken Stock (see page 187)
25 sprigs fresh cilantro

Meatballs (Albondigas)

1 pound coarsely ground beef chuck
1 pound coarsely ground pork
1 medium onion (8 ounces), peeled and finely
    chopped
½ cup cooked white rice
3 extra-large eggs, 1 raw, 2 hard-boiled
2 teaspoons kosher salt
¼ teaspoon ground cumin
¼ teaspoon ground cloves

Garnish

Juice of 2 limes (¼ cup)

Have ready

The Chicken Stock, warm, in a medium
    saucepan over low heat
The cooked rice
The hard-boiled eggs

To prepare the soup: In a large stockpot, over medium-high heat, combine the tomatillos, onion, garlic, jalapeño peppers, cumin, salt, cracked pepper, and the Chicken Stock, and bring to a boil. Reduce the heat and simmer, skimming off any foam that rises to the top, until the tomatillos are tender, about 10 to 15 minutes. Using a colander, strain the vegetables from the broth, reserving both the vegetables and the broth. Puree the tomatillos, onion, garlic, and jalapeño peppers in a blender or food processor fitted with a steel blade, adding ½ cup of broth and about 15 sprigs of cilantro. (This can be done in two or three batches.) Return the pureed vegetables and the remaining soup broth to the stockpot and bring to a simmer.

To make the meatballs: While the soup broth is simmering, in a large mixing bowl, combine the ground meat with the chopped onion, cooked rice, the raw egg, 2 teaspoons kosher salt, ground cumin, and ground cloves and mix gently but thoroughly. Overmixing causes the meatballs to become tough and dense.

Coarsely chop the hard-boiled eggs and set aside. Using a small piece of chopped egg as the center, form the meat into 1-inch meatballs, rolling the meat around the small piece of egg. Keep your hands lightly moistened with cold water to prevent the ground meat from sticking. The mixture should yield about 40 walnut-sized, 1-ounce meatballs. Place the meatballs in the soup and continue to simmer, about 30 minutes longer. Correct the seasoning to taste with kosher salt and black pepper.

Remove the leaves from the remaining 10 sprigs of cilantro, discarding the stems. Place 4 meatballs in each large, warm soup bowl. Ladle about ¾ cup of soup over the meatballs, and squeeze a few drops of fresh lime juice into each bowl. Sprinkle with a few whole cilantro leaves and serve immediately.

Farro and Mushroom Soup

THIS is a wonderful, earthy soup for colder days. Also known as spelt, farro is one of the earliest domesticated strains of wheat. It tastes similar to barley, and in this soup it adds a wholesome, toothy quality. This is delicious topped with Garlic Bread Crumbs (see page 226). To serve 10 to 12, the bread crumb recipe must be doubled.

If you can't find farro, pearl barley or wheat berries can be substituted, but these must be cooked at least 30 minutes longer. For a completely vegetarian soup, the ham hock or bacon can be eliminated and Vegetable Stock (page 196) substituted for Chicken Stock.

¾ pound fresh shiitake mushrooms
12 ounces fresh crimini mushrooms
Vegetable oil
1 medium carrot, peeled and cut into thick
    slices (¾ cup)
1 medium leek, trimmed, split, and cut into
    thick slices (1 cup)
1 medium celery stalk, peeled and cut into
    thick slices (½ cup)
5 large garlic cloves, peeled and minced
    (5 teaspoons)
½ cup dry sherry
1 small ham hock, or 4-ounce slab of bacon
12 cups Chicken Stock (see page 187)

Bouquet garni (1 sprig rosemary,
    1 sprig marjoram, 2 sprigs Italian parsley,
    and 1 bay leaf)
¼ cup dried porcini mushrooms
Kosher salt
Freshly cracked black pepper
½ cup farro
1 bunch fresh chives

Have ready

The Chicken Stock, warm, in a medium
    saucepan over low heat
The Garlic Bread Crumbs (optional)

WIPE the shiitakes clean with a damp towel. Remove and reserve the stems from the shiitakes. Cut each shiitake cap into thin slices and reserve. Quickly rinse the crimini mushrooms and dry them thoroughly. Remove and reserve the stems from the crimini mushrooms. Cut each crimini cap into quarters and reserve.

In a large stockpot, over medium heat, preheat 2 tablespoons of vegetable oil. Sweat the mushroom stems, carrot, leek, celery, and garlic until wilted and beginning to brown, about 10 minutes. Deglaze the pan with the sherry. Add the ham hock or bacon, Chicken Stock, and bouquet garni, and bring to a simmer. Continue to simmer, skimming as necessary to remove any foam that rises to the surface, until the stock has good color and a strong mushroom flavor, about 1 hour.

While the broth is simmering, in a small mixing bowl, combine the dried porcini mushrooms with ½ cup of warm water. Allow about 30 minutes for the mushrooms to reconstitute adequately.

In a large sauté pan, over medium-high heat, preheat 2 tablespoons of vegetable oil just to smoking. Sauté the sliced shiitake caps without stirring until almost charred, about 1 to 2 minutes. Continue to sauté, stirring to brown evenly, about 3 more minutes, adding a little more oil as necessary. As the shiitakes brown, season them lightly with kosher salt and black pepper. Remove the pan from the heat, remove the shiitake mushrooms, and reserve them in a small mixing bowl.

Remove the reconstituted porcini mushrooms from the soaking water, gently squeezing them to remove excess water. Reserve the soaking water. Wipe the sauté pan clean with a paper towel, reduce the heat to medium, and preheat 2 tablespoons vegetable oil. Sauté the quartered crimini caps and the reconstituted porcini mushrooms until lightly browned, about 3 to 4 minutes, seasoning with kosher salt and black pepper and adding more oil as necessary. Remove the pan from the heat, remove the crimini mushrooms, and reserve them in the small mixing bowl with the shiitakes.

After the soup has simmered for about 1 hour, using a fine-mesh, stainless-steel strainer, strain the soup, pressing the vegetables to remove as much liquid as possible. Remove and discard the vegetables. Pick out the ham hock, allow it to cool, and shred the meat, discarding the skin and bone. (If you're using bacon, chop it coarsely.) Return the broth and the ham or bacon to the large stockpot, and bring back to a simmer.

Add the farro to the stockpot. Add the porcini soaking water, taking care not to pour into the stockpot any of the grit from the porcinis that will have collected on the bottom of the bowl. (Dried porcini come with a fine sand that somehow goes through several layers of cheesecloth, but it's heavy, so it stays at the bottom of the bowl if you pour carefully.) Continue to simmer, over medium heat, until the farro is tender, about 15 minutes. Add the reserved sautéed shiitake and crimini mushrooms, and continue to simmer about 15 minutes.

Mince the chives as needed for garnish.

Spoon the soup into large, warm bowls. Top with Garlic Bread Crumbs, if desired, and chopped chives. Serve immediately.

Gazpacho

Serves 8 to 10

THE origins of this cold raw vegetable soup date back to medieval Spain. The original soup was made of chopped cucumbers, onions, and other vegetables. The chopped vegetables would be lightly salted, marinated with vinegar and olive oil, and allowed to exude their natural juices. Slices of bread would then be soaked in the vegetable broth, and the whole mixture then pureed. What we know as gazpacho now is made the same way, but the ingredients are slightly different. Few recipes include the bread, and the tomato is now the most prominent ingredient. This means gazpacho is perfect for summer, when the tomatoes and most of the other ingredients are at their peak.

2 Japanese cucumbers (12 ounces), split and seeded
1 small fennel bulb (6 ounces), trimmed
1 medium red onion (6 ounces), peeled and trimmed
1 medium red bell pepper (6 ounces), cored and seeded
1 small green bell pepper (4 ounces), cored and seeded
1 large celery stalk, peeled
3 pounds ripe tomatoes, cored, seeded, and quartered
1 small jalapeño pepper, split, seeded, and diced
½ cup extra-virgin olive oil
1 bunch fresh basil leaves, 8 leaves reserved
¼ cup red wine vinegar
4 large garlic cloves, peeled and crushed in 1 teaspoon olive oil
Kosher salt
Freshly cracked black pepper
½ cup crème fraîche (optional)

CHOP the cucumbers, fennel, red onion, red bell pepper, green bell pepper, and celery into 2-inch pieces. Combine with the tomatoes, jalapeño, olive oil, basil, vinegar, garlic, 1 tablespoon kosher salt, and 1½ teaspoons black pepper in a large plastic or stainless-steel container. Cover the container with plastic wrap and refrigerate for between 12 and 24 hours, tossing once or twice, to ensure that all the vegetables are marinated thoroughly.

"GAZPACHO IS A GREAT VEGETARIAN DISH, BUT EVEN THE MOST DEDICATED CARNIVORE WILL DEVOUR IT."

Using a grinder with a ¼-inch die, grind the vegetables twice. The soup should have a well blended but chunky consistency. Mix the soup thoroughly in a large mixing bowl, and correct the seasoning to taste with kosher salt and black pepper. If you do not have a grinder, use a food processor fitted with a steel blade and pulse the machine until the vegetables are finely chopped but not pureed and completely smooth.

Julienne the reserved basil leaves, ladle the gazpacho into chilled soup bowls, and top each portion with a little julienne of fresh basil and, optionally, 1 tablespoon of crème fraîche. Serve immediately.

Roasted Parsnip Soup

Serves 8 to 10

IN this warming winter soup we use roasted parsnips, because the sweet, earthy flavor of the parsnips is wonderfully accentuated by the thorough browning. The garlic and onion benefit from a little deep-roasted color as well. This soup is fairly thick and hearty, so it leads perfectly into a lighter main course, such as fish.

Soup

2¾ pounds parsnips, peeled
1 large onion, peeled and cut into chunks
2 heads garlic, peeled and cut in half
    horizontally
2 stalks celery, cut into chunks
¼ cup vegetable oil
Kosher salt
Freshly cracked black pepper
2 teaspoons chopped fresh or 1 teaspoon dried
    thyme
11 cups Chicken Stock or Vegetable Stock
    (see page 187 or 196)
1 large russet potato, peeled and cut into 1-inch
    dice
Bouquet garni (3 sprigs each thyme and
    parsley)

Garnish

Extra-virgin olive oil
10 sprigs fresh chervil
Freshly cracked black pepper

Have ready

The Chicken Stock or Vegetable Stock, warm,
    in a large stockpot over low heat

PREHEAT the oven to 400 degrees.

Cut each parsnip in half crosswise, then each half into 3 or 4 lengths, keeping the sizes similar to ensure even roasting. Combine the pieces of parsnip, onion, garlic, and celery in a large mixing bowl. Toss with the vegetable oil, season lightly with kosher salt and black pepper, and sprinkle with chopped thyme.

Spread out the vegetables in a single layer in a large roasting pan. Roast the vegetables in the oven, turning them 2 or 3 times, until they are cooked through and lightly browned, about 30 to 45 minutes. Remove the pan from the oven and reserve. If any of the vegetables, particularly the garlic, blackens, trim and discard the burned part.

Transfer the roasted vegetables to the large stockpot containing the warm stock. Add the potato and bouquet garni and bring to a boil. Decrease the heat to medium low, and simmer until the potatoes are tender, about 30 minutes.

Remove the bouquet garni and puree the soup in batches through a food mill into a large mixing bowl. When all the soup has been pureed, return it to the stockpot and correct the seasoning to taste with kosher salt and black pepper. If the soup is too thick, simmering stock can be added in small amounts to thin it as necessary.

Warm the soup over low heat, if needed. Ladle the soup into large, warm soup plates. Top each serving with a drizzle of extra-virgin olive oil; add a sprig of chervil and a pinch of cracked black pepper, and serve immediately.

Tomato Soup

Serves 10 to 12

THIS is a rich, dense soup for early in the fall, when the tomatoes are still good and the nights are just getting cool. The sweet tomatoes will make a richly flavored soup that still has lingering hints of summer.

This soup freezes very well, so if you make large batches, you can always have a warm reminder of summer, even when the tomatoes at the market are hard, pink, and unworthy of your attention.

10 large ripe tomatoes (5 to 6 pounds)
½ cup extra-virgin olive oil
Kosher salt
Freshly cracked black pepper
5 large garlic cloves, peeled and minced
    (5 teaspoons)
1 teaspoon chopped fresh thyme
1 teaspoon chopped fresh rosemary
2 ounces pancetta
1 medium carrot, peeled and coarsely chopped
    (¾ cup)
1 small leek, trimmed and coarsely chopped
    (¾ cup)
1 celery stalk, coarsely chopped (½ cup)
½ small onion, peeled and coarsely chopped
    (¾ cup)
1 head of garlic, peeled and cut in half
    horizontally
1 cup dry white wine
8 cups Chicken Stock (see page 187)
¼ cup extra-virgin olive oil
4 cups soft insides of unseeded rye bread, torn
    into large pieces
Bouquet garni (2 sprigs fresh basil, 2 sprigs fresh
    thyme, 1 sprig fresh rosemary)

Have ready

The Chicken Stock, warm, in a medium
    saucepan over low heat

PREHEAT the oven to 325 degrees.

Using a paring knife, remove the cores from the tomatoes. Cut the tomatoes in half horizontally and remove the seeds. In a large mixing bowl, toss the tomato halves in the olive oil with 1 teaspoon of kosher salt, ½ teaspoon of black pepper, 3 teaspoons of the minced garlic, the thyme, and the rosemary.

Spread the tomatoes on a large baking pan in one layer, cut side down, and roast in the oven until tender and the tops are lightly browned, about 1 hour. (Use more than one pan if the tomatoes will not all fit in a single layer.) Remove the baking pan(s) from the oven and allow tomatoes to cool. When cool enough to handle readily, peel off and discard the tomato skin, reserving the tomatoes and the juice.

In a large stockpot, over medium-low heat, sauté the pancetta about 3 minutes to render some of the fat. Increase the heat to medium, and add the carrot, leek, celery, onion, and head of garlic, and lightly sweat the vegetables, about 4 or 5 minutes. Add the wine and reduce until about ¼ cup remains, about 10 minutes. Pour in the stock. Increase the heat, bring to a simmer, and cook, uncovered, until about 6 cups remain, about 45 minutes. Using a colander, strain this double-enriched stock into a large mixing bowl, discarding the vegetables and pancetta.

In the same large stockpot, over medium heat, preheat 2 tablespoons of the olive oil.

Sauté 2 cups of the rye bread pieces until the edges are lightly brown and crisp, stirring occasionally, about 3 or 4 minutes. Add the tomatoes with their juice, the double-enriched stock, and the bouquet garni, and bring to a gentle simmer. Continue to simmer, uncovered, skimming as necessary to remove any fat or foam, until the soup begins to thicken, about 1 hour.

Preheat the oven to 325 degrees.

In a medium mixing bowl, toss the remaining 2 cups of rye bread pieces with the remaining 2 tablespoons olive oil and the remaining 2 teaspoons minced garlic. Season lightly with kosher salt and black pepper and spread out in a baking pan. Bake until golden on all sides, about 10 or 12 minutes, turning or tossing after 3 or 4 minutes. Remove the pan from the oven, and allow the croutons to cool.

When the soup has thickened slightly, after about 1 hour, discard the bouquet garni, remove the soup from the heat, and allow it to cool for about 15 minutes. Puree the soup in batches through a food mill into a large mixing bowl. When all the soup has been pureed, return it to the stockpot and adjust the seasoning to taste with kosher salt and black pepper. If the soup is too thick, simmering stock can be added in small amounts to thin it as necessary.

To serve, ladle a portion of the soup into each large warm soup plate, add a few garlic rye croutons on top, and serve immediately.

Tuscan Minestrone

THE white beans in this soup give it a definitive Tuscan flavor. We add polenta, rather than
rice or some other grain, because it adds a satisfying density to the body of the soup instead of
simply sinking to the bottom of the bowl.

It does take a while to put this soup
together, but it stores quite well in the refrigerator or freezer, and it warms up perfectly. It can
be kept refrigerated, covered, for up to 3 days.

1 tablespoon dried porcini mushrooms, crushed
2 tablespoons vegetable oil
2 large garlic cloves, peeled and minced
    (2 teaspoons)
2 large carrots, peeled and cut into ¼-inch dice
    (2 cups)
1 medium fennel bulb, peeled, trimmed, and
    cut into ¼-inch dice (1½ cups)
4 large stalks celery, trimmed and cut into
    ¼-inch dice (2 cups)
1 large leek, well washed, trimmed, and cut
    diagonally into ¼-inch slices (1½ cups)
1 small red bell pepper (4 ounces), cored,
    seeded, and cut into ¼-inch dice (¾ cup)
Kosher salt
Freshly cracked black pepper
1 cup sherry wine
½ medium (¾ pound) green cabbage, cored,
    trimmed, and sliced thinly
¼ teaspoon ground red chile pepper
12 cups Chicken Stock (see page 187)
Bouquet garni (1 sprig fresh rosemary,
    1 sprig fresh thyme, 3 sprigs fresh parsley,
    1 sprig fresh basil, 1 bay leaf)
½ cup dry polenta
1½ cups cooked white beans (see Cannellini
    Beans, page 246)
3 large Slow-roasted Tomatoes, peeled (2 cups)
    (see page 241)
1 large bunch fresh basil, rinsed and dried
¼ pound prosciutto, cut into julienne

Have ready

The Slow-roasted Tomatoes
The Chicken Stock, warm, in a medium
    saucepan over low heat
The Cannellini Beans

In a small mixing bowl, combine the dried
porcini mushrooms with ½ cup of warm water.
Allow about 30 minutes for the mushrooms to
reconstitute adequately.

While the porcini mushrooms are soaking,
in a large stockpot, over medium heat, preheat
the vegetable oil. Sauté the garlic for 1 or 2
minutes. Add the carrots, fennel, celery, leek,
and red bell pepper, and season with 1 tablespoon kosher salt and ½ teaspoon black pepper.
Sauté the vegetables for about 3 to 5 minutes.

Pour in the wine and reduce by half, about
10 minutes. Add the cabbage, red chile pepper,
stock, and the bouquet garni, and bring to a
simmer.

Add the reconstituted porcini mushrooms
to the stockpot. Add the porcini soaking water,
taking care not to pour into the stockpot any of
the grit from the porcinis that will have collected on the bottom of the bowl.

Reduce the heat to low and simmer,
uncovered, for 30 minutes, stirring occasionally
and skimming as necessary to remove any fat or
foam that rises to the surface.

In a slow, steady stream, pour in the
polenta, stirring constantly. Simmer for
20 minutes longer, stirring often to prevent the
polenta from sticking to the bottom of the pot.
Stir in the beans and the tomatoes; heat
through, about 10 minutes. Remove from the
heat and correct the seasoning to taste with
kosher salt and black pepper. Remove and discard the bouquet garni.

To serve, ladle the soup into large, warm
soup plates. Garnish each serving with 1 large
perfect basil leaf and about 6 pieces of julienne
of prosciutto. As an option, this soup is delicious with a drizzle of basil pesto over the top
of each portion.

Garlic Soup

Serves 8 to 10

THIS is an easy and quick soup to make. It is garlicky, but in a refined and understated way, as the garlic is tempered by the cooking and sweetened by the light caramelization of the other vegetables. Rapini, also called broccoli rabe, adds a slightly bitter counterpoint to the sweet richness of the soup.

¼ cup plus 1 tablespoon vegetable oil
2 large brown onions (2 pounds), peeled and coarsely chopped
3 celery stalks (12 ounces), trimmed and coarsely chopped
1 large carrot (4 ounces), trimmed, peeled, and coarsely chopped
1 large parsnip (3 ounces), trimmed, peeled, and coarsely chopped
10 cups Chicken Stock or Vegetable Stock (see page 187 or 196)
2 russet potatoes (1¼ pounds), peeled and cut into chunks
4 large heads (1 pound) garlic, cut in half horizontally
Bouquet garni (5 sprigs Italian parsley, 3 sprigs thyme, 1 sprig rosemary)
Kosher salt
Freshly cracked black pepper
1 bunch rapini (8 ounces)
Extra-virgin olive oil

Have ready

The Chicken Stock or Vegetable Stock, warm, in a medium saucepan over low heat

IN a large stockpot, over medium-high heat, preheat ¼ cup of vegetable oil. Sauté the onions, celery, carrot, and parsnip until the vegetables are lightly colored, about 10 minutes. Stir the vegetables frequently to prevent uneven browning. Pour in the warm stock. Add the potatoes, garlic, and bouquet garni, and gently simmer until the vegetables are softened, about 1 hour. It is important that the garlic be soft enough to puree smoothly.

Remove the bouquet garni and puree the soup, in batches, using a food mill or blender. Using a coarse-mesh, stainless-steel strainer, strain into a clean stockpot and correct the seasoning to taste with kosher salt and black pepper. Keep warm over low heat until needed, or allow to cool and refrigerate, covered, for up to 3 days.

Using a sharp knife, cut off the top 2 inches of each rapini stalk, reserving the tops and discarding the remaining portion. In a medium sauté pan, over high heat, preheat 1 tablespoon vegetable oil to smoking. Sauté the rapini tops until lightly browned, about 2 minutes. Season the rapini with about ¼ teaspoon of kosher salt.

Warm the soup over low heat if necessary. Ladle about 8 ounces into each large, warm soup plate. Add a few sprigs of seared rapini and a drizzle of extra-virgin olive oil to each portion, and serve immediately.

Pastas, Risottos, and Polenta

Chapter 6

Fresh Pasta

PASTA is in many ways similar to bread, in that they are both made from the same few humble ingredients—flour, water, and salt—and they are both extremely versatile and nutritious. And as with bread, there is an astounding variety of different tastes, textures, and shapes that can be created from those few ingredients. Pasta can be served for lunch or dinner, as an appetizer or a main course. It is inexpensive, yet not at all unrefined or coarse.

Pasta generally can be separated into two distinct types: fresh and dried. The ease of storage, handling, and use of dried pasta has caused it to eclipse fresh pasta in popularity in homes. However, in many fine restaurants not too long ago, the only acceptable pasta to use was fresh. This was a reaction to the overwhelming predominance of dried pasta, rather than a well-conceived pairing of pasta and sauce. As a result, there were many bad pasta dishes made and served in otherwise good restaurants. Although there are no absolute rules about fresh as opposed to dried pasta, there are some good general guidelines.

Fresh pasta, because it is more tender, is best served with lighter sauces. Fresh pasta works well with a very delicate but flavorful sauce such as one made with lobster, fava beans, and currant tomatoes. We serve this sauce with fresh pasta that is simply torn into pieces after being rolled out into flat sheets. Though this sauce wouldn't be ruined if served with a good dried penne, it would not have the same subtle balance of tender texture and delicate flavor. The lobster, fava beans, and currant tomatoes would be lost in the bulk of the penne.

Different types of pasta have different cooking requirements. Fresh pasta is cooked very briefly, but it cannot ever be cooked al dente. The high moisture content makes it softer than cooked dried pasta. As with dried pasta, it is crucial not to overcook fresh pasta, because it can quickly turn into a soft, flavorless paste.

Pasta Machines

Avoid extruder-type pasta machines. In an extruder, the pressure compacts the dough as it is pushed through the die. As the extruded shape exits the die, the pressure is released and the pasta surface scales and fractures. The small pieces that lift up like fish scales are very thin, and as a result, cook more quickly than the interior of the pasta shape. This results in the outside of the pasta becoming overcooked and mushy by the time the inside is cooked through. This will be particularly evident in extruded pasta made from any flour other than durum semolina.

A simple hand-operated pasta machine with rollers produces firm, smooth sheets of pasta that can be used for a variety of pasta shapes. It can be cut into thin strips for linguine, wide strips for pappardelle, torn by hand, or formed into ravioli. The kneading action of the rollers produces a uniform pasta with a well-developed gluten, which is necessary to achieve the proper texture.

Pasta Shapes and Sauces

The whole argument about various shapes and sizes and ridges and holes gripping sauces of differing viscosity has some level of merit. A hearty sauce needs a hearty form of pasta, while a light sauce of subtle flavor requires a delicate pasta. The combination of flavors and textures in a fresh cheese ravioli tossed with a light sauce of ripe September tomatoes and tender leaves of basil, and drizzled with extra-virgin olive oil, is inspiring. Perfect ravioli like this can bring out a little childish glee in just about anyone. In addition, of course, to make ravioli or tortellini, one must have fresh pasta because it must be formed around the filling.

Pasta Dough

For ravioli, torn pasta, pappardelle, or any dish needing fresh pasta, this is a wonderfully simple recipe. A properly prepared pasta dough can easily be made into almost any flat noodle, from linguini to lasagna. The only consideration is to match the shape of the pasta with the sauce and accompaniment.

With a little experience in making fresh pasta, you will be able to tell the quality and condition of your dough from its feel and appearance. You will be able to determine when it has rested adequately, and when it is sufficiently developed to be rolled out.

To preserve the beautiful texture of the fresh pasta, don't add colored vegetable purees for pretty tints; put the color in the sauce instead. Cooked fresh pasta will still have some resistance to your teeth, but not to the same extent as dried pasta. Fresh pasta cooks far more quickly than dried pasta; take care not to overcook it.

If you feel confident making this by hand, do so. It will give you a better feel for the dough and a superior texture in the pasta. At the restaurant, we knead all the fresh pasta by hand. If you are using an electric mixer, you may need the extra teaspoon of water, but when made by hand, it might not be necessary. Do not make this dough in a food processor, as it will not be kneaded properly, and thus the gluten will not develop. Fresh pasta dough will keep, wrapped

in plastic in the refrigerator, for up to 5 days. It takes so little time to make, there isn't any benefit in preparing large batches and freezing it for future use.

2 cups (10 ounces) unbleached bread flour
2 extra-large eggs
1 tablespoon olive oil
1 tablespoon plus 1 teaspoon cold water
1½ teaspoons kosher salt

To prepare the dough by hand: Place the flour in a mound on a large work surface, at least 18 × 24 inches. Make a depression in the center of the mound and crack the eggs into it. Add the olive oil, 1 tablespoon of water, and kosher salt into the depression. Using a fork, gently blend together the eggs, oil, and water, and then begin to incorporate the flour. Work from the center out, a small amount at a time, until most of the flour has been incorporated, using the remaining teaspoon of water only if necessary. When most of the flour has been incorporated, start kneading the dough, using the heel of your hand, forming a smooth ball of dough.

Knead for about 5 minutes, until the dough is stiff but malleable and consistent in color and texture. Cover with plastic wrap and let rest, at room temperature, 30 minutes to 1 hour.

To prepare the dough in an electric mixer: In a small mixing bowl, whisk together the olive oil and the eggs. Using an electric mixer fitted with a dough hook, on low speed, combine the flour and kosher salt. When the dry ingredients are completely combined, slowly add the oil-and-egg mixture to the flour in the electric mixer. Add the water to the dough. Start with 1 tablespoon and, if necessary, add the remaining teaspoon. The dough is ready when small pieces will hold together when pinched with your fingers.

Turn the dough out onto a lightly floured work surface and knead for 2 or 3 minutes, using the heel of your hand, and dusting your hands with flour as needed. Cover the kneaded dough with plastic wrap and allow it to rest, at room temperature, for 30 minutes to 1 hour.

To roll out the dough: After the dough has rested, divide it in half. Cover one half with plastic wrap, and allow it to rest, refrigerated, until needed. Using your hands, flatten the remaining half to a thickness of about ½ inch, and put it through the rollers of a pasta machine on the widest setting.

Put the dough through the rollers a second time. Set the pasta machine to two positions thinner and roll the dough through a third time.

Fold the dough in thirds. Turn it 90 degrees relative to the pasta machine, reset the pasta machine to the widest setting, and put the pasta dough through the rollers a fourth time.

Set the pasta machine to two positions thinner and put the dough through the rollers a fifth time. Fold the dough in thirds, turn it 90 degrees, and set the pasta machine to the widest setting. Roll the dough through a sixth time. Dust with flour as necessary if the dough becomes sticky.

Continue to roll the dough through, reducing the opening each time the dough is put through the rollers, one setting at a time, until the thinnest setting is reached. At this point the dough should have a smooth, even, and elastic consistency.

If you prefer a thicker noodle, you may stop one position back from the thinnest setting. For a thinner noodle and for ravioli, run the dough through the pasta machine on the thinnest setting a second time. Using a sharp knife, cut the pasta dough to the desired size.

To prevent the pasta noodles from sticking together, dust lightly with flour after cutting. Use cut pasta immediately, or refrigerate, covered, for up to one day.

Basic Procedure for Making Ravioli

THE procedure for making ravioli may seem long and involved at first glance, but after you have done it once, you shouldn't ever need to read the instructions again.

Finished ravioli can be frozen on a baking sheet. When they are frozen through they can be transferred to a sealed container for storage. They must be separate when first put in the freezer or they will stick together.

This procedure uses 13 ounces of pasta dough to make 36 ravioli.

To roll out the pasta dough: The pasta dough must be run through the machine several times to complete the kneading. Thorough kneading is necessary for a smooth, even texture.

Divide the chilled pasta dough in half. Cover one half with plastic wrap and return it to the refrigerator until needed. Using your hands, flatten the remaining half to a thickness of about ½ inch, and put it through a pasta machine on the widest setting. Put the dough through a second time. Set the pasta machine to two positions thinner, and roll the dough through a third time.

Fold the dough in thirds. Turn 90 degrees relative to the pasta machine, reset the pasta machine to the widest setting, and put the pasta dough through a fourth time. Set the pasta machine to two positions thinner and put the dough through a fifth time. Fold the dough in thirds, turn 90 degrees, and reset the pasta machine to the widest setting. Put the pasta

dough through a sixth time. At this point the dough should have a smooth, even, and elastic consistency.

Continue to put the pasta through the machine, narrowing the opening each time the dough is put through, until the thinnest setting is reached. Put the dough through the pasta machine on the thinnest setting a second time to roll out to a rectangle approximately 60 inches long and 6 inches wide. Fold the dough over lengthwise to make a 2-layer rectangle measuring about 30 × 6 inches. Trim away about ¼ inch from the folded end to make two separate pieces measuring about 30 × 6 inches. Lightly dust one sheet with flour and carefully fold it down to a manageable size, wrap in plastic wrap, and reserve.

To prepare the ravioli: Put about 1 cup of cold water in a small mixing bowl. Using approximately 1 heaping teaspoonful of chilled filling for each ravioli, make 18 mounds of filling on the remaining rectangle of dough in 2 rows, each mound placed about 1½ inches apart, starting 1 inch in from the edge. Using a pastry brush moistened with the cold water, lightly brush the dough around each portion of filling.

Unwrap the reserved sheet of dough and carefully place it on top to cover the mounds of filling. Align the edges of the pasta sheets, and press down gently around each covered mound to seal in the filling, and to expel any air between the pasta layers and the filling. This is important, as air pockets in the ravioli can cause them to come apart during the cooking process, resulting in a watery disaster.

When all the air has been pressed out, seal the ravioli by pressing the edges of the pasta sheets together to secure them firmly. Using a fluted pastry wheel, separate the ravioli by cutting straight lines between them to make each ravioli about 2 inches square. Press down on the edges after the ravioli have been cut to ensure a good seal. Place the cut ravioli on a baking pan that has been sprinkled with flour, and dust a little flour over the ravioli to prevent them from sticking to one another. If you need to stack them, use parchment paper dusted with flour in between the layers and stack only 2 layers deep. If the ravioli stick to the paper and become dif-

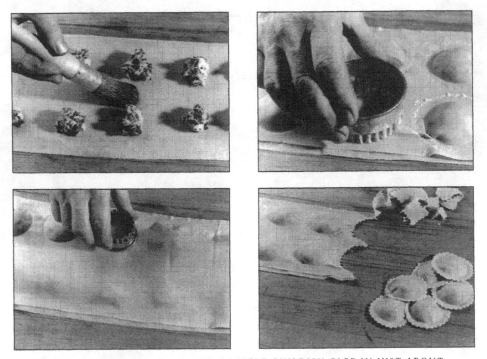

"PERFECT RAVIOLI CAN BRING OUT A LITTLE CHILDISH GLEE IN JUST ABOUT ANYONE."

ficult to work with, put them in the freezer for up to 30 minutes to firm up.

Repeat the procedure with the remaining dough and filling, and refrigerate the ravioli until needed.

To cook the ravioli: Cook the ravioli in three batches. Quickly but carefully add about 12 ravioli to a large stockpot of boiling water (at least 4 quarts), and cook until tender, about 3 to 5 minutes. With a slotted spoon, remove the ravioli, place on a warm platter, and splash a little of the pasta water over the ravioli to prevent them from sticking to one another. Repeat the procedure to cook the remaining ravioli.

Torn Pasta with Lobster, Fava Beans, and Currant Tomatoes

Serves 6

THE pieces of lobster, the fava beans, and the currant tomatoes are similar in size, but quite different in taste and texture, and it is the combination that makes this dish interesting. It is time-consuming in preparation, but the finishing steps—combining all the ingredients—can be accomplished in about ten minutes. You can cook the lobster, blanch the fava beans, and prepare the pasta in advance and then pull it all together just before serving. Currant tomatoes are small, sweet, and intense in flavor. If they are difficult to find, quartered cherry tomatoes can be substituted. Chicken stock can be substituted for fish stock if it is more convenient; the flavor will be different, but not inferior.

⅔ cup fresh fava beans, shelled
Pasta Dough (see page 97) (13 ounces)
1½ cups Fish Stock or Chicken Stock (see page 194 or 187)
1 tablespoon unsalted butter
1 large garlic clove, peeled and thinly sliced
6 ounces lobster meat, cooked
½ cup currant tomatoes
1 cup whole Italian parsley leaves
Kosher salt
Freshly cracked black pepper
Fresh lemon juice (optional)

Have ready

The Pasta Dough
The cooked lobster meat
The fava beans, shelled
The Fish Stock or Chicken Stock, warm, in a small saucepan over low heat

Torn Pasta with Lobster, Fava Beans, and Currant Tomatoes *(cont.)*

In a large saucepan, bring approximately 1 quart of water to a boil and add 1 teaspoon of kosher salt. Fill a large mixing bowl with ice water.

Blanch the shelled fava beans in the saucepan of boiling water for about 30 seconds. Drain the fava beans in a colander, and then plunge them into the ice water for about 30 seconds. When they are cool, drain them a second time in the colander. Using your fingers, remove the peel of the fava beans by pinching off one end of the skin and gently squeezing the bean out of the skin. Reserve the beans in a small bowl.

Roll out the pasta dough according to the instructions in Pasta Dough (see page 97). Roll the dough out to a rectangle approximately 60 × 6 inches. Cut it in the center to make two 30- × 6-inch pieces. Set one piece aside.

To make the torn pasta, use one hand to hold down the strip of pasta against the work surface and slide the other hand under the end of the strip. Grasp a large (1½- × 3-inch) piece between your thumb and your fanned-out fingers beneath the pasta, and tear the piece off, pulling horizontally away from the pasta strip. Place the torn pasta pieces on a baking sheet lined with parchment paper and dusted with flour. The pieces should be irregular in size and shape, but not crumpled or folded. Repeat the procedure with the remaining pasta.

In a large stockpot, bring approximately 4 quarts of water to a boil, and add 1 tablespoon of kosher salt.

In a medium sauté pan, over medium heat, combine the Chicken Stock or Fish Stock, butter, and the garlic, and simmer for about 5 minutes. Add the lobster meat, currant tomatoes, and the fava beans. Stir, and simmer to heat through, about 2 minutes. Remove the sauté pan from the heat, add the parsley, and stir to just wilt the parsley, about 1 minute. Correct the seasoning to taste with kosher salt and black pepper. A squeeze of fresh lemon juice could be added for a little more tartness, if desired. Remove the sauce from the heat and keep it warm.

Cook the pasta in the large stockpot of boiling water for no more than 2 to 3 minutes. Drain the pasta in a colander, then add it to the sauce and toss gently but thoroughly.

Ladle the sauce and pasta into 6 large, warm soup plates, distributing all the ingredients (especially the lobster) equally, and serve immediately.

Potato and Black Olive Ravioli

Serves 6 to 8

POTATOES make a wonderful ravioli filling because they are soft and mildly flavored; they function like a canvas on which other flavors can be displayed. In this case the strong, salty black olives are the dominant element, supported by the subtle flavors of the steamed garlic and the Parmesan cheese.

Ravioli

2 medium russet potatoes (1 pound), peeled
    and cut into 1-inch chunks
12 large garlic cloves, peeled
½ cup black oil-cured olives
1 stick (4 ounces) unsalted butter
½ cup heavy cream
⅓ cup freshly grated Parmesan cheese
¼ cup extra-virgin olive oil
½ cup chives, finely chopped
Pasta Dough (see page 97) (13 ounces)

Sauce

2 sticks (8 ounces) butter
1 cup Chicken Stock or Vegetable Stock
    (see page 187 or 196)
1 large garlic clove, peeled and minced
    (1 teaspoon)
2 large shallots, peeled and minced
    (2 tablespoons)
⅓ cup pale celery leaves
Kosher salt
2 teaspoons fresh lemon juice

Have ready

The Chicken Stock or Vegetable Stock
The Pasta Dough, well wrapped and
    refrigerated

To prepare the ravioli filling: In a large saucepan, bring approximately 1 quart of water to a boil. Using a vegetable steamer, steam the potatoes and garlic cloves over the boiling water until very tender, about 20 minutes.

Remove and discard the olive pits. Coarsely chop the olives and reserve them in a small mixing bowl. In a medium saucepan, over medium heat, melt the butter and add the cream, stirring briefly, about 3 to 5 minutes. Mash the potatoes and garlic using a food mill or electric mixer.

In a large mixing bowl, blend the potatoes and garlic with the melted butter and cream. Fold in the Parmesan cheese and olive oil, and then fold in the chopped olives, mixing just to combine. Refrigerate, covered, until firm, about 1 hour.

Stir in the chopped chives. (The mixture may have discolored a bit from the juice in the olives.)

To prepare the ravioli: Follow the instructions in Basic Procedure for Making Ravioli (see page 99).

In a large stockpot bring approximately 4 quarts of water to a boil, and add 1 tablespoon of kosher salt to the water.

To prepare the sauce: In a medium sauté

Potato and Black Olive Ravioli *(cont.)*

pan, over medium heat, melt and lightly brown the butter, about 10 minutes. Add the stock to the butter, then add the garlic and the shallots. Bring to a simmer. Remove the pan from the heat and keep warm.

Cook the ravioli according to the instructions in Basic Procedure for Making Ravioli (see page 99).

To serve, add the celery leaves to the reserved and browned-butter mixture, and correct the seasoning to taste with kosher salt and fresh lemon juice. Divide the ravioli and sauce among 8 large, warm soup plates, and serve immediately.

Five-Cheese Ravioli with Braised Lettuce, Celery Leaves, and Brown Butter Sauce

Serves 6 to 8

THE five cheeses—ricotta, Gorgonzola, fontina, Gruyère, and Parmesan—used in this recipe are commonly available, but most good-quality cheeses could be used to make ravioli filling. Just don't include more than one pungent cheese such as Gorgonzola or blue. The distinct tastes of ripe cheeses don't combine well with one another and will make the filling too strongly flavored. The ingredients for this dish are always in season, but the flavors and the colors remind me of fall.

Ravioli

1 pound ricotta cheese
3 ounces Gorgonzola cheese, hand crumbled
3 ounces fontina cheese, grated
3 ounces Gruyère cheese, grated
3 ounces Parmesan cheese, grated
½ cup heavy cream
1 egg, beaten
1 teaspoon kosher salt
½ teaspoon freshly cracked black pepper
1 large garlic clove, peeled and minced
    (1 teaspoon)
2 teaspoons finely chopped fresh thyme
Pasta Dough (see page 97), chilled (13 ounces)

Sauce of Celery Leaves and Brown Butter

1 cup Chicken Stock or Vegetable Stock
    (see page 187 or 196)
2 sticks (8 ounces) butter
8 large leaves iceberg lettuce
Kosher salt
2 large garlic cloves, peeled and minced
    (2 teaspoons)
2 large shallots, peeled, trimmed, and minced
    (2 tablespoons)
Pale celery leaves from 1 bunch (1 loose cup)
Fresh lemon juice

Have Ready

The Chicken Stock or Vegetable Stock, warm,
    in a small saucepan, over low heat
The Pasta Dough

To prepare the ravioli filling: In a large mixing bowl, combine the ricotta, Gorgonzola, fontina, Gruyère, and Parmesan, and stir just to combine. Gently fold in the cream, egg, kosher salt, black pepper, garlic, and the chopped thyme, and stir just to combine.

Refrigerate the filling, covered, for 1 hour, or until firm.

To prepare the ravioli: Follow the instructions in the section Basic Procedure for Making Ravioli (see page 99).

In a large stockpot bring approximately 4 quarts of water to a boil, and add 1 tablespoon of kosher salt to the water.

To prepare the sauce and lettuce: In a medium sauté pan, over medium-high heat, melt and lightly brown the butter, about 10 minutes.

While the butter is browning, carefully remove the large outer leaves from a head of iceberg lettuce. In a medium sauté pan, over high heat, bring 1 cup of water to a simmer and reduce the heat to medium. Add the lettuce and 1 teaspoon of kosher salt, and stir briefly. Braise the lettuce for 2 to 3 minutes. Remove the pan from the heat, remove the lettuce, drain thoroughly, and place each leaf in a large, warm soup plate.

Add the stock and garlic to the browned butter and stir briefly, about 1 minute. Add the shallots, stirring to combine, for about 1 minute. Add the celery leaves, about ½ teaspoon kosher salt, and 2 teaspoons lemon juice. Stir to combine, about 1 minute. Remove the pan from the heat, and correct the seasoning to taste with salt and lemon juice; keep warm.

Cook the ravioli according to the instructions in Basic Procedure for Making Ravioli (see page 99).

Divide the ravioli equally and place on the braised lettuce in each of the large, warm soup plates. Stir the sauce briefly and drizzle over the ravioli, ensuring that each portion receives some garlic, shallots, and celery leaves, and serve immediately.

Roasted Garlic and Potato Ravioli with Chanterelle Sauce

This is a robust fall dish with the earthiness of mushrooms, potatoes, and the deep flavor of garlic. The ingredients for this dish should be available late August through mid-December. This is meaty, although there is no actual meat in it, so as a first course it sets up the appetite for a lighter main course, such as striped bass.

Ravioli

2 large russet potatoes (1½ pounds), peeled and cut into 1-inch chunks
½ stick (2 ounces) unsalted butter
½ cup heavy cream
⅓ cup Roasted Garlic Puree (see page 245)
1 tablespoon chopped fresh thyme
Kosher salt
Freshly cracked black pepper
Pasta Dough (see page 97) (13 ounces)

Sauce

1 whole head fresh garlic
2 tablespoons vegetable oil
½ pound fresh chanterelle mushrooms, wiped clean
1 large shallot, peeled and minced (1 tablespoon)
½ cup dry white wine
1 cup Brown Veal Stock (see page 190)
1 tablespoon (½ ounce) unsalted butter
Kosher salt
Freshly cracked black pepper
About 25 whole Italian parsley leaves

Have Ready

The Brown Veal Stock
The Pasta Dough

To prepare the ravioli filling: In a large saucepan, bring approximately 1 quart of water to a boil. Using a vegetable steamer, steam the potatoes over the boiling water until very tender, about 20 minutes.

In a medium saucepan, over medium heat, melt the butter and the cream together and bring to a boil, about 3 to 5 minutes, and remove from the heat.

Using a food mill, electric mixer fitted with a paddle attachment, or a potato masher (but not a food processor), puree the potatoes; mix in the Roasted Garlic Puree. In a large mixing bowl, blend the potatoes with the melted butter and cream and chopped thyme. Correct the seasoning to taste with kosher salt and black pepper. Refrigerate until cool and firm, about 1 hour.

To prepare the ravioli: Follow the instructions in the Basic Procedure for Making Ravioli (see page 99).

To prepare the sauce: Separate and peel the cloves of garlic. In a medium sauté pan, over very low heat, preheat 1 tablespoon vegetable oil. Sauté the garlic until nicely browned and tender, about 15 minutes. Do not rush this or the garlic will burn and turn bitter. Remove the garlic from the pan and set aside.

While the garlic is sautéing, using your fingers, shred the chanterelles vertically into large, bite-sized pieces. In the same medium sauté pan, heat the remaining tablespoon of vegetable oil. Over medium heat, sauté the chanterelles until most of the moisture has evaporated, about 5 to 7 minutes.

Add the shallot and ½ teaspoon kosher salt and continue to sauté 30 seconds longer. Deglaze the pan with the wine and reduce by two thirds, about 5 minutes.

Add the stock and reduce until the sauce lightly coats the back of a spoon, about 5 more minutes. Whisk in the butter, stir in the reserved garlic cloves, and correct the seasoning to taste with kosher salt and black pepper. Keep the sauce warm while cooking the ravioli.

In a large stockpot bring approximately 4 quarts of water to a boil, and add 1 tablespoon of kosher salt to the water. Cook the ravioli according to the instructions in the Basic Procedure for Making Ravioli (see page 99).

Divide the ravioli and sauce among 8 large, warm soup plates, ensuring that each serving receives both chanterelles and garlic. Sprinkle a few parsley leaves on each serving, and serve immediately.

Sweet Potato, Prosciutto, and Kale Ravioli with Brown Butter Sauce and Black-eyed Peas

Serves 8

THIS dish has the flavors of the American South—ham, sweet potatoes, kale, and black-eyed peas—presented in an Italian fashion. The firm toothiness of the black-eyed peas is complementary to the supple texture of the freshly made ravioli. The ham, in this case prosciutto, adds a salty, meaty flavor that blends with the butter to produce a sauce that is highly flavored, but still light.

Ravioli

2 large sweet potatoes (1½ pounds)
5 large leaves of kale
2 tablespoons extra-virgin olive oil
2 large garlic cloves, peeled and minced
   (2 teaspoons)
Kosher salt
1 stick (4 ounces) unsalted butter
6 medium sage leaves, finely chopped
   (1 teaspoon)
3 ounces prosciutto, finely chopped
Juice of ½ medium lemon
Pasta Dough (see page 97) (13 ounces)

Sauce

Brown Butter Sauce with Black-eyed Peas
   (see page 206)

Have ready

The Pasta Dough, well wrapped and
   refrigerated
The ingredients necessary to prepare Brown
   Butter Sauce with Black-eyed Peas

PREHEAT the oven to 400 degrees.

To prepare the ravioli filling: Prick the sweet potatoes all over with a fork to prevent them from rupturing in the oven. Roast the sweet potatoes until soft, about 1½ hours. Remove the sweet potatoes from the oven and allow to cool until they can be handled comfortably.

Wash the kale thoroughly, and pat dry with a clean kitchen towel. Using a sharp knife, cut the stems, or main rib, out of each kale leaf, reserving both the stems and the leaves. Slice the stems diagonally on the bias into ¼-inch pieces. Coarsely chop the kale leaves.

In a medium sauté pan, over medium heat, preheat the olive oil. Gently sauté the chopped kale stems and the minced garlic until softened, about 10 minutes. Add the chopped kale leaves and 1 teaspoon of kosher salt and continue to sauté for about 5 more minutes. Remove the sautéed kale and garlic from the pan. Make a small mound of the chopped kale mixture on a clean kitchen towel, fold up the corners, and squeeze out the moisture. The kale and garlic mixture should yield about ¾ cup.

Cut each sweet potato in half lengthwise. With a spoon, scoop out the soft insides and transfer to a medium mixing bowl. Discard the skins. Using a fork, mash the butter into the sweet potato puree to remove any lumps.

Add the sautéed kale and garlic mixture, chopped sage, prosciutto, and the lemon juice to the sweet potato puree, and mix to combine. Correct the seasoning to taste with kosher salt.

Refrigerate, covered, until firm, about 1 hour.

To prepare the ravioli: Follow the instructions in the Basic Procedure for Making Ravioli (see page 99).

In a large stockpot bring approximately 4 quarts of water to a boil, and add 1 tablespoon of kosher salt to the water.

Prepare the Brown Butter Sauce with Black-eyed Peas (see page 206).

Cook the ravioli according to the instructions in the Basic Procedure for Making Ravioli (see page 99).

Divide the ravioli equally among warm plates. Spoon the sauce on and around the ravioli, ensuring that each serving receives some black-eyed peas and fresh herbs, and serve immediately.

Duck Confit and Cannellini-bean Ravioli with Port Wine Sauce

Serves 6 to 8

IF you have the Duck Confit, be sure to try this ravioli. It is wonderful for a cold winter night; it has the sort of flavor that sets a leisurely pace for the rest of the evening. The confit is essential; it brings texture and big flavor to the dish. Because this is time-consuming to prepare, it isn't something to start from scratch. This is a dish that should be made from leftover confit and beans. In the restaurant, we always have these ingredients on hand, so it comes together easily. At home you could use a different kind of stock or substitute another kind of bean.

Ravioli

1 tablespoon extra-virgin olive oil
1 large leek (¼ pound), well washed, trimmed, and thinly sliced
2 large shallots, peeled, trimmed, and thinly sliced (2 tablespoons)
⅓ cup tawny port
2 tablespoons balsamic vinegar
½ cup Duck Stock (see page 188)
1 cup (½ pound) shredded Duck Confit (see page 164)
1 cup cooked Cannellini Beans (see page 246)
¼ teaspoon freshly cracked black pepper
Pasta Dough (see page 97) (13 ounces)

Sauce

½ cup tawny port
½ cup dry red wine
2 large shallots, peeled and minced (2 tablespoons)
2 cups Duck Stock (see page 188)
1 tablespoon unsalted butter
1 cup cooked Cannellini Beans (see page 246)
Kosher salt
1 teaspoon freshly cracked black pepper
2 teaspoons fresh chopped Italian parsley or chervil

Have ready

The Duck Confit, shredded
The Duck Stock, warm, in a small saucepan over low heat
The Pasta Dough, wrapped in plastic, refrigerated
The Cannellini Beans, cooked, and refrigerated, covered

To prepare the ravioli filling: In a medium sauté pan, over medium-low heat, preheat the olive oil. Gently sauté the leek and shallots until just wilted, 2 to 3 minutes. Add the port and vinegar and reduce by two thirds, about 10 minutes. Add the stock and reduce by one fourth, about 5 minutes. Add the shredded duck confit and the beans, and cook just until most of the liquid is absorbed, about 10 minutes. Season to taste with freshly cracked pepper. Refrigerate, uncovered, in a small mixing bowl until well chilled, at least 1 hour.

To prepare the ravioli: Follow the instructions in the Basic Procedure for Making Ravioli (see page 99).

In a large stockpot, bring approximately 4 quarts of water to a boil, and add 1 tablespoon of kosher salt to the water.

To prepare the sauce: In a medium saucepan, over medium heat, combine the port, red wine, and shallots, and reduce by two thirds, about 5 to 8 minutes. Pour in the stock and reduce by one fourth, about 5 to 8 minutes. Using a fine-mesh, stainless-steel strainer, strain the sauce into a clean medium saucepan and whisk in the butter. Stir in the beans and heat through, about 10 minutes. Season to taste with salt and pepper. Remove the pan from the heat and keep warm.

Cook the ravioli according to the instructions in the Basic Procedure for Making Ravioli (see page 99).

Divide the ravioli equally among large, warm soup plates. Spoon the sauce, including some beans, on and around the ravioli. Sprinkle with the chopped herbs, and serve immediately.

Potato Gnocchi with Asparagus

THIS is especially good in the spring when asparagus is at its best. We use russet potatoes, as they are best for baking, mashing, and making gnocchi. Truffle oil is expensive and hard to find, but it is a lot more affordable than actual white truffles. The aroma of white truffle oil is wonderful and enticing; it transforms this simple dish into an elegant sensation.

The tips of the asparagus are the only part used for this dish. Making the gnocchi will be a little messy at first, but practice will eventually make perfect and the investment in time will be well justified. To prepare gnocchi with the proper firm but tender texture, it is important to avoid overworking the dough when mixing and shaping it. The gnocchi should be cooked very soon after they are shaped; if allowed to rest for longer than about 15 minutes, they will fall apart in the boiling water. After they are cooked, they can be reserved on a lightly oiled baking sheet for up to a few hours and briefly warmed when needed in boiling water.

Potato Gnocchi

1¾ pounds (2 or 3 large) russet potatoes
1 extra-large egg
3 tablespoons melted unsalted butter, clarified
¼ cup (1 ounce) freshly grated Parmesan cheese
Unbleached all-purpose flour
¾ teaspoon kosher salt
½ teaspoon freshly cracked black pepper

Sauce

¼ stick (1 ounce) unsalted butter
3 large shallots, peeled, trimmed, and minced (3 tablespoons)
1½ cups Chicken Stock (see page 187)
30 asparagus tips, 2½ inches long, from medium asparagus stalks
2 tablespoons fresh lemon juice
Pinch of chopped fresh thyme
Kosher salt
Freshly cracked black pepper
3 teaspoons truffle oil

Have ready

The melted, clarified, unsalted butter
The Chicken Stock, warm, in a small saucepan over low heat

PREHEAT the oven to 400 degrees.

To prepare the gnocchi: Bake the potatoes until tender, about 45 minutes. Cool slightly (enough to be able to handle), cut the potatoes in half, and scoop out the insides. Pass the flesh of the potatoes through a food mill. You should have 2 cups, packed, of pureed potatoes.

Mound the cooled pureed potatoes on a clean work surface and make a well in the center of the mound. Crack the egg into a small mixing bowl, whisk briefly, and pour the egg and the melted butter into the well. Using a fork, work the egg and butter into the pureed potatoes.

Sprinkle the grated Parmesan cheese over the potato mixture and knead into a consistent dough, adding enough flour to make a smooth ball, between ½ and ¾ of a cup. Work the kosher salt and black pepper into the dough as you knead. (You should have about 1¼ pounds of dough.)

In a large stockpot, bring approximately 4 quarts of water to a boil and add 1 tablespoon of kosher salt.

Lightly dust a work surface and your hands with flour. Cut the dough into 6 equal pieces, about 3 ounces each. Using the palms of your hands, roll out one of the balls of dough on the work surface until it forms an 8-inch-long rope. It should be about ½ inch in diameter. Then cut the rope into eight 1-inch sections.

For each piece, using the side of the thumb, make a shallow indentation in one side of the

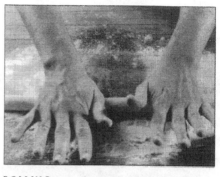

ROLLING . . .

. . . CUTTING . . .

. . . AND SHAPING THE GNOCCHI.

dough while rolling it off the tines of a fork or a gnocchi board. (The indentation allows the sauce to be absorbed more easily, as do the markings of the tines.) Reserve the finished gnocchi on a lightly floured baking sheet. Repeat this procedure with the remaining balls of dough.

To prepare the sauce: In a medium saucepan, over medium heat, heat the butter. Sweat the shallots, just to soften, about 2 minutes. Add the stock; bring to a simmer. Add the asparagus tips and simmer about 2 minutes. Add the fresh lemon juice and thyme, and correct the seasoning to taste with kosher salt and black pepper. Remove from the heat and keep warm.

Cook the gnocchi in two batches. Gently put the gnocchi in the large stockpot of boiling water. When the gnocchi rise to the top, after about 4 minutes, remove them with a slotted spoon to warm bowls. Repeat the procedure until all the gnocchi are cooked.

Spoon about ¼ cup of the sauce over each serving, dividing the asparagus evenly. Then drizzle a little truffle oil over, and serve immediately.

Dried Pasta

Wɪᴛʜ the introduction of electric pasta machines, many people have allowed themselves to be misled into the notion that fresh pasta is always superior to dried commercially manufactured pasta. In many cases it simply isn't true. Fresh pasta can be wonderful for certain types of dishes, but other pasta dishes require the texture and flavor of a dried pasta. Any pasta that you desire to be al dente—that is, with a perceptible resistance to the bite, such as spaghetti or penne—should be made from commercially manufactured dried pasta. With a little experimentation, you should be able to find at a reasonable price a high-quality dried pasta that suits your tastes.

Dried penne with an arrabbiata or puttanesca sauce is a time-proven combination. The thick tomato sauces coat the pasta both inside and out to produce a very hearty dish. Dried spaghetti or linguini is great for supporting meatballs, clams, or mussels. The dense tangle of pasta keeps the pieces from slipping through to the bottom of the bowl.

Chicken Meatballs with Fusilli

THIS is a variation on classic spaghetti and meatballs, the difference being that the relationship between the pasta and the meat is more balanced by the use of a heartier pasta and a lighter chicken meatball. Fusilli comes in two shapes: One looks like an auger, and one resembles a long telephone cord. The telephone-cord shape is preferred for this dish because the curlicue shape holds the sauce and provides support for the chicken meatballs.

2 teaspoons whole coriander
2 teaspoons fennel seed
2 hot red chile peppers
Vegetable oil
1 small onion, peeled and finely diced (½ cup)
4 large garlic cloves, peeled and minced
    (4 teaspoons)
2 pounds ground chicken
1 cup fresh bread crumbs
5 ounces pancetta, diced fine
1 bunch chopped fresh Italian parsley leaves
    (¾ cup)
2 tablespoons chopped fresh marjoram
2 tablespoons chopped fresh sage
Kosher salt
½ cup tawny port
Unbleached all-purpose flour for dusting
1 cup Chicken Stock (see page 187)
1½ cups Slow-roasted Tomatoes (see page 241)
Freshly cracked black pepper
1 pound dry fusilli
Freshly grated Parmesan cheese

Have ready

The Chicken Stock, in a medium saucepan,
    simmering over low heat
The Slow-roasted Tomatoes

Chill the bowl and paddle of an electric mixer in the refrigerator for at least 30 minutes.

To prepare the meatballs: In a small sauté pan, over low heat, combine the coriander, fennel, and chiles, and toast until the mixture becomes aromatic and the ingredients begin to turn slightly brown, about 8 to 10 minutes, stirring constantly. Take care not to burn any of the spices. Remove the spices from the pan and allow to cool. Grind the cooled mixture in a spice grinder, or mortar and pestle, and reserve.

In a medium sauté pan, preheat 1 tablespoon of vegetable oil. Sauté the onion and garlic just to soften, about 3 to 4 minutes. Remove from the heat and reserve.

Put the ground chicken in the chilled bowl of the electric mixer. Add the bread crumbs, pancetta, parsley, marjoram, sage, 2 teaspoons of salt, and the reserved onion and the toasted spice mixtures. Mix on low speed until well combined, about 3 minutes. Increase the speed to medium and slowly add the port and mix for about 2 minutes more. Return the meat to the refrigerator to chill for 1 hour to firm before rolling.

Lightly moisten your hands with cold water to prevent the ground meat from sticking. Form the meat into thirty 1½-inch-diameter meatballs. Each meatball should weigh about 1½ ounces.

In a large stockpot, bring approximately 4 quarts of water to a boil and add 1 tablespoon of kosher salt.

In a large sauté pan, over medium-high heat, preheat 2 tablespoons of vegetable oil almost to smoking. Sprinkle a little flour over the meatballs and brown them thoroughly, about 5 minutes. The meatballs should be browned in 2 batches. When all the meatballs are browned, remove them from the pan, discard the oil, and reduce the heat to low. Return the meatballs to the pan and add the stock and Slow-roasted Tomatoes, and simmer about 15 minutes. Correct the seasoning to taste with kosher salt and black pepper.

While the meatballs are simmering, cook the pasta al dente according to the manufacturer's directions, in the large stockpot of boiling water. Using a colander, drain the pasta.

Divide the pasta equally among 6 large warm soup plates. Distribute 5 meatballs and about ⅓ cup of sauce over each portion, top with freshly grated Parmesan cheese, and serve immediately.

Spaghetti with Artichokes, Endive, and Fennel

Serves 4

EARLY spring is the best time to prepare this dish; the artichokes and fennel are both at the peak of their season, and the endive is readily available. We normally think of spring dishes as being comprised of tender, young vegetables, with mild and sweet flavors. This dish is more robust, because the sautéed endive adds a sharp, slightly bitter flavor. The Garlic Bread Crumbs add a crunchy and flavorful contrast to the braised artichokes and fennel, and the soft pasta.

4 small artichokes (1½ pounds)
Juice of 1 medium lemon
2 medium fennel bulbs (1½ pounds), trimmed
3 cups Chicken Stock (see page 187)
Kosher salt
¼ cup vegetable oil
2 endive heads (8 ounces), trimmed and cut in
    half lengthwise
Freshly cracked black pepper
3 large garlic cloves, peeled and minced
    (1 tablespoon)
12 ounces dry spaghetti
¼ stick (1 ounce) unsalted butter
2 ounces (1½ cups) Italian parsley leaves
Fresh lemon juice
Garlic Bread Crumbs (see page 226)

Have ready
The Chicken Stock
The Garlic Bread Crumbs

PREHEAT the oven to 400 degrees.

Using your hands, peel off most of the artichoke leaves, leaving the last few atop the heart. Using a sharp knife, trim the bottom and stems and cut each artichoke in half lengthwise. Cut out the choke, and then cut each half into thin slices, lengthwise. Place the artichoke pieces in a small mixing bowl filled with cold water. Squeeze the lemon juice into the water and add the 2 halves of the lemon as well. Reserve.

Cut the fennel bulbs in half vertically. In a medium sauté pan, over medium-high heat, combine the fennel halves and 2 cups of the Chicken Stock, and bring to a simmer. Reduce the heat to low, cover, and simmer until tender, about 20 to 30 minutes. Remove the fennel from the pan; allow to cool until the fennel can be handled comfortably. Reserve the cooking liquid. Using a sharp knife, cut the fennel bulb into long, thin strips.

In a large stockpot, bring approximately 4 quarts of water to a boil, and add 1 tablespoon of kosher salt.

While the fennel is simmering, in a large cast-iron skillet, over medium-high heat, preheat 2 tablespoons of the vegetable oil. Sauté the endive, cut side down, until lightly browned, about 3 minutes. Add 1 cup of the Chicken Stock. Reduce the heat to low and season lightly with kosher salt and black pepper; cover and simmer until tender, about 15 minutes. Remove the endive from the pan, discard the cooking liquid, and cut the halves lengthwise to make quarter sections.

Drain the artichoke slices thoroughly. Pat dry with a clean kitchen towel. Wipe the large cast-iron skillet clean, and over medium-high heat, preheat the remaining 2 tablespoons of vegetable oil. Sauté the artichokes until lightly brown, about 5 minutes. Add the reserved fennel cooking liquid and the garlic, and simmer about 3 minutes.

In the large stockpot of boiling water, cook the pasta al dente, according to the manufacturer's instructions. Drain the pasta in a colander. Divide the pasta among 4 large, warm soup plates.

While the pasta is cooking, whisk the butter into the cooking liquid of the artichokes in the large cast-iron skillet. Add the fennel, endive, and parsley, and toss gently to combine and heat through, about 2 minutes. Adjust the seasoning to taste with kosher salt and black pepper.

Ladle the sauce and vegetables over the pasta in the soup plates. Garnish with a squeeze of lemon juice and a generous sprinkling of Garlic Bread Crumbs, and serve immediately.

Duck Confit Ragout

Serves 6

THIS ragout of pasta, beans, mushrooms, and duck is complex, hearty, and too much trouble to serve as an appetizer, so at Campanile we generally serve it as a main course. As a variation you could add some greens, such as arugula or spinach, as a contrast to the richness of the confit. Another option is to garnish the ragout with wedges of sweet, caramelized onion. If you don't include the pasta, this can be made into a warm main-course salad just by tossing the ragout with a mixture of bitter greens and baby escarole. Fresh pasta is preferred, but 12 ounces of dry pappardelle or fettuccine may be substituted.

Pasta Dough (see page 97) (13 ounces)
6 duck legs from Duck Confit (see page 164)
2 large garlic cloves, peeled and thinly sliced
4 ounces fresh shiitake mushrooms, stemmed
    and sliced
6 large shallots, peeled, trimmed, and finely
    sliced (6 tablespoons)
Kosher salt
Freshly cracked black pepper
½ cup tawny port
½ cup balsamic vinegar
2 cups Duck Stock or Chicken Stock
    (see page 188 or 187)
½ teaspoon chopped fresh thyme
½ teaspoon chopped fresh rosemary
½ cup Cannellini Beans (see page 246)

Have ready

The Duck Confit
The Duck Stock or Chicken Stock, warm, in a
    small saucepan over low heat
The Pasta Dough

PREPARE pappardelle (6-by-1-inch pieces) according to the instructions in the Pasta Dough recipe (see page 97).

Remove the duck legs from the fat and place them in a large sauté pan. Over low heat, warm the duck legs just to melt the fat, taking care not to start frying the duck legs, about 10 minutes. Remove the duck legs from the pan and let them cool on a large baking pan. Pour all but 3 tablespoons of the duck fat into a small mixing bowl, and allow it to cool. When it has reached room temperature, pour it back into the container of confit. Reserve the 3 tablespoons of duck fat in the large sauté pan.

Shred the meat from the legs into bite-sized pieces, to make about 3¼ cups of shredded duck meat. Reserve the shredded duck meat in a small mixing bowl.

In a large sauté pan, over medium heat, preheat the 3 tablespoons of duck fat. Sauté the garlic until it just begins to color, about 1 minute. Add the mushrooms and the shallots and sauté until softened, about 3 to 4 minutes. Season lightly with kosher salt and black pepper. Deglaze the sauté pan with the port. Add the vinegar and reduce by half, about 10 minutes. Pour in the stock, add the thyme and rosemary, and reduce by one quarter, about 5 to 8 minutes. Stir in the shredded duck and the beans and heat through, about 10 minutes. Correct the seasoning to taste with kosher salt and black pepper.

In a large stockpot, bring approximately 4 quarts of water to a boil and add 1 tablespoon of kosher salt.

Cook the pappardelle in the stockpot of boiling water about 1 to 2 minutes. Using a colander, drain the pasta and place it in a large mixing bowl.

Toss the cooked pasta and the confit mixture in the large mixing bowl and correct the seasoning to taste with kosher salt and black pepper. Divide equally among 6 large, warm plates and serve immediately.

Pasta al Ceppo with Wild Mushrooms and Duck Confit

Serves 6

THE very name of this dish would seem to epitomize fall. When this is served with a simple salad of fennel and arugula, you have a complete and filling autumn meal. Pasta al ceppo is a rolled sheet pasta that is shaped something like a cinnamon stick. It is more substantial in texture than penne; it holds sauce well and has a toothy bite.

12 ounces assorted fresh mushrooms (button, shiitake, chanterelle)
2 tablespoons vegetable oil
Kosher salt
Freshly cracked black pepper
2 tablespoons balsamic vinegar
¾ cup leeks, well washed and trimmed
2 large shallots, peeled, trimmed, and minced (2 tablespoons)
½ cup port
1 cup Duck Stock or Brown Veal Stock (see page 188 or 190)
½ teaspoon chopped fresh rosemary
½ teaspoon chopped fresh thyme
½ ounce dried porcini mushrooms, soaked for 15 minutes in ½ cup warm water (optional)
¾ pound dry pasta al ceppo
½ pound shredded (1 cup packed) Duck Confit (see page 164)

Pasta al Ceppo with Wild Mushrooms and Duck Confit (cont.)

Have ready

The Duck Confit, cooked and shredded
The Duck Stock or Brown Veal Stock, warm, in a small saucepan over low heat

THE button mushrooms can be washed, but the shiitakes and chanterelles should be gently wiped clean with a damp kitchen towel, as washing will make them soggy. Using a sharp knife, trim the stems of the button and shiitake mushrooms. Then cut the button and shiitake mushrooms into quarters. Using your fingers, pull the chanterelles into thick shreds.

In a large sauté pan, over high heat, preheat 1 tablespoon of the vegetable oil. Sauté the mushrooms, turning to brown on all sides, about 5 minutes, and season lightly with kosher salt and black pepper. Transfer the mushrooms to a medium mixing bowl and reserve. Add the balsamic vinegar to the sauté pan, and cook for 1 or 2 minutes to deglaze the pan. Pour the deglazed liquid over the mushrooms in the mixing bowl, and reserve.

Wipe the sauté pan clean, and over medium heat, preheat the remaining 1 tablespoon of vegetable oil. Add the leeks and shallots, and sauté lightly, about 2 minutes. Add the port, deglaze the pan, and reduce by half, about 5 to 8 minutes. Add the stock, the rosemary, and thyme. If the dried mushrooms are to be used, add them at this point, including the soaking water, taking care to prevent any dirt from the dried mushrooms from pouring into the sauce. Reduce until the sauce thickens slightly, about 10 minutes. Season to taste with kosher salt and black pepper, and keep warm.

In a large stockpot, bring approximately 4 quarts of water to a boil, and add 1 tablespoon of kosher salt. Cook the pasta al dente, according to the manufacturer's instructions. Drain the pasta in a colander.

Add the pasta, the mushrooms, and the Duck Confit to the sauce, and stir to heat through, about 3 minutes. Correct the seasoning to taste with kosher salt and black pepper. Divide equally among 6 large, warm plates, and serve immediately.

Gnocchette with Beans, Bacon, and Fall Vegetables

THIS hearty dish can be interpreted as an evolution of the venerable minestrone or as a refreshing change from the usual brown stews of fall. We use a wide variety of beans and vegetables to produce a dish of beautiful colors, subtle tastes, and many different textures. This can be prepared as a purely vegetarian meal; simply substitute Vegetable Stock (see page 196) or water for the Chicken Stock, omit the bacon, and add some sliced sun-dried tomatoes at the same time as the beans.

4 ounces bacon, cut into 4 slices
¼ cup vegetable oil
8 ounces butternut or kabocha squash, peeled, seeded, and cut into ⅜-inch dice (1 cup)
1 large carrot, peeled and cut into ⅜-inch dice (1 cup)
1 medium onion, peeled and cut into ⅜-inch dice (1 cup)
4 stalks of celery, cut into ⅜-inch dice
3 large garlic cloves, peeled and minced (1 tablespoon)
2 bay leaves
Kosher salt
Freshly cracked black pepper
¼ cup balsamic vinegar
4 cups Chicken Stock (see page 187)
½ teaspoon chopped fresh rosemary

1 teaspoon chopped fresh thyme
2½ cups cooked beans (black runners, cannellini, flageolet), using a combination of 2 or 3 varieties
8 ounces dry gnocchette (or other shell pasta of your choice)
2 cups arugula or spinach leaves, washed and stemmed

Garnish

1 cup Garlic Bread Crumbs (see page 226)

Have ready

The Chicken Stock, warm, in a medium saucepan over low heat
The cooked beans
The Garlic Bread Crumbs

IN a large saucepan, bring 2 quarts of water to a simmer.

Cut each slice of bacon into ¾-inch pieces. Blanch the bacon in a fine-mesh, stainless-steel strainer in the simmering water to cover for about 5 minutes, to reduce the amount of fat in the bacon. Remove the bacon from the pan, drain well, and reserve. Discard the water.

In a large saucepan, over medium heat, preheat the vegetable oil. Sauté the squash and carrot for about 2 minutes, then add the onion, celery, and garlic and continue to sauté 1 to 2 minutes longer, stirring occasionally. Add the bay leaves and the blanched bacon and season lightly with kosher salt and black pepper. Continue to sauté until the onion is translucent, about 5 minutes. Take care not to brown the vegetables and bacon too much, as only a little color is desired at this point.

Add the vinegar and deglaze the pan over medium heat. Continue to cook to reduce by half, about 2 to 3 minutes. Add the stock and bring to a boil. Reduce the heat until the stock is just simmering. Stir in the rosemary, thyme, and the beans. Continue to simmer until the vegetables are al dente, about 10 minutes longer. Using a ladle, skim off any foam or fat that rises to the top.

Meanwhile, in a large stockpot, bring approximately 4 quarts of water to a boil, and add 1 tablespoon kosher salt.

Add the gnocchette to the boiling water and cook al dente, according to the manufacturer's directions. Using a colander, drain the pasta well, and add it to the stew. Correct the seasoning to taste with kosher salt and black pepper.

Before serving, warm the stew over medium heat and stir in the arugula or spinach leaves in the final few seconds, stirring just until they wilt.

Divide among 8 large, warm soup plates, making certain that some of each of the ingredients is included in each portion. Sprinkle the Garlic Bread Crumbs over the top and serve immediately.

Penne alla Puttanesca

Serves 4 to 6

THIS classic dish, made famous by the prostitutes of Rome, will be at its peak in summer, when the best tomatoes are available. In this recipe, we roast the tomatoes differently than in Slow-roasted Tomatoes (see page 241). We roast tomatoes for puttanesca quickly at a high temperature, because it isn't important that they retain their shape. This recipe makes a large quantity because it keeps so well. The sauce can be refrigerated in a covered container for up to 5 days. It can be kept frozen for months, to always have a taste of summer available.

5 pounds (6 or 7 large) ripe tomatoes, cut in half
4 tablespoons extra-virgin olive oil
3 large shallots, peeled, trimmed, and minced (3 tablespoons)
6 large garlic cloves, peeled and minced (6 teaspoons)

Kosher salt

1½ teaspoons chopped fresh rosemary

1½ teaspoons chopped fresh thyme

1 teaspoon freshly cracked black pepper

1 large onion, peeled, trimmed, and diced
(1¼ cups)

3 ounces pancetta, diced

5 anchovy fillets, chopped fine

1 small garlic clove, peeled and minced
(1 teaspoon)

1 cup dry white wine

3 cups Chicken Stock (see page 187)

5 ounces (1 cup) black oil-cured olives, pitted

3 tablespoons drained capers

½ teaspoon ground dry red chile pepper

Bouquet garni (1 small sprig fresh rosemary,
1 sprig fresh thyme, 1 bay leaf)

1 pound dry penne

Have ready

The Chicken Stock

PREHEAT the oven to 400 degrees.

Place the tomatoes, 3 tablespoons olive oil, shallots, garlic, 1 tablespoon kosher salt, rosemary, thyme, and black pepper in a large mixing bowl, and toss to combine. Arrange the tomatoes, cut side down, on 1 or 2 baking pans, and then scrape the ingredients from the bowl over the tomatoes. Roast the tomatoes until tender, 50 to 60 minutes (depending on their size).

Remove the baking pans from the oven and allow the tomatoes to cool slightly. Then put the tomatoes and pan juices through a food mill to remove the skins and seeds. Discard the skins and seeds, and reserve the tomato puree until needed.

In a large saucepan, over medium heat, preheat 1 tablespoon of olive oil. Gently sauté the onion, pancetta, anchovies, and garlic for 2 or 3 minutes, taking care not to color. Add the wine and cook for 2 to 3 minutes. Add the reserved puree, Chicken Stock, olives, capers, ground chile pepper, and the bouquet garni, and simmer gently until the sauce thickens, about 30 minutes longer. Remove and discard the bouquet garni.

In a large stockpot, over high heat, bring approximately 4 quarts of water to a boil and add 1 tablespoon of kosher salt.

Add the penne and cook al dente, according to the manufacturer's directions. Drain the pasta in a colander.

To serve, divide the penne among 4 to 6 plates, then ladle the desired amount of sauce over it. Serve with freshly shaved Parmesan, if desired.

Veal Bolognese with Pappardelle

Serves 8 (yields about
10 cups)

AMERICAN-STYLE spaghetti sauce (canned
tomatoes and ground beef) is a poor, simplified
version of Bolognese sauce. Good Bolognese is
complex, very rich and flavorful, and has a
chewy texture. The sauce must simmer long
and slow, just barely bubbling, each ingredient
releasing the essence of its flavor to the whole.

This recipe produces more sauce than is
needed for eight portions, but it freezes well
and can be used for lasagna or perhaps, if you
cook it down a little, as a stuffing for ravioli. We
serve it with pappardelle, because such a robust
sauce requires a substantial pasta to complement
it. If you wish to use equal amounts of Brown
Veal Stock (see page 190) and Chicken Stock,
instead of only Chicken Stock, the sauce will
be even richer. It is more luxurious, but certainly not necessary.

6 or 7 large ripe tomatoes (5 pounds) cut in half
3 tablespoons extra-virgin olive oil
3 large shallots, peeled, trimmed, and minced
   (3 tablespoons)
6 large garlic cloves, peeled and minced
   (6 teaspoons)
Kosher salt
1½ teaspoons chopped fresh rosemary
1½ teaspoons chopped fresh thyme
Freshly cracked black pepper
2 pounds shoulder of veal

¼ cup vegetable oil
2 large carrots (½ pound) peeled, and cut into
   ¼-inch dice
1 medium onion (½ pound) peeled, and cut
   into ¼-inch dice
4 or 5 large ribs celery (½ pound) peeled, and
   cut into ¼-inch dice
1 small fennel bulb (½ pound) trimmed, and cut
   into ¼-inch dice
6 large garlic cloves, peeled and minced
   (2 tablespoons)
3 ounces pancetta, cut into ¼-inch dice
   (optional)
1 cup port
1 cup dry red wine
6 cups Chicken Stock (see page 187)
Bouquet garni (1 sprig rosemary, 1 sprig thyme,
   2 bay leaves, 2 sprigs parsley, 4 whole
   cloves, zest of 1 medium lemon)
Ground dried red chile pepper flakes
1 pound dry pappardelle
Freshly grated Parmesan cheese for garnish

Have ready

The Chicken Stock

PREHEAT the oven to 400 degrees.

Place the tomatoes, olive oil, shallots, garlic, 1 tablespoon of kosher salt, the rosemary, thyme and 1 teaspoon of the black pepper in a large mixing bowl, and toss to combine. Arrange the tomatoes, cut side down, on 1 or 2 baking pans, and then scrape the ingredients from the bowl over the tomatoes. Roast the tomatoes until tender, 50 to 60 minutes (depending on size).

Remove the baking pans from the oven and allow the tomatoes to cool slightly. Put the tomatoes and pan juices through a food mill to remove the skins and seeds. Discard the skins and seeds, and reserve the tomato puree until needed.

Using a large, sharp knife, trim the veal shoulder of excess fat. Discard the fat, and cut the meat into 1½-inch cubes. Season the veal lightly with kosher salt and black pepper.

In a large stockpot, over high heat, preheat the vegetable oil. Sauté the veal pieces until browned, about 10 to 15 minutes. Reduce the heat to medium and stir in the carrots, onion, celery, fennel, garlic, and, if desired, pancetta. Sauté until lightly browned, about 5 minutes. Deglaze the pot with the port, add the red wine, and reduce by half, about 10 minutes. Add the stock, the roasted tomato puree, and the bouquet garni. Season with kosher salt, black pepper, and a pinch of dried red chile flakes.

Bring to a boil, then reduce to very low heat and simmer gently, about 1½ to 2 hours, stirring occasionally to prevent the bottom from burning, until the veal becomes fork tender. Skim as necessary, using a ladle to remove any foam or excess fat that rises to the surface.

Using a slotted spoon, remove the veal pieces from the sauce and place them in a medium mixing bowl. Continue to simmer the sauce over very low heat. Using two forks, coarsely shred the veal pieces, and return the shredded meat and juices to the sauce. Continue to simmer the sauce over very low heat for about 30 minutes longer, stirring occasionally to prevent the sauce from burning on the bottom of the pot. Correct the seasoning to taste with kosher salt, black pepper, and red chile pepper. Remove and discard the bouquet garni. Use the sauce as needed, or freeze in sealed plastic containers.

In a large stockpot, over high heat, bring 4 quarts of water to a boil and add 1 tablespoon of kosher salt.

Cook the pasta until it is al dente, according to the manufacturer's directions. Drain the pasta in a colander, then place it in a large mixing bowl and toss with a ladleful of the Bolognese sauce. To serve, divide the pasta equally among 8 large, warm soup plates and add about ½ cup of the Bolognese sauce to each portion. Serve immediately with freshly grated Parmesan. This is even more delicious with a little basil pesto drizzled over the top.

Penne with Gorgonzola, Walnuts, and Spinach

Serves 4

WHEN selecting a Gorgonzola for this dish, be sure to get one that is young and firm as opposed to one more aged, soft, and pungent. Heating accentuates flavors and aromas, so an older Gorgonzola will be too pungent and will overwhelm all other flavors. This is a good lunchtime dish; it is rich and flavorful but still light, and can be put together in about 20 minutes.

½ cup walnut halves
8 ounces dry penne
1 cup Chicken Stock or Vegetable Stock
    (see page 187 or 196)
½ stick (2 ounces) unsalted butter
1 teaspoon fresh savory leaves
3 cups loosely packed spinach leaves
4 ounces Gorgonzola cheese, broken or cut
    into chunks
Kosher salt
Freshly cracked black pepper
Juice of ½ medium lemon

Have ready

The Chicken Stock or Vegetable Stock

PREHEAT the oven to 325 degrees.

Spread the walnut halves on a baking pan and toast in the oven about 8 to 10 minutes, stirring with a spatula halfway through. Take care not to brown the walnuts, as it will produce a bitter flavor. Remove the walnuts from the oven, allow them to cool, and reserve.

In a large stockpot, over high heat, bring approximately 4 quarts of water to a boil and add 1 tablespoon of kosher salt. Add the penne and cook al dente, according to the manufacturer's directions. Drain the pasta in a colander.

While the pasta is cooking, in a large saucepan, over medium heat, combine the stock, butter, and the savory leaves. Cook until the butter is completely dissolved, about 3 to 5 minutes.

Stir in the walnuts, then the spinach, and cook about 1 minute longer. Add the cooked penne and about three quarters of the cheese, reserving a little to crumble over the pasta as a garnish, and heat through, about 1 minute. (The Gorgonzola should not completely melt.) Adjust the seasoning to taste with kosher salt, black pepper, and fresh lemon juice.

Divide the penne among 4 large, warm soup plates. Spoon the sauce over, equally dividing walnuts and spinach leaves among the plates. Crumble the reserved Gorgonzola over, and serve immediately.

Risotto

ALL the romantic mystery and second-generation folklore about risotto cooking techniques can be so daunting that even experienced cooks will opt for something else. The big secret is that there is no secret. Simply buy the best Italian rice—large, unbroken grains of arborio rice—and follow the simple, proper steps. That's it, and maybe a little practice to refine your perception of the risotto as it cooks, learning to read the rice to know when to add more stock. It is important to have all the ingredients ready beforehand, as risotto is a high-maintenance dish. If you neglect it for more than a few moments, it can burn. This isn't to say that it will go wrong as soon as the baby cries or the phone rings, just that there is a significant possibility for error if the cook's attention is diverted for too long at the wrong time. If risotto is to be prepared properly, it must be stirred not necessarily vigorously, but certainly with at least some level of numbing regularity so the broth becomes creamy while the rice is absorbing the stock. The variations in added ingredients and flavorings won't change the procedure drastically, so feel free to experiment once you understand the basic technique.

For our preferred procedure, please refer to our basic Risotto with Sweet Onion and Parmesan (next page).

Risotto with Sweet Onion and Parmesan

Serves 6

WITH risotto, you can't wing it. It's not diffi-cult to make good risotto, but it does require attention. Basic risotto is very versatile; with the addition of a few simple ingredients, risotto can be transformed into anything from a simple first course to almost a full meal.

3 tablespoons extra-virgin olive oil
1 medium sweet onion (Vidalia, Maui, or Walla
    Walla) (8 ounces), peeled and finely diced
1 pound (2 cups) arborio rice
1 cup dry white wine
Kosher salt
1 large garlic clove, peeled and finely chopped
    (1 tablespoon)
6¼ cups Chicken Stock or Vegetable Stock
    (see page 187 or 196)
½ stick (2 ounces) unsalted butter, cut into
    small pieces
¼ cup (1 ounce) freshly grated Parmesan cheese

Have ready

The Chicken Stock in a medium saucepan, at a
    gentle simmer over low heat

IN a large sauté pan, over medium-high heat, preheat 1 tablespoon of the olive oil. Sauté the sweet onion until it becomes translucent but still crunchy, about 2 minutes.

In the same large sauté pan, over medium heat, preheat the remaining olive oil. Add the rice and stir to coat with the oil. Using a wooden spoon, stir the rice continuously for about 5 minutes. Do not let the rice start to brown.

When the rice turns opaque and begins to give off a nutty aroma, add the white wine and 1 teaspoon of kosher salt. Reduce the heat to medium low and cook, stirring slowly but con-stantly, just until the wine is almost absorbed. The risotto should begin to appear creamy at this point; keep stirring. Stir in the chopped garlic, and add 1 cup of the simmering stock. Cook until the stock is almost absorbed, about 2 to 4 minutes.

Continue to add the simmering stock, ½ cup at a time, stirring continuously, until each ½ cup is absorbed, about 15 to 18 minutes total, and 1¼ cups stock remain.★

Season with about 2¼ teaspoons of kosher salt. Pour in ¾ cup more of the stock, and when that has been absorbed, after about 2 minutes,

★ When 1¼ cups stock remain, the risotto can be scraped out of the saucepan and spread over a baking tray and refrigerated until just before serving time. When almost ready to serve, scrape the rice back into a clean sauté pan, pour in ½ cup of the simmering stock, and continue to stir over low heat. Finish as described above.

add the remaining ½ cup of stock. The rice should be creamy, but not runny, and firm, but not hard. Stir in the butter and Parmesan cheese, and continue to stir off the heat for about 1 minute longer. The total cooking time for the risotto should be about 18 to 22 minutes. Correct the seasoning to taste with kosher salt and serve immediately.

SIMPLE VARIATIONS

Grains

A number of different grains can be added to risotto for a chewier texture and nuttier flavor. Add ¼ cup of toasted flax or ½ cup of cooked faro or barley at the same time as the onions, and finish the risotto normally.

Beans

Beans can be added to impart a hearty, smokey quality to risotto. This is perfect for a warm, filling winter lunch. Add 1 teaspoon chopped fresh thyme at the same time as the onions; 5 minutes before serving, add ½ cup of cooked cranberry beans and ¼ cup of rendered and diced bacon, and finish the risotto normally.

Potatoes

Adding spring potatoes and asparagus will bring the light flavor of spring to risotto. Add ½ cup of steamed, diced red or white rose potatoes and ½ cup of blanched asparagus tips at the very last moment; simply stir in before serving.

Sausage

Just adding a little meat will transform risotto into a main course. Add 8 ounces of cooked crumbled sausage and 2 cups of roughly chopped raw spinach in the last 2 minutes; simply stir in before serving.

Radicchio

A little julienne of radicchio and a few tender celery leaves add sharp flavor and beautiful color without bulk. Add ¼ cup of thinly sliced radicchio and tender yellow celery leaves at the very last moment, and simply stir in before serving.

Squash and Peas

Bright and summery risotto is a simple matter of adding fresh peas, diced squash, and fresh mint. Sauté ½ cup of diced yellow squash (acorn or butternut) in 1 tablespoon of olive oil until just tender. Add the squash and 1 cup of shelled raw peas about 5 minutes before serving, and finish the risotto normally, with 1 teaspoon of chopped fresh mint added just before serving.

Saffron Risotto with Clams, Spanish Sausage, and Borlotti Beans

Serves 4 to 6

THIS dish is a simple version of paella, a meal in a single pan. It is creamy and not as heavy as a traditional paella. The meat and beans add flavoring and textural elements rather than large masses of protein. A good first course for this dish is a simple fig and fennel salad. Then just bring the big pot of risotto out and place it in the middle of the table on your best trivet.

A pinch of saffron threads

6¼ cups Chicken Stock (see page 187)

2 tablespoons extra-virgin olive oil

1 medium sweet onion (Vidalia, Maui, or Walla Walla) (8 ounces), peeled and finely diced

1 pound (2 cups) arborio rice

1 cup dry white wine

Kosher salt

1 large garlic clove, peeled and finely chopped (1 tablespoon)

1 tablespoon (½ ounce) unsalted butter

8 medium (8 ounces) asparagus stalks, trimmed, peeled, and cut into 1-inch pieces

½ cup cooked borlotti or cranberry beans (see Marinated Bean Salad, page 65)

¼ pound thin Spanish sausage, cooked and cut into 1-inch pieces

24 manila clams, scrubbed clean

Freshly cracked white pepper

Chopped Italian parsley

Have ready

The Chicken Stock in a medium saucepan, at a gentle simmer over low heat

ADD the saffron threads to the simmering Chicken Stock.

In a large sauté pan, over medium-high heat, preheat 1 tablespoon of the olive oil. Sauté the sweet onion until it becomes translucent but still crunchy, about 2 minutes.

In the same large sauté pan, over medium heat, add the remaining olive oil. Add the rice and stir to coat with the oil. Using a wooden spoon, stir the rice continuously for about 5 minutes. Do not let the rice start to brown.

When the rice turns opaque and begins to give off a nutty aroma, add the white wine and 1 teaspoon of kosher salt. Reduce the heat to medium low and cook, stirring slowly but constantly, just until the wine is almost absorbed. The risotto should begin to appear creamy at this point; keep stirring. Stir in the chopped garlic, and add 1 cup of the simmering stock. Cook until the stock is almost absorbed, about 2 to 4 minutes.

Continue to add the simmering stock, ½ cup at a time, stirring continuously, until each ½ cup is absorbed, about 15 to 18 minutes total, and 1¼ cup remains.★

★ When 1¼ cups stock remain, the risotto can be scraped out of the saucepan and spread over a baking tray and refrigerated until just before serving time. When almost ready to serve, scrape the rice back into a clean sauté pan, pour in ½ cup of the simmering stock, and continue to stir over low heat. Finish as described above.

Add ¾ cup more stock, the butter, asparagus, beans, and sausage, and stir briefly just to combine. Add the remaining ½ cup of stock, and stir briefly to combine. Add the clams to the top of the risotto, cover the pan with the lid, reduce the heat to very low, and steam the clams until the shells open, about 4 to 5 minutes. Remove and discard any clams that do not open. The total cooking time should be about 19 to 22 minutes. Correct the seasoning to taste with kosher salt and white pepper. Garnish the top of the risotto with chopped parsley.

Bring the pan to the table, place it on a heatproof surface or trivet, and serve immediately.

Risotto with Mussels, Peas, and Parsley

Serves 4

In this risotto there is wonderful texture and flavor contrast between the rich, soft mussels and the fresh sweet peas. It is a dish to welcome the bounty of spring. Accompanied by a bottle of good white wine and a loaf of crusty bread, it makes a great lunch. We use Chicken Stock or Vegetable Stock rather than fish stock because the juice of the mussels is distinctive, and the addition of fish stock would make the seafood flavor in the rice too prominent.

Mussel Stock

24 mussels (12 ounces), Prince Edward Island variety preferred
2 tablespoons extra-virgin olive oil
2 ounces button mushrooms, diced (stems can be used for this)
2 large shallots, peeled, trimmed, and minced (2 tablespoons)
3 large garlic cloves, peeled and minced (1 tablespoon)
½ small fennel bulb, diced (¼ cup)
1 sprig fennel fronds
1 sprig fresh thyme
1 sprig fresh Italian parsley
1 sprig fresh basil
1 cup dry white wine

Risotto

3½ cups Chicken Stock or Vegetable Stock (see page 187 or 196), plus additional as necessary
¼ teaspoon saffron threads
2 tablespoons extra-virgin olive oil
12 ounces (1½ cups) arborio rice
1 cup dry white wine
Kosher salt
1 cup shelled fresh peas
¼ stick (1 ounce) unsalted butter
¼ cup chopped fresh Italian parsley leaves
1 tablespoon fresh lemon juice
Freshly cracked white pepper
½ cup fresh whole Italian parsley leaves

To prepare the mussel stock: Scrub the mussels well under cold running water and then remove the beard found on the side of each mussel. Do not use any mussels that have broken or opened shells.

In a medium sauté pan, over medium heat, preheat the olive oil. Stir in the mushrooms, shallots, garlic, fennel, and herbs. Sweat the vegetables and herbs about 3 to 4 minutes. Add the white wine and simmer for 2 or 3 minutes. Add the mussels, and cover and steam until they open, about 3 to 5 minutes. After the majority of the mussels have opened, remove the open ones to a warm platter. Continue to cook any unopened mussels for 1 additional minute to determine if any more will open. Remove all opened mussels to the platter, and discard any unopened mussels.

Strain the stock into a medium mixing bowl through a clean, moist cloth to remove any sand. Discard the vegetables and herbs. Refrigerate the mussels and the stock separately until needed. While the rice is cooking, remove the mussels from their shells, reserving 8 of the nicest mussels in the half shell.

To prepare the risotto: Combine the Chicken Stock and the reserved mussel stock and bring to a simmer, stirring in the saffron threads as the stock heats. In a large sauté pan, over medium heat, preheat the olive oil. Using a wooden spoon, stir in the rice and keep stirring until the rice becomes opaque and begins to give off a nutty aroma, about 5 minutes. Add the wine, reduce the heat to medium low, and season with 1 teaspoon of kosher salt. Cook, stirring all the while, until the wine is almost absorbed.

Pour ½ cup of the stock mixture into the rice and cook over low heat, stirring, until the stock is almost absorbed. Continue adding the stock mixture to the rice, ½ cup at a time, reserving ¼ cup, until the rice is almost cooked, about 14 to 17 minutes. Stir in the shelled peas and cook about 5 minutes longer, until the rice is creamy and a little runny. (When you bite into a grain of rice there should be a tiny white dot in the center.)

Stir the reserved shelled mussels into the risotto. Stir in the butter, the chopped parsley leaves, and the lemon juice; correct the seasoning to taste with kosher salt and white pepper. In a small covered saucepan, over medium heat, warm the reserved 8 mussels in the shells with the reserved ¼ cup of stock.

Spoon the risotto into 4 large, warm soup bowls, making certain that the shelled mussels are divided equally. Arrange 2 mussels in the half shell in each bowl and garnish with a few whole parsley leaves, and serve immediately.

Risotto Cakes

As is the case with risotto itself, many variations are possible with risotto cakes. You are only limited by the availability of good ingredients. Because both risotto and risotto cakes are time intensive, yet simply flavored, it is important that you don't waste your time and degrade the dish by using poor ingredients.

For variety in taste and texture, small amounts of other cooked grains can be added to the risotto. Add ¼ cup of toasted flax, or ½ cup of cooked farro or barley can be added a few minutes before the risotto is finished.

2 tablespoons extra-virgin olive oil
1 small onion, peeled, trimmed, and diced
 (¾ cup)
1 large garlic clove, peeled and minced
 (1 teaspoon)
12 ounces (1½ cups) arborio rice
½ cup dry white wine
3½ to 4 cups Chicken Stock (see page 187)
¼ cup freshly grated Parmesan cheese
1½ teaspoons kosher salt
1 teaspoon freshly cracked white pepper
¼ cup vegetable oil

Have ready

The Chicken Stock, simmering, in a medium
 saucepan over low heat

In a large saucepan, over medium heat, preheat the olive oil. Sauté the onion and garlic for 1 to 2 minutes. Using a wooden spoon, stir in the rice, coating well. Cook the rice, stirring, until the rice begins to turn opaque, about 5 minutes. Reduce the heat to low, add the wine, and stir until it is almost completely absorbed. Add 1 cup of stock, stirring until the stock is absorbed.

Continue to add stock, ½ cup at a time, stirring constantly, until the rice is tender and the stock is almost completely absorbed, about 20 minutes.

When 3½ cups of stock have been absorbed, check the rice by biting a few grains; it should be cooked through, but still have a slight firmness in the center.

Stir in the grated cheese and correct the seasoning to taste with kosher salt and white pepper. Scrape the risotto out onto a tray, or baking sheet, to cool.

When cool, refrigerate, covered, for at least 1 hour. The rice must be cold and firm before it can be properly formed into cakes.

To form the risotto cakes, moisten your hands in cold water and shape the risotto into 12 patties, each about 3 inches in diameter and ½ inch thick. Place them on a large platter or baking sheet and refrigerate, covered, until needed.

Before sautéing the risotto cakes prepare any accompaniments.

In 1 or 2 sauté pans large enough to hold the risotto cakes in one layer, over medium heat, preheat the vegetable oil until almost smoking. Sauté the risotto cakes until golden brown on one side, about 3 to 5 minutes. Turn and brown on the other side, about 3 to 5 minutes. Remove the risotto cakes from the pans and keep warm.

Creamed Corn, Crab, and Asparagus
(accompaniment for Risotto Cakes)

CREAMED fresh corn is a strong declaration of summer, and paired with blue crab and young asparagus, this is a great opener for a summer dinner on the veranda. The sweetness of the creamed corn and the crab contrasts with the crisp richness of the risotto cake. Pea tendrils, which can be purchased in Oriental markets, are a delicious substitute for the asparagus. Peas are one of the easiest vegetables to grow in home gardens, and you just pick off the tender shoots when needed.

½ recipe (1⅓ cups) Creamed Corn (see page 239)
4 tablespoons (½ stick) unsalted butter
2 large garlic cloves, peeled and thinly sliced
¼ pound thin asparagus tips or pea tendrils
¾ pound cooked crabmeat
Kosher salt
Freshly cracked white pepper

IN a small saucepan, over low heat, warm the Creamed Corn. In a second small saucepan, over medium heat, melt the butter. Sweat the garlic, but do not brown it. Add the asparagus tips or pea tendrils and the crab and cook until the tips are just tender, and the crabmeat is heated through, about 5 minutes. Adjust the seasoning to taste with kosher salt and white pepper.

Divide the Creamed Corn among 6 or 12 warm plates. Place 1 or 2 risotto cakes on the corn and spoon the asparagus or pea tendrils and crabmeat around the cakes evenly; serve immediately.

Polenta

POLENTA is extremely versatile. It can be served soft and warm directly from the pot; it can be chilled, cut into portions, and sautéed; it can be deep fried or even grilled. You can add fresh herbs, spices, or just cracked pepper and salt to make a soothing, filling foundation for any dish with a flavorful broth or sauce. Braised meats, grilled or sautéed fish, stews, and soups can be raised above the level of simple meals with just the addition of polenta.

Dry polenta can be purchased in markets that specialize in Italian foods, and it is becoming more available in everyday supermarkets as well. Avoid instant polenta; it doesn't have the character or the quality of the real stuff. Though polenta can be cooked with just water, cooking it with butter, milk, and stock adds flavor and complexity. Leftover soft polenta should be poured into a shallow pan and allowed to chill until firmly set into a layer about ¾ inch thick.

For a twist (but a logical one if you think of it), polenta is delicious served for breakfast, like oatmeal, with maple syrup. Be sure to omit the Parmesan cheese and herbs if you prepare polenta for breakfast.

3 cups whole milk
3 cups Chicken Stock or Vegetable Stock
    (see page 187 or 196)
½ stick (2 ounces) unsalted butter

1½ cups dry polenta
1½ teaspoons kosher salt
¼ teaspoon freshly ground white pepper
2 teaspoons chopped fresh sage
2 teaspoons chopped fresh thyme
½ teaspoon chopped fresh rosemary
¼ cup freshly grated Parmesan cheese

½ cup unbleached all-purpose flour (for crisp
    polenta)
⅓ cup vegetable oil (for crisp polenta)

Have ready

The Chicken Stock or Vegetable Stock

COMBINE the milk and the stock in a large saucepan and bring to a boil, about 5 minutes. Add the butter, then reduce the heat so that the liquid just simmers. Stir in the polenta, adding it slowly in a steady stream. If you add the polenta all at once, you will end up with uncooked lumps. Season with the kosher salt, white pepper, sage, thyme, and rosemary.

Reduce the heat to medium low, and continue to cook for about 40 minutes, until the polenta is thick and cooked. The polenta should be stirred frequently to prevent it from sticking to the bottom and burning. The frequent stirring performs the same function as it does with risotto; it makes the polenta creamier by releasing some of the starch in the grain. This creamy texture is what is missing in instant polenta.

Stir in the Parmesan cheese and correct the seasoning to taste with additional kosher salt and white pepper. At this point you have soft polenta, and if desired it can be served this way.

To make crisp polenta: Line the bottom of a 13 × 9 × 2-inch baking pan with parchment or waxed paper.

Spread the polenta in the lined baking pan (it should be about ¾ inch deep). Smooth the top with a rubber spatula. Cover with a second sheet of parchment paper and put a second pan on top. Place a few pounds of canned goods (or something of similar mass) on the second tray to weigh it down and level the polenta. Allow to cool to room temperature, about 1 hour, and then refrigerate until very firm, at least 4 hours.

Remove the canned goods, the second tray, and the parchment paper. The polenta should be quite firm and well formed. Cut the firm polenta into 12 approximately 3-inch squares. Then cut each square in half diagonally. Dust each half in flour, shaking off any excess.

In a large sauté pan, over medium heat, preheat 2 tablespoons of oil and put 4 to 6 pieces of polenta in the pan. Brown the polenta on one side, turn, and brown the second side, about 5 minutes on each side. Repeat with the remaining pieces of polenta, adding more oil as necessary. Drain the sautéed polenta pieces on absorbent paper and keep them warm until needed.

To make grilled polenta: Follow the setup and chilling instructions for crisp polenta, but do not flour the polenta. Don't cut the chilled polenta into pieces smaller than 3 inches, as it will be too troublesome to move on the grill.

You must be sure the polenta is well chilled, and the grill is clean and well oiled. Brush the polenta pieces with a little vegetable oil just before grilling.

Grill the chilled polenta over medium heat for about 5 minutes on each side. Don't be impatient to turn the polenta on the grill; only when it begins to brown at the bottom edges will it hold together for turning. If the bottom isn't browned when you try to flip it, the slice will crumble into little pieces and disappear through the grill.

Grilled polenta should be served hot and crisp from the grill.

Polenta Serving Suggestions

Sautéed polenta with puttanesca sauce
Soft polenta with grilled portobello
    mushrooms and sautéed spinach, with a
    teaspoon of pesto drizzled over the top
Sautéed polenta substituted for the pasta in the
    Duck Confit Ragout (see page 120)
Sautéed polenta substituted for the pasta in
    Gnochette with Beans, Bacon, and Fall
    Vegetables (see page 123)
Soft polenta with Grilled Scallops with Warm
    Leek and Bacon Salad (see page 144)

Main Courses

Chapter 7

THE food at Campanile is sometimes described as "simple rustic fare." The perception is that of food, largely in its natural state, quickly grilled and turned out deliciously as bounty of the earth. The reality is that using fresh ingredients means a lot of manual labor.

No dish in this book requires a level of devotion on a par with a religious calling, but the main courses usually have a few ingredients that can take on a life of their own in terms of labor. The guiding philosophy at work here is that a really good thirty-dollar piece of meat can suffer greatly under a sauce based on a sixty-five-cent can of stock. This logic holds true when buying all your ingredients. If you have prepared a brown veal sauce and reduced it down to a sublime level of richness, you don't buy frozen chuck steak at the supermarket because it's on special. Follow this philosophy through to the grill. Use hardwood charcoal, and don't be frugal when building the fire; a slow-cooked, dried out, beef fillet is not a wise tradeoff for the savings on the price of a few pounds of charcoal.

Grilled Scallops with Warm Leek and Bacon Salad

Serves 4

THE smokey flavor of the bacon and the sweetness of the leeks are the perfect complement to the flavor of grilled fresh scallops. The textures of the chewy bacon and the soft scallops contrast wonderfully as well. Fresh scallops should be firm, translucent, and have the distinct scent of the sea. If the scallops are parchment white, flabby, and lacking any scent, they have been soaked in a chemical bath, which adds to the weight and shelf life, but not the quality.

1½ pounds sea scallops
1 tablespoon vegetable oil
Kosher salt
Freshly cracked black pepper
1 tablespoon extra-virgin olive oil
4 ounces bacon, thick-cut slices cut into lardons
2 large leeks, well washed and trimmed, split, and cut into julienne
¼ cup Chicken Stock (see page 187)
2 tablespoons whole grain mustard
Fresh lemon juice

Have ready

The Chicken Stock, warm, in a small saucepan over low heat

SOAK twelve 6-inch wooden skewers in water for about 30 minutes.

Start a fire in the grill and allow it to burn to medium-high temperature.

Clean the scallops, removing the small ligament on the side of each scallop. The scallops should be skewered through the sides, so the flat surfaces line up and come in even contact with the grill. You need to use two 6-inch wooden skewers to hold each group of 5 or 6 scallops, to prevent them from rotating on the skewer. Brush both sides of the scallops with vegetable oil, and season them lightly with kosher salt and black pepper.

In a large sauté pan, over low heat, render the fat from the bacon lardons, about 5 to 8 minutes. Remove the pan from the heat and remove the bacon with a slotted spoon, discarding all but 1 tablespoon of the bacon fat. Drain the bacon on absorbent paper and reserve.

Add the 1 tablespoon of olive oil to the 1 tablespoon of bacon fat in the large sauté pan, and preheat over medium heat, but not to smoking. Add the leeks, season lightly with kosher salt and black pepper, and sauté about 2 to 3 minutes. Return the bacon to the pan, stir, and continue to sauté for 2 minutes longer. Add the Chicken Stock, stir, and cook for about 2 minutes. Remove the pan from the heat, add the mustard, and stir to mix thoroughly. Correct the seasoning to taste with

"THE SMOKEY FLAVOR OF THE BACON AND THE SWEETNESS OF
THE LEEKS ARE THE PERFECT COMPLEMENT TO THE FLAVOR
OF GRILLED FRESH SCALLOPS."

kosher salt, black pepper, and fresh lemon juice, and keep warm.

Grill the skewered scallops over medium-high heat, about 3 to 4 minutes on each side.

Divide the warm leeks and bacon evenly among 4 large, warm plates. Remove the scallops from the skewers, place them on the leeks and bacon, and serve immediately.

Steamed Clams with Pancetta and Borlotti Beans

Serves 4

IF you have chicken stock and some cooked borlotti beans, this can be put together in about 10 minutes. Clams are available year round, but this is a summer meal. The broth is light, the parsley is sharply refreshing, and the clams are meaty, but not too filling.

2 pounds Manila clams, in the shells
4 ounces pancetta, cut into slices ¼ inch thick
3 large garlic cloves, peeled and minced
    (1 tablespoon)
½ cup dry white wine
½ cup Chicken Stock (see page 187)
½ cup cooked borlotti or cranberry beans
    (see Marinated Bean Salad, page 65)
½ stick (2 ounces) unsalted butter, cut in small
    pieces
¼ cup Italian parsley leaves, coarsely chopped
Juice of ½ medium lemon
Kosher salt
Freshly cracked black pepper

Have ready

The Chicken Stock

SCRUB the clams well under cold running water. Do not use any clams that have broken or opened shells. In a large sauté pan, over low heat, render the fat from the pancetta, about 10 to 15 minutes. Drain and discard the fat, then cut the pancetta into lardons, pieces ¼ × 1 inch. Return the pancetta lardons to the sauté pan. Increase the heat to medium, add the garlic to the pan, stir, and cook about 1 minute. Add the white wine and cook about 1 minute. Add the Chicken Stock, and when it comes back to the boil, add the clams; cover the pan and cook about 5 minutes. When the majority of the clams have opened, remove them to warm, large soup bowls. Continue to cook any unopened clams for 1 additional minute to determine if any more will open. Remove any opened clams to the soup bowls, and discard any unopened clams. When all the clams have been removed, add the borlotti beans to the sauté pan and cook just to warm them through, about 2 to 3 minutes. Remove the pan from the heat, stir in the butter and chopped parsley, and season to taste with the lemon juice, kosher salt, and black pepper.

Splash the broth equally over the clams in the bowls, ensuring that the parsley and beans are distributed evenly, and serve immediately.

Black Cod with Brown Butter Sauce and Fresh Herbs

Serves 4

BLACK cod is a West Coast fish. It is white fleshed and very tender. The toasty, nutlike flavor of the brown butter is a wonderful complement to the mild flavor of the black cod. The fish sautés well but is difficult to grill, so this quick preparation is ideal. The fish has a number of small bones, but they are all in a line down the center of the fillet. The best technique to remove the bones is to simply eat half the fillet, then scrape the bones away with your fork and finish eating. This recipe works well with other types of fish, such as rock cod or a true cod from the East Coast.

Four 6-ounce black cod fillets, skin removed
Kosher salt
Freshly cracked black pepper
Unbleached all-purpose flour for dusting
2 tablespoons vegetable oil
1 bunch chives cut 1 inch long (½ cup)
1 bunch fresh Italian parsley, stemmed (1 cup)
1 bunch fresh chervil, stemmed (½ cup)
5 sprigs fresh dill, stemmed (⅓ cup)
1 bunch fresh tarragon, stemmed (⅓ cup)
1 stick (4 ounces) unsalted butter
1 large shallot, peeled, trimmed, and minced
    (1 tablespoon)
Juice of 1 lemon

PREHEAT the oven to 400 degrees.

Lightly season the black cod fillets with kosher salt and black pepper. Then lightly dust the fillets in flour, and shake off any excess flour.

In a large, ovenproof cast-iron skillet, over medium-high heat, preheat the vegetable oil until just smoking. Sear the fillets on the side that was connected to the bone until lightly browned, about 5 minutes. Using a wide stainless-steel spatula, turn the fillets over, and transfer to the oven to cook for about 5 minutes more.

In a large mixing bowl toss together the parsley, chervil, dill, tarragon, and chives.

To serve, divide the herb salad equally among 4 large, warm plates. In a small saucepan, over medium heat, melt and brown, not blacken, the butter, about 3 to 4 minutes. Remove the pan from the heat. Add the shallot and the fresh lemon juice. Adjust the seasoning to taste with kosher salt and black pepper. On each plate, place a fillet next to each portion of herb salad, and splash the brown butter sauce over the salad and the fillet. Serve immediately.

Soft-shell Crabs with Beer Batter

Serves 4 or 8

In many great dishes there are elements that appeal to people's affinity for junk food. Spicy, salty, and sharp flavors, and crisp, deep-fried textures tempt you into eating more than you really want to. At Campanile, when soft-shell crabs are in season, April through August, we can't ever seem to make enough. The intent here is to combine the crisp salty crust, the sharpness of lemon, the sweet taste of the crab, and the zest of the Celery Root Slaw into one intricate but accessible puzzle of flavor and texture. It is very important to keep the batter well chilled, and the oil very hot, to produce a light, crisp, bubbly coating.

Crabs should be purchased live and used the same day. The fishmonger can remove the gills, tail, and eyes of the crabs for you. The terms *prime* and *hotel* are designations for larger-sized crabs. Serve soft-shell crabs with Celery Root Slaw (see page 56), Roasted Garlic Tartar Sauce (see page 208), and wedges of freshly cut lemon.

8 soft-shell crabs, prime or hotel size

Batter

1½ cups unbleached all-purpose flour
1½ cups cornstarch
1 teaspoon crushed dried red chile pepper
2 teaspoons paprika
1 teaspoon baking powder
1 teaspoon kosher salt

1 12-ounce bottle dark beer, chilled
1 cup soda water, chilled
Vegetable oil for deep frying
Celery Root Slaw (see page 56) (½ recipe)
1 lemon, cut into wedges
Roasted Garlic Tartar Sauce (see page 208)

Have ready

The Celery Root Slaw
The Roasted Garlic Tartar Sauce

If the crabs have not been cleaned, using kitchen shears, remove the gills, eyes, and tails. Rinse the crabs under cold water. Refrigerate until needed.

To prepare the batter: In a medium mixing bowl, combine the flour, cornstarch, chile pepper, paprika, baking powder, and kosher salt. Whisk in the beer and as much of the soda water as necessary to make a smooth batter that is a little thinner than pancake batter. Keep the mixing bowl containing the batter in a larger mixing bowl half filled with ice (chilled batter is necessary to make a crisp, lacy crust).

In a deep, heavy saucepan or deep-fat fryer, over high heat, preheat 3 inches of oil to 350 degrees. A deep-fat frying thermometer is necessary to determine the oil temperature. Dip each crab into the batter and coat well. Carefully place the crabs, two at a time, in the hot oil and cook until golden brown on both sides, about 2 minutes per side. The crabs tend to float to the surface of the oil, so they will need to be turned to cook evenly. Using long, stainless-steel tongs, rather than a spoon, turn the crabs over gently, taking care not to damage the coating or splash the hot oil out of the pan. Using a slotted spoon, remove the crabs, allowing the majority of the oil to drain back into the fryer, and place on paper towels to finish draining. Check the temperature of the oil to make sure it is hot enough to add the second batch of crabs. Keep the cooked crabs warm while frying the remaining crabs.

Spoon ½ cup of Celery Root Slaw onto each plate. Place 1 or 2 crabs on the side of the slaw with 1 or 2 lemon wedges and about 2 tablespoons of Roasted Garlic Tartar Sauce per crab, and serve immediately.

Grilled Tuna with White Bean Sauce

Serves 8

THIS dish is similar to the grilled prime rib recipe on page 180 because tuna is in many ways similar to steak. They are both hearty, rich in flavor, and enhanced by robust sauces and strongly flavored accompaniments. Don't be confused by the cooking of already cooked beans. We do it to make the sauce.

1½ cups cooked flageolet beans (see Marinated Bean Salad, page 65)
1¼ cups Chicken Stock (see page 187)
2 tablespoons Roasted Garlic Puree (see page 245)
1 teaspoon chopped fresh thyme leaves
¼ cup extra-virgin olive oil
¼ cup balsamic vinegar
Kosher salt

Freshly cracked black pepper
2 heads curly endive
3 pounds fresh tuna, in 8 steaks, at least ½ inch thick
¼ cup vegetable oil

Have ready

The Chicken Stock, warm, in a medium saucepan over low heat
The Roasted Garlic Puree

START a fire in the grill and allow it to burn to medium-high temperature.

In a medium saucepan, over medium heat, combine the flageolet beans and the Chicken Stock, saving some stock in reserve. Bring them to a gentle simmer, reduce the heat to low, and cook for about 30 minutes, to thoroughly soften the beans. Stir the beans occasionally, and add a little stock if necessary. The beans should have about ½ cup of liquid remaining after cooking for 30 minutes. Remove the beans from the heat.

In a food processor, combine the beans, Roasted Garlic Puree, and chopped thyme; process until smooth. Transfer the puree back to the medium saucepan, add the olive oil and all but 2 tablespoons of the balsamic vinegar, and mix thoroughly. Correct the seasoning to taste with kosher salt and black pepper; reserve over very low heat.

Trim the coarse outer leaves from the two heads of curly endive, leaving just the tender inner leaves, and cut each head in half.

Brush the endive and the tuna steaks with vegetable oil, and season with kosher salt and cracked black pepper. Grill the endive on a medium-temperature part of the grill for about 3 to 4 minutes on each side, until browned on the edges and softened. Grill the tuna steaks on a medium-high temperature part of the grill, and sear for about 1 minute on each side. The tuna should be well colored, but not blackened. Remove the endive and the tuna from the grill. Using a sharp knife, slice the endive into quarters, cutting through the root and severing it to separate the leaves.

Scatter a quarter of a head of endive leaves over each of 8 large warm plates. Drizzle the remaining 2 tablespoons balsamic vinegar over. Put a tuna steak on top of the endive on each serving. Divide the white bean sauce evenly among the 8 portions, spooning some over and around each steak, and serve immediately.

Roasted Monkfish

Serves 4

A whole monkfish, which you will probably never see in a market, is a really ugly creature. It is also a really delicious fish. The meat from the tail has the firm texture of lobster and a delicate flavor that you won't find in other fish.

When purchasing monkfish, be sure to buy it fully trimmed and cleaned, with the cartilage removed.

2 ripe tomatoes (¾ pound)
4 pieces caul fat, about 8 inches square each★
8 very thin slices (2 to 3 ounces) pancetta
¼ cup Italian parsley leaves, plus extra whole
    leaves for garnish
¼ cup fresh basil leaves

★ Caul fat is a thin, gauzelike membrane used for wrapping sausages, roasts, and fish, to keep the meat moist during cooking. It can be purchased from most good service butchers.

2 tablespoons fresh marjoram leaves
Freshly cracked black pepper
Kosher salt
4 monkfish tails, about 8 ounces each, well
  trimmed
1 tablespoon vegetable oil
1 recipe Green Lentils (see page 248)
Fresh lemon wedges

Have ready

The Green Lentils

Cut each tomato in half through the core,
then cut each half into thirds. Using a very sharp
paring knife, cut away the inside (seeds and
pulp) of each third, leaving only the outer flesh.

Place a piece of caul fat on your work surface, gently stretching it until it is spread out as
much as possible. Start layering the ingredients.
Arrange 2 slices of pancetta, one slice overlapping another, down one side of the caul fat.
Arrange a quarter of the tomato slices on top of
the pancetta, then a quarter of the parsley, a
quarter of the basil, 1½ teaspoons marjoram,
and a pinch of black pepper and kosher salt.
Arrange 1 piece of fish on top and wrap the
caul fat around, leaving just the tip of the tail
exposed. As you wrap, gently pull to make certain the wrapping is secure and the fish is well
enclosed. Repeat with the remaining caul fat,
pancetta, tomato, parsley, basil, marjoram, pepper, kosher salt, and fish, to make 4 bundles,
each approximately 3 × 6 inches.

Preheat the oven to 400 degrees.

In an ovenproof sauté pan or cast-iron skillet, large enough to hold the 4 wrapped fish
bundles in one layer, over medium-high heat,
preheat the oil until almost smoking. Place the
fish in the pan, ensuring that there is at least
1 inch of clearance around each bundle. Sauté
the bundles on one side, about 5 minutes.
Using a long metal spatula, carefully turn the
bundles over. Transfer the sauté pan to the oven.
Roast the monkfish about 12 to 15 minutes,
turning it over about halfway through.

While the monkfish is in the oven, warm
the lentils and reserve.

Remove the monkfish from the oven,
transfer the bundles to a warm platter, and let
them rest for 10 minutes. Using a very sharp
knife, slice each fish bundle into 1-inch-thick
medallions.

Divide the lentils among 4 large, warm
plates. Distribute the medallions equally among
the plates. Garnish with whole leaves of Italian
parsley and fresh lemon wedges, and serve
immediately.

Thyme-charred Whole Striped Bass with Confit of Lemon, Garlic, and Thyme

Serves 4

THIS fish is roasted under a covering of fresh thyme, which chars in the oven. This gives the fish a smokey flavor, but when serving the fish, the large pieces of charred thyme should be carefully removed and discarded. Have the fish-monger remove the guts, fins, gills, and spines from the fish; it is easier and safer.

4 ounces fresh thyme sprigs
2 whole striped bass, 2 pounds each, scaled and
    gutted, and fins and gills removed
Kosher salt
Freshly cracked black pepper
½ cup Fish Stock or Chicken Stock
    (see page 194 or 187)
½ cup Lemon and Garlic Confit (see page 223)
¼ cup Lemon Oil (see page 219)
1 teaspoon grated lemon zest
1 tablespoon fresh lemon juice

Have ready

The Fish Stock or Chicken Stock
The Lemon and Garlic Confit, warm, in a small
    saucepan over low heat
The Lemon Oil

PREHEAT the oven to 400 degrees.

Fill a medium mixing bowl with water. Remove enough leaves from the thyme sprigs to yield about 2 tablespoons finely chopped. Reserve the chopped thyme (discard the stems), and soak the remaining sprigs of thyme in the water for at least 10 minutes.

Cut 5 or 6 shallow, diagonal lines, spaced about 1 inch apart, across 1 side of the body of each fish. Take care not to cut all the way through the flesh, but just to score it, about ⅛ of an inch or less. The other side of each fish is left uncut. The scoring of the flesh allows the essence of the charred thyme to penetrate the fish.

Season the fish inside and outside with kosher salt and black pepper. Spread about half of the thyme sprigs over the bottom of a roast-ing pan, place the fish on the thyme, scored-side up, and cover them with the remaining thyme.

Roast the fish until the flesh behind the head can be easily separated from the spine, about 20 minutes.

Remove the roasting pan from the oven. Using two large stainless-steel spatulas, remove the whole fish from the roasting pan and trans-fer them to a platter. Remove the larger pieces of charred herbs.

"A WHOLE FISH WILL BE MORE FLAVORFUL THAN INDIVIDUALLY COOKED FILLETS."

Meanwhile, in a medium saucepan, over medium-high heat, combine the Fish Stock or Chicken Stock and the Lemon and Garlic Confit with ¼ cup of the Lemon Oil in which it was cooked. Bring to a rapid boil, and cook about 1 minute. Stir in the lemon zest, chopped fresh thyme, and fresh lemon juice. Season with kosher salt and black pepper to taste, and remove from the heat.

Place the fish on a large platter with ramekins of Lemon and Garlic Confit on the side.

Sautéed Salmon with Red Onion Vinaigrette

Serves 4

THE freshest salmon and an onion bursting with spring flavor will make this dish memorable, but frozen salmon and a shriveled onion from the back of the pantry will render it less than inspiring. Spring is the best time for onions and fennel, and the difference in flavor can be quite remarkable. A good spring onion should be heavy for its size and dense with sweet juice.

Vinaigrette

1 tablespoon plus 1 teaspoon kosher salt
1 medium red onion, peeled (8 ounces)
1 medium fennel bulb, trimmed (8 ounces)
¼ cup coarsely chopped, tender, pale green
    fennel fronds
Kosher salt
⅓ cup extra-virgin olive oil
2 tablespoons fresh lemon juice
2 tablespoons white wine vinegar
1 teaspoon freshly cracked black pepper

Salmon

1½ pounds salmon fillet, cut into four 6-ounce
    portions, 1 inch thick, skin on one side
2 tablespoons vegetable oil
Kosher salt
2 tablespoons Aromatic Spice Rub
    (see page 221)
8 small fennel fronds

Have ready

The Aromatic Spice Rub

To prepare the vinaigrette: In a large stockpot, over high heat, bring approximately 2 quarts of water to a boil, and add 1 tablespoon of the kosher salt. Fill a large mixing bowl with ice water. Using a sharp knife, cut the onion in half and then into ¼-inch dice. Rinse the diced onion under cold water and drain well; dry thoroughly and transfer to a medium mixing bowl. (The rinsing will make the onion milder.) Cut the fennel bulb in half and then into ¼-inch dice. Put the diced fennel in a fine-mesh, stainless-steel strainer. Blanch the fennel for 30 seconds in the boiling water, then plunge the strainer in the large mixing bowl of ice water and chill for about 2 minutes. Using a clean kitchen towel, dry the fennel thoroughly and add it to the onion. Add the chopped fennel fronds. Season the vegetables lightly with kosher salt and toss to combine. Add the olive oil, lemon juice, and vinegar, toss well, and correct the seasoning to taste with kosher salt and black pepper. This vinaigrette should be served at room temperature.

To prepare the salmon: Brush each portion of the salmon, on both sides, with a little vegetable oil. Season each lightly with kosher salt and about 1½ teaspoons of the Aromatic Spice Rub. In a large cast-iron skillet, over medium-high heat, preheat 1 teaspoon vegetable oil just to smoking. Place the salmon in the skillet, skin side down. Sauté the salmon 3 to 4 minutes, and turn, using a stainless-steel spatula. Sauté 1 or 2 minutes longer for medium rare.

Divide the vinaigrette equally among 4 large, warm plates. Using the spatula, place 1 fillet of salmon, skin side up, on the vinaigrette. Garnish each portion with 2 small fennel fronds, and serve immediately.

Salmon Grilled in Grape Leaves

Serves 4

WRAPPING a fish in grape leaves accomplishes two things. The enclosed fish actually steams rather than grills, and the charred grape leaves produce a smokey, tart flavor. Mature raw grape leaves are tough and very sour in flavor, so it is important to use young, tender leaves to impart the best flavor. The grape leaf may be eaten or not, depending on whether or not the charred flavor is too intense. It is intended as a method of adding flavor to the salmon and preserving moisture during the cooking process.

Currant tomatoes are difficult to find, but their delicious flavor makes the search worthwhile. If you simply can't find them, omit them from the recipe, and simply spoon a bit of Slow-roasted Tomatoes (see page 241) on each fillet.

½ cup currant tomatoes
2 tablespoons extra-virgin olive oil
1 teaspoon chopped fresh thyme
1 teaspoon chopped fresh Italian parsley
Kosher salt
8 young grape leaves, 6 inches across
1 stick (4 ounces) unsalted butter
16 large basil leaves
Four 6-ounce salmon fillets, without skin
Freshly cracked black pepper
1 large sweet onion (Walla Walla, Vidalia, or Maui), diced
¼ cup Chicken Stock (see page 187)
Juice of 1 medium lemon
¼ cup whole Italian parsley leaves

Have ready

The Chicken Stock

PREHEAT the oven to 350 degrees. Start a fire in the grill and allow it to burn to medium temperature.

In a baking pan, toss the tomatoes with the olive oil, chopped thyme, and chopped parsley. Roast the tomatoes in the oven for about 20 minutes. Remove the pan from the oven and reserve the tomatoes and any liquid.

In a large stockpot, bring approximately 4 quarts of water to a boil and add 1 tablespoon of kosher salt. Fill a large mixing bowl with ice water.

Blanch the grape leaves in a fine-mesh, stainless-steel strainer for about 30 seconds. Remove the strainer from the stockpot and plunge it into the large mixing bowl of ice water for about 1 to 2 minutes. Drain and, using a clean kitchen towel, pat dry and reserve.

In a small saucepan, over low heat, melt ½ stick (2 ounces) of the butter. Remove it from the heat and reserve.

Spread 4 of the reserved grape leaves out, rib side up, on a work surface. Put 4 basil leaves in the center of each grape leaf. Lightly brush each salmon fillet with the reserved melted butter, and season moderately with kosher salt and black pepper. Place a salmon fillet in the center of a grape leaf, on top of the basil, and fold the leaf up over the top to enclose the fillet as completely as possible. Spread the remaining 4 grape leaves out, rib side up, and lightly brush with melted butter. Turn each partially covered fillet over and place it on a second grape leaf.

Fold the edges of the second grape leaf up over the fillet to completely cover the salmon.

Grill the wrapped salmon fillets, folded side down, for about 5 minutes. Using stainless-steel tongs, carefully turn each fillet over and grill about 4 to 5 minutes more. Remove from the heat and keep warm.

In a large sauté pan, over medium heat, preheat the remaining ½ stick of butter. Sauté the diced onion until translucent, about 5 to 8 minutes. Add the roasted currant tomatoes and any of their cooking liquid, and the stock, and bring to a simmer, stirring occasionally. Remove from the heat, season the sauce to taste with kosher salt, black pepper, and fresh lemon juice, and gently stir in the parsley leaves.

Place a wrapped salmon fillet on each of 4 large, warm plates. Using a small, sharp knife, split open the grape leaves and pull to the side to expose the salmon fillets. Spoon the currant tomato sauce over the salmon fillets, and serve immediately.

Crisp Flattened Chicken with Wilted Parsley Salad

Serves 2 to 4

"CHICKEN with a brick" is the literal translation of the colloquial Italian name for this dish. We first saw this technique used at a small, family-run restaurant near the city of Lucca, in Tuscany. In that fine establishment they used a paint can filled with cement to flatten the chicken in a hot cast-iron skillet, but we recommend using a second cast-iron skillet as the weight.

It is important that you cook the chicken in a cast-iron skillet. The chicken will not brown well or crisp properly in a nonstick pan. Do not crowd the pan; no more than two halves of chicken should be cooked in each skillet. The Beurre Fondue can be made about 1 hour before needed and kept warm in a double boiler. This is delicious with Potato-Parsnip Puree (see page 237).

Boning a chicken, by the way, is an acquired skill. You may wish to have your service butcher do it for you.

One 3½-pound chicken, cut in half and boned
4 large garlic cloves, peeled and cut into thin slices
2 tablespoon fresh marjoram leaves
Kosher salt
Freshly cracked black pepper
2 tablespoons vegetable oil

Parsley Salad

2 large garlic cloves, peeled
¼ cup extra-virgin olive oil
4 cups curly parsley, large stems removed, leaving just the florets, washed and well dried
Kosher salt
1 tablespoon fresh lemon juice

Beurre Fondue (see page 203)

Have ready

The Beurre Fondue
The Potato-Parsnip Puree (if desired)

CAREFULLY lift, but do not remove, the skin from the meat of each chicken half. Divide the garlic slices and marjoram leaves equally and stuff them under the skin of the chicken halves. Refrigerate, covered, for 2 to 3 hours. Just before sautéing, season the chicken pieces lightly with kosher salt and black pepper.

In a large cast-iron skillet, over medium-high heat, preheat the vegetable oil. When the oil is almost smoking, put the 2 halves of chicken in the skillet, skin side down. Place a second cast-iron skillet of the same size as the first, unheated, on top, with the bottom pressing down on the chickens. Cook over medium-high heat until the chicken is nicely browned and the skin is crispy, about 12 to 15 minutes. Do not cook over high temperature or the chicken skin will burn before the meat will be cooked through. Remove the top skillet and turn the chicken halves over. Cook, uncovered, until the underside loses its pink color, about 6 to 7 minutes longer. Remove the chicken from the skillet, and if the chicken juices are not burned, set the skillet aside for use in preparing the parsley salad. If the pan juices are burned, prepare the parsley salad in the other clean cast-iron skillet.

To prepare the parsley salad: Using the flat of a cleaver or heavy knife, gently crush the garlic cloves. In the same skillet the chicken was cooked in, over medium heat, preheat the olive oil. Gently sauté the garlic until tender and lightly colored, about 2 to 3 minutes. Increase the heat to medium high, add the parsley, and sauté until it just begins to wilt, about 30 to 60 seconds. Season to taste with kosher salt and a few drops of fresh lemon juice.

To serve, spoon about ½ cup Potato-Parsnip Puree on each plate and place the chicken halves on top. Divide the parsley salad equally among the plates. Spoon about ¼ cup of the Beurre Fondue on each plate and serve immediately.

Grilled Chicken with Confit of Lemon and Garlic

Serves 4

EVERYBODY needs at least one great grilled chicken dish in their repertoire, and this recipe fulfills that need. The Confit of Lemon and Garlic is cooked long and slowly, so the strong flavor is tempered. The Lemon Oil, Preserved Lemon Peel, and the fresh lemon juice give this dish a very summery and light character. The confit and sauce can be made in saucepans on the edge of the grill. That way, you don't need to use your stove at all.

Confit of Lemon and Garlic

2 whole garlic heads, cloves separated and
    peeled
1 cup Lemon Oil (see page 219)
Bouquet garni (3 small sprigs each thyme and
    savory)

Chicken

2 chickens, about 3 pounds each, boned, wing
　　bone kept in
Leaves from 4 sprigs fresh thyme, chopped
2 teaspoons kosher salt
Freshly cracked black pepper

Sauce

1 cup Chicken Stock (see page 187)
¼ cup Preserved Lemon Peel (see page 222),
　　cut into julienne
¼ cup chopped fresh Italian parsley
2 teaspoons fresh lemon juice
Kosher salt
Freshly cracked black pepper

Have ready

The Lemon Oil
The Chicken Stock
The Preserved Lemon Peel

START a fire in the grill and allow it to burn to
medium-high temperature.

To prepare the Confit of Lemon and Garlic: In a medium saucepan, over medium heat,
combine all the ingredients for the confit and
bring them to a simmer. Reduce the heat to
low and simmer until the garlic is very tender,
about 25 minutes. (If the oil is simmering too
quickly, take the pan off the heat for 1 or 2 minutes, then return it to the heat. You will find

that the oil will continue to simmer for those
1 or 2 minutes.)

To prepare the chicken: Season the chickens with chopped thyme, kosher salt, and a few
grinds of black pepper. Grill the chickens, skin
side down, until the skin is browned and crispy,
almost charred, about 6 to 8 minutes. Turn the
chickens over and place on a moderate-
temperature part of the grill so as not to burn.
Continue to grill the chickens until they are
firm to the touch and cooked through, about
15 to 20 minutes longer.

To prepare the sauce: Meanwhile, in a
medium saucepan, over medium-high heat,
combine the Chicken Stock and the confit with
a ¼ cup of the Lemon Oil in which it was
cooked. Bring to a rapid boil, and cook about
1 minute. Stir in the Preserved Lemon Peel,
chopped fresh parsley, and fresh lemon juice;
season with kosher salt and black pepper to
taste, and remove from the heat.

Arrange half a chicken on each of 4 large,
warm plates. Spoon ¼ cup of the sauce over the
chicken, making certain that some garlic,
lemon peel, and parsley are in each serving, and
serve immediately.

Herbed Baby Chicken (Poussin) with Lemon-Thyme Butter

Serves 4

THIS recipe came about backward; we had a wonderful, crisp, buttery Potato Galette and wanted a tender and flavorful chicken dish to complement it. A poussin (a six-week-old chicken) has the perfect tender texture for this dish but is quite mildly flavored, so a quick splash of Lemon-Thyme Butter is tossed on to add an intense accent. To butterfly the chickens, the backbone must be removed, but with a little practice, it isn't a difficult procedure.

Poussin is available from a good butcher.

Chicken

4 baby chickens (about 1 pound each)
¼ cup extra-virgin olive oil
3 tablespoons chopped fresh herbs (parsley and thyme)
Kosher salt
Freshly cracked black pepper

2 Potato Galettes (see page 234)

Lemon-Thyme Butter

6 tablespoons (3 ounces) unsalted butter
2 large garlic cloves, peeled and chopped (2 tablespoons)
Zest of 1 medium lemon, finely chopped (2 tablespoons)
2 tablespoons fresh lemon thyme leaves
Kosher salt
Freshly cracked black pepper
2 tablespoons fresh lemon juice

Have ready

The ingredients and equipment for the Potato Galette

To prepare the chicken: Using a large, very sharp knife, remove the backbones and ribs from the chickens. Place each chicken, breast side up, on a cutting board. Insert the tip of the knife into the cavity as far as it will go. Line the knife blade up parallel to the backbone and cut through the ribs on both sides of the backbone. Remove and discard the backbone of each chicken. Spread each chicken out on the cutting board, and press down on it with the heel of your hand until the breastbone cracks and the chicken will lie flat. Turn each chicken over and, using your fingers, pull out and discard the ribs.

In a large mixing bowl, marinate the chickens, refrigerated, in the olive oil and the chopped herbs for 2 to 3 hours. Remove the chickens from the refrigerator about 15 minutes before cooking. Just prior to cooking, season the chickens lightly with kosher salt and black pepper.

Start a fire in the grill and allow it to burn to medium-high temperature.

Prepare the Potato Galettes.

While the galettes are cooking, grill the chickens, skin side down, until the skin is browned and crispy, almost charred, about 6 to 8 minutes. Turn the chickens and place them on a moderate-temperature part of the grill so as not to burn them. Continue to grill the chickens until they are firm to the touch all the way through, about 15 to 20 minutes longer. When the thigh is pierced and the juices run clear, the chicken is done.

Remove the Potato Galettes from the oven and turn them out onto a cutting board. Cut each galette in half and transfer the halves to 4 large warm plates.

To prepare the Lemon-Thyme Butter: In one of the cast-iron skillets used for making the galettes, melt the butter over medium heat. When the butter begins to sizzle and foam, just before it browns, stir in the garlic and lemon zest, remove the pan from the heat, add the lemon thyme, and swirl briefly. Correct the seasoning to taste with kosher salt, black pepper, and up to 2 tablespoons of fresh lemon juice.

Put 1 chicken, skin side up, on each galette half and splash a little of the Lemon-Thyme Butter over the chicken and the galette. Serve immediately.

Whole Roasted Chicken Charred with Rosemary

Serves 2 to 4

ROSEMARY and chicken are wonderfully complementary, but it is possible to overwhelm the subtle flavor of the poultry with too much rosemary, so a level of caution is warranted.

2 tablespoons vegetable oil
2 medium onions, peeled and coarsely chopped
    (1½ cups)
1 head of garlic, cloves separated, peeled, and
    thinly sliced
Kosher salt
Freshly cracked black pepper
2 dozen fresh rosemary sprigs, each 6 inches
    long
1 whole chicken, about 4 pounds
½ cup Italian parsley leaves, finely chopped

PREHEAT the oven to 500 degrees.

In a large sauté pan, over medium heat, preheat the vegetable oil. Sauté the chopped onions and the garlic until they soften, about 8 to 10 minutes. Remove the pan from the heat, season with about 1 teaspoon each of kosher salt and black pepper, and allow to cool.

Remove the leaves from one sprig of rosemary and finely chop them to make 1 tablespoon. Mix the chopped rosemary with the sautéed onions and garlic, and stuff the large cavity of the chicken, taking care not to pack the vegetables in too tightly. Season the chicken moderately all over with kosher salt and black pepper.

In a large roasting pan, put the chicken on a roasting rack or a bed of carrots and celery (see page 13). Heap the remaining rosemary sprigs all over the chicken, transfer the pan to the oven, and reduce the heat to 400 degrees. Roast the chicken for 50 to 60 minutes, until the rosemary is quite charred and the chicken skin is golden brown. Remove the pan from the oven, take the roasting pan and chicken outside, and ignite the charred rosemary with a match. Let the rosemary burn completely. Allow the chicken to rest for 10 to 15 minutes before serving. Brush the excess charred rosemary off the chicken.

To serve, remove and discard the stuffing, then carve the chicken as desired, and serve with a potato dish. It goes particularly well with the Campfire Roasted Potatoes (see page 231) or the Celery Root Puree (see page 236).

Roasted Squab with Foie Gras and Onion Soubise

Serves 4

THE only trick to this simple dish is to find good, fresh foie gras. It is available at gourmet shops, usually by special order. The onion soubise is simple to prepare, but deeply flavored and very delicious. Its sweet, sharp taste is a perfect counterpoint to the richness of the squab and the foie gras.

4 squabs, each about 1 pound
Extra-virgin olive oil
¼ cup chopped parsley
Kosher salt
Freshly cracked black pepper
4 ounces goose or duck foie gras, cut in 4 pieces
1 tablespoon vegetable oil
Onion Compote (Soubise) (see page 242)
Fresh chervil, for garnish

Have ready

The Onion Compote

IN a large mixing bowl, rub the squabs with olive oil and sprinkle with parsley. Marinate, refrigerated, about 5 hours. Before cooking, season the squabs lightly with kosher salt and black pepper.

Preheat the oven to 400 degrees.

In a large ovenproof sauté pan, large enough to hold the squabs, over high heat, preheat 3 tablespoons olive oil. Sauté the squabs, turning to brown all sides, about 5 minutes. Transfer to the oven and cook until tender, 8 or 9 minutes. The squabs should still be slightly pink on the inside. Remove from the oven, transfer to a platter, and allow the squabs to rest for 10 minutes. Using a sharp knife, cut away the legs and separate the breast from the bone of each squab, and keep warm.

Lightly season the pieces of foie gras with kosher salt and black pepper. In a large sauté pan, over high heat, preheat the vegetable oil until just smoking. Sauté the foie gras until browned and crispy on the first side, about 30 seconds; turn the foie gras over and continue to sauté about 10 seconds longer. Remove the foie gras from the pan and reserve.

Using a sharp boning knife, cut the squab breasts into thin slices. Spoon about ¼ cup of the onion compote onto each of 4 large, warm plates and top with the foie gras. Place the sliced squab breasts and the legs around the foie gras, garnish with fresh chervil, and serve immediately.

Duck Confit

Serves 10 or more

Wʜᴇɴ you're making confit, make a lot. It works better in a large batch; a big vat of confit, bubbling slowly, is less likely to burn, and it will fill your house with enticing aromas. It's always good to have a jar of confit in the refrigerator; you'll never go hungry again. Use only legs and thighs because they have the most flavor. You can buy these, as well as the duck fat, fresh or frozen, from a good butcher or meat company; fresh is better. Do not substitute table salt for the kosher salt. Small-grained table salt is denser than kosher salt, so a teaspoon of table salt actually contains more salt than a teaspoon of kosher salt. The finished confit can keep for up to 2 months in the refrigerator. (Refer to the index for recipes using confit.)

Dry Cure

8 bay leaves
2 tablespoons whole black peppercorns
1 tablespoon whole coriander
2 teaspoons juniper berries
5 whole allspice (¼ teaspoon)
⅓ cup kosher salt
⅓ cup granulated sugar
½ cup coarsely chopped fresh rosemary
2 tablespoons dried thyme

Duck

10 whole duck legs and thighs (5 pounds)
4 pounds duck fat

Iɴ a large mixing bowl, crumble the bay leaves. In a spice grinder, combine the peppercorns, coriander, juniper berries, and allspice. Grind the spices coarsely, and add them to the mixing bowl with the kosher salt, sugar, rosemary, and thyme, and mix well.

Place the duck legs in the mixing bowl and completely coat all sides of the meat with the dry cure ingredients. Cover and refrigerate for 48 hours.

Render the duck fat. In a large saucepan, over high heat, combine 4 cups of cold water and the duck fat and bring to a boil, about 30 minutes. Reduce the heat to low and simmer for 2 hours, to clarify the fat. Skim off any foam or scum that rises to the top.

Remove the saucepan from the heat and allow the mixture to cool for at least 30 minutes, to let all the fat rise to the surface and any particles to sink to the bottom of the pan. Refrigerating the mixture for an hour will make removing the fat from the water somewhat easier. Ladle the fat off the water, and reserve in a container. Discard the water.

Remove the duck legs from the dry cure and rinse under cold water, removing most of the dry ingredients (some will stick to the skin, but that's okay). Pat the meat dry with a kitchen towel.

Pour half the rendered duck fat into a large stockpot. Put the duck legs in the pot and pour the remaining fat over. Pour 1 cup of cold water into the pot and place a heavy plate in the pot on top of the duck legs. The water is added to prevent the duck fat from becoming too hot at the bottom of the pot. The fat should cover the legs and the plate. Bring to a boil, turn the heat down to very low, and simmer until the meat is tender and begins to separate from the bone, about 1½ hours. Remove the pot from the heat and let it rest for about 10 minutes, then test the duck meat for tenderness; if the meat is not cooked enough, return the pot to the heat for up to 30 minutes longer.

Using stainless-steel tongs, remove the duck legs from the pan and arrange them in a deep plastic or glass container. Using a ladle, pour the fat over the duck legs, covering them completely. Take care not to ladle up any remaining water from the bottom of the pot. Allow the confit to cool for about 1 hour, and then refrigerate, covered, until the fat is solid around and on top, at least 24 hours. At this point the confit is ready to be used, but it will keep, refrigerated, for up to 2 months. If you use a few legs at a time, make certain that the remaining legs are completely covered with the fat by pressing it back down around the duck legs with a spoon.

Sautéed Leg Lamb Chop with Potato-Onion Galette

Serves 6

THIS is a rough, flavorful country dish that should be enjoyed with close friends since it's a somewhat messy meal. Lamb chops cut from the leg are not as tender as loin or rib chops, but they are very flavorful, and they go perfectly with the Potato-Onion Galette. The procedure is a little complicated, but the dish is well worth all the effort.

Lamb Chops

3 leg lamb chops, each about ¾ pound, bone in
2 tablespoons extra-virgin olive oil
1 sprig fresh sage
1 sprig fresh rosemary
1 sprig fresh thyme
1 large garlic clove, peeled and minced (1 teaspoon)
½ teaspoon freshly cracked black pepper
Kosher salt
2 tablespoons vegetable oil
2 tablespoons balsamic vinegar (optional)

Potato-Onion Galette

4 tablespoons vegetable oil
1 medium red onion (8 ounces), peeled and cut into ⅛-inch slices
Kosher salt
Freshly cracked black pepper
1 medium trimmed fennel bulb (8 ounces), cut into thin slices
¼ cup dry white wine
5 medium russet potatoes (2½ pounds), peeled
2 tablespoons extra-virgin olive oil
2 teaspoons chopped fresh thyme
½ stick (2 ounces) unsalted butter

To prepare the lamb: In a large mixing bowl, rub the lamb chops with the 2 tablespoons of olive oil, sage, rosemary, thyme, garlic, and cracked pepper. Refrigerate, covered, for 2 to 4 hours.

To prepare the galette: In a large, ovenproof cast-iron skillet, over medium heat, preheat 2 tablespoons of the vegetable oil. Sauté the onion until it begins to brown, about 5 minutes. Season lightly with kosher salt and black pepper. Add the sliced fennel and sauté for 1 or 2 minutes longer. Reduce the heat to low, and cook, stirring occasionally, until the onion is very soft, about 10 minutes longer. Deglaze with the white wine and continue to cook just until the wine is absorbed, about 5 minutes.

Remove the pan from the heat and transfer the onion-fennel mixture to a medium mixing bowl.

Using a mandolin or a very sharp knife, cut the potatoes into ⅛-inch rounds. In a large mixing bowl, toss the potatoes with the 2 tablespoons of olive oil and the fresh thyme, and reserve.

Preheat the oven to 400 degrees.

Lightly season the lamb chops with kosher salt. Using paper towels, wipe out the cast-iron skillet. Over medium-high heat, preheat 2 tablespoons vegetable oil until almost smoking. Sear the chops until brown on one side, about 3 to 4 minutes. Turn the chops and continue to cook until medium rare, 3 minutes longer. Transfer to a warm platter and keep in a warm spot while cooking the potatoes.

In a small saucepan, over low heat, melt the butter. Remove the pan from the heat and keep warm. Scrape out the skillet as necessary to remove any burned remnants of lamb and, over medium heat, preheat the remaining 2 tablespoons of vegetable oil. Quickly arrange 2 layers of potatoes in the pan (see Potato Galette, page 234) in a circle. Drizzle 2 tablespoons of melted butter over the potatoes and cook for about 5 minutes. Spoon the onion-fennel mixture over the potatoes, leaving a 1-inch space around the perimeter of the circle. Arrange the remaining potatoes in a circle over the filling,

drizzle the remaining 2 tablespoons of melted butter over, and transfer the skillet to the oven. Bake the galette until the top is slightly brown and the potatoes are cooked through, about 20 minutes. Remove the galette from the oven, place the chops on top of the potatoes, and sprinkle with the balsamic vinegar, if desired. Return the whole assembled dish to the oven to heat the chops through, about 10 minutes.

Remove the skillet from the oven and transfer the chops to a cutting board. Cut into ½-inch slices, discarding the bone. Pour off the excess oil from the potatoes and turn the galette out on a large round platter. (To pour out the oil, place a large plate on top of the potatoes and carefully invert over a bowl.)

Arrange the slices of meat on a platter. Any juice that has collected on the cutting board from slicing the chops should be drizzled over the sliced meat. Bring both platters to the table and serve immediately.

Lamb Stew

THIS lamb stew follows the age-old Provençal method of preparing a daube. The meat is marinated overnight with wine, herbs, spices, and aromatic vegetables. The marinade is the key to the success of this dish; the meat is tenderized, and the flavor of the whole stew is improved by the red wine, fresh herbs, and strong garlic. The odd ingredient here is the pig's foot. It gives a marvelous richness and intensity to the stew but it can be eliminated. Lamb stew is especially good served over a portion of soft Polenta (see page 138), which adds a stick-to-your-ribs quality that fills this dish out into a full meal in one bowl.

Marinated Lamb

2 tablespoons vegetable oil
2 medium onions, peeled and coarsely chopped
    (3 cups)
1 celery stalk, coarsely chopped (½ cup)
1 medium carrot, peeled and coarsely chopped
    (¾ cup)
¼ cup coarsely chopped fresh parsley leaves
1 head of garlic, cut in half horizontally
2 bay leaves
2 sprigs fresh thyme, stemmed
1 sprig fresh rosemary, stemmed
6 to 8 whole allspice, crushed
6 to 8 whole juniper berries, crushed
¼ cup red wine vinegar

1 bottle (750 ml) dry red wine
5 pounds lamb shoulder or stew meat, cut in
    1½-inch cubes

Stew

2 tablespoons vegetable oil
Kosher salt
Freshly cracked black pepper
2 medium onions, peeled and coarsely chopped
    (3 cups)
1 celery stalk, coarsely chopped
1 carrot, peeled and coarsely chopped
4 cups Lamb Stock or Veal Stock
    (see page 192 or 190)
1 bottle (750 ml) dry red wine
Bouquet garni (3 or 4 sprigs each of Italian
    parsley, thyme, tarragon, and rosemary, and
    1 bay leaf)
2 heads of garlic, cut in half horizontally
1 pig's foot
Sprigs of fresh Italian parsley for garnish

Have ready

The Lamb Stock or Veal Stock

To prepare the marinated lamb: In a large stockpot, over medium-high heat, preheat the vegetable oil. Sauté the onions, celery, and carrot until softened and lightly browned, about 5 to 8 minutes. Reduce the heat to medium. Add the parsley, garlic, bay leaves, thyme, rosemary, allspice, and juniper berries, and continue to sauté about 2 to 3 minutes. Add the red wine vinegar and the red wine, bring to a simmer, and cook for about 20 minutes. Remove the pot from the heat and allow to cool to room temperature. Transfer the marinade to a large mixing bowl, and then refrigerate until chilled, about 1 hour.

When the marinade is well chilled, add the lamb meat, stirring to coat well, and refrigerate for at least 12 hours. The meat should be tossed midway through the marination period to ensure that it is evenly coated.

Remove the lamb meat from the marinade; discard the marinade and vegetables. Pat the meat dry with absorbent paper or a clean kitchen towel.

To prepare the stew: In a large stockpot, over medium-high heat, preheat the vegetable oil. Season the meat lightly with kosher salt and cracked black pepper, then brown the lamb meat in 3 batches, turning the pieces to brown evenly on all sides, about 5 to 8 minutes per batch.

When the last batch is browned, remove the meat from the stockpot. Add the second batch of onions, celery, and carrot, and sauté until softened and lightly browned, about 5 to 8 minutes.

Add the lamb or veal stock, red wine, the bouquet garni, garlic heads, and the pig's foot, and bring to a simmer. Simmer for about 5 minutes. Return all the browned lamb meat to the pot. Cover the stockpot, reduce the heat to very low, and gently simmer the stew until the meat is tender, about 2 to 3 hours, skimming occasionally to remove any fat or foam. Remove the bouquet garni and the pig's foot, and correct the seasoning to taste with kosher salt and black pepper.

Ladle the stew over soft Polenta (if desired) in large, warm bowls. Garnish with leaves of fresh Italian parsley, and serve immediately.

Braised Lamb Shanks

Serves 6

WHEN the nights begin to have a hint of chill and the leaves start to change color, people seem to be hungrier. That desire for a big, filling meal, for succulent meat and long-cooked broth, must be instinctually driven. The slow braising of this dish pulls the essence from the shank bone, producing an intense flavor. We use a braising liquid that is half water and half stock, so it won't become too heavy and strongly flavored. This dish can be done without lighting a grill by searing the shanks in a cast-iron skillet. We just like the flavor the grill imparts. Yam Puree (see page 238) is a wonderful accompaniment for this dish.

Lamb and Marinade

6 lamb shanks, about 1 pound each
6 to 8 whole allspice, crushed (⅛ teaspoon)
6 to 8 whole juniper berries, crushed
    (⅛ teaspoon)
¼ cup extra-virgin olive oil
¼ cup chopped fresh Italian parsley leaves
5 large garlic cloves, peeled and crushed
2 or 3 anchovy fillets, finely mashed (optional)
1 tablespoon chopped fresh thyme
1 tablespoon chopped fresh rosemary
Kosher salt
Freshly cracked black pepper

Braising Ingredients

2 tablespoons vegetable oil
2 large carrots (½ pound), peeled and coarsely
    chopped
2 medium celery stalks (¼ pound), coarsely
    chopped
1 leek (¼ pound), well washed and coarsely
    chopped
1 small (¼ pound) parsnip, peeled and coarsely
    chopped
½ small (¼ pound) turnip, peeled and coarsely
    chopped
10 large garlic cloves, peeled
3 or 4 whole allspice
2 sprigs fresh rosemary
2 sprigs fresh thyme
1 bay leaf
4 cups Lamb Stock or Brown Veal Stock
    (see page 192 or 190)
2 cups Chicken Stock (see page 187)

Preserved Lemon Peel (see page 222), cut into
    julienne
Caramelized Browned Root Vegetables
    (see page 240)
Yam Puree (see page 238)

Have ready

The Lamb Stock or Brown Veal Stock and the
    Chicken Stock, combined and warm, in a
    large saucepan over low heat
The Preserved Lemon Peel
The Caramelized Browned Root Vegetables
    (these can be prepared while the lamb
    shanks are braising)
The Yam Puree

PLACE the lamb shanks in a bowl, or bowls, large enough to hold them in one layer. The allspice and juniper berries can be crushed together and then combined with the other marinade ingredients (everything but the salt and pepper). Rub each shank with the olive oil first, then with the marinade, ensuring that the lamb shanks are well coated. Refrigerate the shanks, lightly covered, and marinate for 1 to 2 days.

Start a fire in the grill and allow it to burn to medium-high temperature.

Preheat the oven to 350 degrees.

Season the shanks with kosher salt and black pepper. On the preheated grill, brown the shanks on all sides, about 10 to 15 minutes.

(You can also brown the shanks by sautéeing them: In a large sauté pan, over medium-high heat, preheat 1 tablespoon of the vegetable oil. Brown the shanks, about 10 to 15 minutes, taking care not to crowd the pan or to burn the pan glaze while browning.)

Before chopping the vegetables, wash them all quite well, especially the leek, as sand tends to hide between the individual stalks.

Using a large sauté pan (if the shanks were pan browned, and the glaze is not burned, use the same pan to sauté the vegetables), over medium heat, preheat the remaining 1 tablespoon of vegetable oil. Lightly sweat the carrots, celery, leek, parsnip, turnip, garlic, allspice, rosemary, thyme, and bay leaf about 5 to 10 minutes. Remove the vegetables, herbs, and spices from the sauté pan, and distribute them evenly in a large roasting pan. Add 4 cups of the combined stock to the sauté pan and, over medium-high heat, bring to a simmer. As the stock simmers, scrape up any browned particles from the bottom of the pan.

Arrange the shanks in and around the vegetables in the large roasting pan. Add the simmering stock to halfway cover the lamb shanks. Simmer and add the remaining stock as needed. (The amount of stock needed depends on the size of the pan.) Put the roasting pan in the oven and braise the lamb shanks, uncovered, until the meat is very tender, about 3 hours.

Prepare the Yam Puree and the Caramelized Browned Root Vegetables while the meat is braising in the oven.

Remove the large roasting pan from the oven and let the shanks cool for a half an hour in the liquid to firm up. (If you remove the shanks too soon, they might fall apart.) When the shanks are cool, remove them to a large platter. Using a colander, strain the braising liquid into a large container, pressing down on the vegetables to extract as much liquid as possible. Discard the herbs and vegetables. Allow the braising liquid to cool about 10 minutes, and then, using a ladle, skim off and discard the fat. Clean the roasting pan and arrange the shanks in one layer. Pour the braising liquid over the shanks. At this point, the shanks and braising liquid can be stored in a large container, covered, in the refrigerator for up to 3 days.

Before serving, warm the shanks and liquid in the large roasting pan, in a 350-degree oven, about 15 to 25 minutes. If the shanks and liquid have been refrigerated, it will take 25 minutes to warm them through. Correct the seasoning to taste with kosher salt and black pepper.

Place 1 lamb shank in the center of each of 6 warm soup plates, ladle about ½ cup of broth over each portion, and sprinkle with a few pieces of the julienne of Preserved Lemon. Surround each shank with Browned Root Vegetables, and serve immediately, accompanied with Yam Puree.

Braised Oxtails

Serves 6

Like braised brisket of beef, or lamb stew, this is a hearty, savory dish that is cooked slowly to tenderize a tough but very flavorful cut of meat. Oxtails are delicious, but so very bony that people usually end up eating them with their fingers. So perhaps this isn't the best choice of recipes for a formal dinner. It is perfect for a family dinner during the colder seasons.

1 bottle (750 ml) dry red wine
¼ cup red wine vinegar
1 bay leaf
10 sprigs fresh thyme
5 sprigs fresh rosemary
1½ teaspoons freshly cracked black pepper
1 teaspoon kosher salt
1 head of garlic, cut in half horizontally
4 pounds oxtails, cut into 1½-inch sections
2 tablespoons vegetable oil
Kosher salt
Freshly cracked black pepper
1 medium onion, peeled and cut into 1-inch
    pieces
1 celery stalk, cut into 1-inch pieces

1 medium leek, trimmed, well washed, and cut
   into ½-inch sections (1 cup)
1 medium carrot, peeled and cut into 1-inch
   pieces
5 cups Chicken Stock (see page 187)
Bouquet garni (3 or 4 sprigs each of Italian
   parsley, thyme, and rosemary)
10 large garlic cloves, peeled
Salsa Verde (see page 211)
Garlic Mashed Potatoes (see page 233)

Have ready

The Chicken Stock

The ingredients necessary to prepare the Salsa
   Verde

The ingredients necessary to prepare the Garlic
   Mashed Potatoes

In a large saucepan, combine half the red wine,
the vinegar, bay leaf, thyme, rosemary, black
pepper, and kosher salt, and bring to a simmer.
Remove the pan from the heat and allow to
cool to room temperature. Transfer to a large
mixing bowl, add the garlic, and then refrigerate until chilled, about 1 hour.

When the marinade is well chilled, add the
oxtails, stirring to coat well, and refrigerate for
at least 12 hours. The meat should be tossed
midway through the marinating period to
ensure that it is evenly coated.

Remove the oxtails from the marinade, and
discard the liquid and vegetables. Pat the meat
dry with absorbent paper or a kitchen towel.

In a large stockpot, over medium-high
heat, preheat the vegetable oil. Season the
oxtails lightly with kosher salt and black pepper,
then brown the meat in 3 batches, turning the
pieces to brown evenly on all sides, about 5 to 8
minutes per batch.

When the last batch is browned, remove
the meat from the stockpot, add the onion, celery, leek, and carrot, and sauté until softened
and lightly browned, about 5 to 8 minutes.

Add the chicken stock, the remaining red
wine, the bouquet garni, and the garlic cloves,
and bring to a simmer. Simmer for about
5 minutes. Return all the browned oxtails to
the pot, cover the stockpot, reduce the heat to
very low, and gently simmer the stew, until the
meat is tender, about 2 to 3 hours, skimming
occasionally to remove any fat or foam.

During the last hour of the braising period,
prepare the Salsa Verde and the Garlic Mashed
Potatoes.

When the oxtails are tender, remove the
bouquet garni and correct the seasoning to taste
with kosher salt and black pepper.

Divide the oxtails equally among 6 large,
warm soup plates. Spoon ½ cup Garlic Mashed
Potatoes alongside them. Ladle the broth over,
and top each oxtail with a small spoonful of
Salsa Verde. Serve immediately.

Roasted Loin of Pork with Braised Red Cabbage and Port Wine Sauce

Serves 6 to 8

FOR a big, wintry dinner, a properly brined pork roast can rival the most tender, juicy prime rib of beef. Brined pork will come out more tender, juicy, and flavorful when cooked because the brine causes a change in the meat protein that makes it retain more moisture.

Kosher salt
3 tablespoons granulated sugar
2 tablespoons cracked black peppercorns
1 tablespoon dried thyme
4 whole cloves
4 whole allspice, cracked
1 bay leaf
1 center-cut pork loin, rib bones left in
    (2½ to 3 pounds)
1 head (1 pound) red cabbage, cored, split, and
    cut into ¼-inch slices
Freshly cracked black pepper
1 large onion (12 ounces), peeled and cut into
    ½-inch-thick round slices
1 tablespoon vegetable oil
1 large garlic clove, peeled and chopped
    (1 teaspoon)
¼ cup balsamic vinegar
8 fresh sage leaves, chopped fine
1 tablespoon drained capers

Port Wine Sauce

1 tablespoon (½ ounce) unsalted butter
2 large shallots, trimmed, peeled, and chopped
    (2 tablespoons)
¼ cup balsamic vinegar
1 cup ruby port
1 cup Brown Veal Stock (see page 190)

Have ready

The Brown Veal Stock

COMBINE 2 quarts of water, ⅓ cup kosher salt, sugar, peppercorns, thyme, cloves, allspice, and bay leaf in a large stockpot and bring to a boil. Reduce the heat to low and simmer for 15 minutes. Remove the stockpot from the heat, transfer the brine to a large mixing bowl, allow to cool to room temperature, then refrigerate until cold, at least 2 hours. When the brine is thoroughly chilled, add the pork loin, ensuring that it is completely immersed, and refrigerate, covered, for between 2 and 3 days. When ready to roast, remove the meat from the brine, and dry with kitchen towels.

In a large stockpot, bring approximately 4 quarts of water to a boil and add 1 tablespoon of kosher salt.

Fill a large mixing bowl with ice water.

Using a fine-mesh, stainless-steel strainer, blanch the red cabbage for about 30 seconds in the large stockpot of boiling water. (This will help the cabbage retain its color.) After blanching, plunge the strainer containing the cabbage in the ice water for about 30 seconds. Dry the cabbage with a kitchen towel and reserve.

Preheat the oven to 400 degrees.

Season the pork lightly with black pepper. It has enough salt already. In a large cast-iron skillet, over medium-high heat, brown the pork loin on all sides, about 10 to 15 minutes. When properly browned, remove the pork loin to a platter and reserve.

Distribute the onion slices on the bottom of the cast-iron skillet and place the browned pork loin on top. Transfer to the oven and roast until the internal temperature of the pork is 150 degrees, about 20 to 25 minutes.

While the pork is roasting, prepare the Port Wine Sauce: In a small saucepan, over medium-high heat, melt the butter. Sauté the shallots until just wilted, about 5 minutes. Pour in the ¼ cup balsamic vinegar and cook until completely absorbed, about 2 to 3 minutes. Add the port and cook until ½ cup remains, about 5 to 10 minutes. Add the stock and cook until the sauce begins to thicken, about 5 to 10 minutes. Strain the sauce through a fine-mesh, stainless-steel strainer into a double boiler and keep warm.

Remove the cast-iron skillet from the oven, transfer the pork loin from the skillet to a platter and let it rest in a warm spot. Using a stainless-steel spatula, scrape the bottom of the skillet to loosen any browned particles. Remove any of the onions that are burned. Sauté the remaining onions over medium heat until caramelized, about 10 minutes, remove from the pan and reserve.

In a large sauté pan, over high heat, preheat the vegetable oil. Add the garlic and blanched cabbage. Sauté until the cabbage is thoroughly heated through, but still crisp, about 4 to 5 minutes. Add the ¼ cup balsamic vinegar and the caramelized onions from the cast-iron skillet, stir briefly, add the sage and capers, and season with kosher salt and black pepper to taste. Remove from the heat and keep warm.

To serve, cut the pork loin into ½-inch- to 2-inch-thick slices with one bone in each slice. Place the cooked cabbage on a large, warm platter. Arrange the slices of pork on the cabbage, ladle the sauce over, and serve immediately.

Grilled Sweetbreads

Serves 4

WHEN we lived in New York, we went to the festival of San Gennaro in Little Italy. At the festival there was a line of Italian food stalls that seemed to go on for miles. One stall offered sweetbreads that had been skewered, wrapped in caul fat, and grilled. They were not great sweetbreads—in fact, they were rubbery—but they had a delicious, smokey flavor that was unforgettable. This recipe makes them tender but with the same great flavor. At the restaurant we use pancetta instead of caul fat because it has more flavor.

Sweetbreads should be soaked overnight in acidulated water (water with a little white wine vinegar) to whiten them for a uniform appearance. Soak the wooden skewers for about 30 minutes in water before using them on the grill. The sweetbreads can be skewered in advance and refrigerated until needed. This recipe requires the Port Wine Sauce from the Roasted Loin of Pork recipe on pages 174–175.

1 tablespoon white wine vinegar
1½ pounds sweetbreads
½ cup dry white wine
4 cups Court Bouillon (see page 197)
4 thin slices pancetta (3 ounces)
2 tablespoons vegetable oil
Kosher salt
Freshly cracked black pepper
2 tablespoons olive oil
6 ounces dry fettuccine
1 small leek (white part only), cut into julienne
    (1 cup)
1 tablespoon extra-virgin olive oil
Juice of ½ medium lemon
2 tablespoons chopped fresh parsley
1 bunch basil, leaves only
½ cup Port Wine Sauce (see pages 174–175)

Have ready

The Court Bouillon

IN a medium mixing bowl, combine 2 cups of cold water and the white wine vinegar. Add the sweetbreads and refrigerate, covered, for at least 12 hours. Drain and reserve the sweetbreads, discarding the water.

Fill a large mixing bowl with ice water.

Add the white wine to the Court Bouillon and in a 2-quart saucepan bring to a simmer. Add the sweetbreads and cook at a simmer just until the sweetbreads are firm and will hold their shape, about 6 to 8 minutes. Do not cook completely. (The cooking time depends on the size of each sweetbread.) Remove the sweetbreads with a slotted spoon and plunge them in the mixing bowl of ice water to cool for about 10 minutes. Discard the Court Bouillon. Remove the sweetbreads from the ice water and drain on absorbent paper.

Place the sweetbreads in a single layer on a baking pan and place a second baking pan on top to flatten them. Weight the second baking pan with a few 1-pound cans, and refrigerate for about 1 hour. When the sweetbreads are flattened and firm, carefully remove and discard the tendons and membranes from the outsides.

Divide the sweetbreads into 4 equal portions, using about 6 ounces for each serving (try to keep the pieces as large as possible). To ready for grilling, wrap a slice of pancetta around the perimeter of each of the sweetbreads. You need to use two 6-inch wooden skewers to hold each sweetbread and pancetta, to prevent them from rotating on the skewer. Brush both sides of the sweetbreads and pancetta with vegetable oil and season them lightly with kosher salt and black pepper. Repeat with the remaining sweetbreads and pancetta.

Start a fire in the grill and allow it to burn to medium temperature.

In a large stockpot, bring approximately 4 quarts of water to a boil and add 1 tablespoon of kosher salt.

Prepare the Port Wine Sauce, and keep it warm in a double boiler over low heat.

Grill the sweetbreads over medium heat until the sweetbreads and pancetta are crisp on the outside with a deep brown color, about 7 or 8 minutes on each side. Remove from the heat and keep warm.

In the stockpot of boiling water, cook the fettuccine al dente according to the manufacturer's instructions. Using a colander, drain the fettuccine.

While the fettuccine is cooking, in a small sauté pan, over medium heat, preheat the 2 tablespoons of olive oil. Gently sauté the julienned leek, about 5 to 8 minutes. In a large mixing bowl, toss the cooked fettuccine with the extra-virgin olive oil, lemon juice, sautéed leek, and chopped parsley. Correct the seasoning to taste with kosher salt and black pepper.

Divide the fettuccine and leeks equally among 4 large, warm plates and scatter 6 or 7 whole basil leaves around each portion. Remove the sweetbreads from the skewers and arrange on the plates of pasta. Top each portion with about 2 tablespoons of Port Wine Sauce and serve immediately.

Grilled Beef Fillet with Escarole

Serves 4

Beef fillet is very tender, but it is not the most flavorful cut of a steer, so it is usually served with some sort of flavorful sauce or accompaniment. We grill it with a dry spice rub and serve it in a Chicken Stock broth with mushrooms and fresh herbs. This preparation gives the fillet a spicy, well-browned crust that is contrasted by the subtle flavors of the broth. The spice rub mixture is difficult to make in small quantities, as it burns quite quickly when toasting. The amount this recipe produces is more than would be judicious to use on 1½ pounds of meat. Store the excess spice mixture in a sealed container for up to 1 week. It can be used on just about any grilled or roasted meat or poultry. It's also great with grilled ahi tuna steaks.

Spice Mixture

¼ cup whole fennel seeds
2 tablespoons whole coriander seeds
1 tablespoon whole allspice
2 dried red chile peppers
2 tablespoons whole black peppercorns

1½ pounds filet mignon, cut into 8 medallions
    1 to 1½ inches thick
Kosher salt
6 ounces fresh white button mushrooms
Vegetable oil
1 large garlic clove, peeled and minced
    (1 teaspoon)

¼ cup dry white wine
2½ cups Chicken Stock (see page 187)
Bouquet garni (fresh Italian parsley, bay leaf)
2 heads escarole
Freshly cracked black pepper
2 tablespoons chopped fresh Italian parsley
Juice of ½ medium lemon

Have ready

The Chicken Stock

Start a fire in the grill and allow it to burn to medium-high temperature.

In a large sauté pan, over medium heat, toast the fennel seeds, coriander seeds, allspice, dried chiles, and the black peppercorns until lightly done, about 5 to 8 minutes. Remove the spices from the pan and allow to cool, about 10 to 15 minutes. Coarsely grind the toasted spice mixture in a spice grinder. The optimum grind is finer than simply cracked pepper, but coarser than a finely ground commercial spice.

Lightly brush the pieces of beef fillet with vegetable oil. Season them moderately with kosher salt and liberally with the toasted spice mixture, and reserve in the refrigerator.

Wash the mushrooms and dry them with a kitchen towel. Using a sharp knife, stem and then thinly slice the mushrooms. In a large sauté pan, over medium high heat, preheat 1 tablespoon of the vegetable oil until almost smoking. Sauté the mushrooms, without stirring, for about 2 minutes, to color them.

Reduce the heat to medium, and continue to sauté the mushrooms, stirring occasionally, for about 5 minutes longer. Reduce the heat to medium-low, add the minced garlic to the mushrooms, and continue to sauté for about 1 minute more. Add the wine and allow to reduce slightly, 1 to 2 minutes. Add the Chicken Stock and the bouquet garni, and simmer until the broth reduces by one fourth, about 15 minutes.

While the broth is reducing, remove the beef fillets from the refrigerator. Trim the coarse outer leaves from the two heads of escarole, leaving just the tender yellow inner leaves. Brush the escarole lightly with vegetable oil, season lightly with a little kosher salt and black pepper, and grill over a medium-low-temperature part of the grill to color the edges and soften all the way through, about 8 to 10 minutes.

When the escarole has been on the grill about 5 minutes, add the beef fillets, placing them on a medium-high-temperature part of the grill. Grill the beef about 2 minutes on each side for rare, or about 3 minutes on each side for medium rare. Remove the escarole and the beef from the grill. Using a sharp knife, slice the heads of escarole in quarters lengthwise. Add the chopped parsley to the simmering broth and correct the seasoning to taste with kosher salt, black pepper, and fresh lemon juice.

Put 2 quarters of escarole in each of 4 large warm soup plates. Equally divide the broth and mushrooms among the plates, add 2 pieces of beef fillet, and serve immediately.

Grilled Prime Rib Steak with Red Wine Sauce

Serves 4

WHEN Nancy was growing up, her parents were always searching out new, exotic ethnic restaurants, but like any suburban kid, she just wanted a messy, overcooked hamburger. Now that she's all grown up, she still eats hamburgers (with a little Gorgonzola), but a great steak, served rare, is Nancy's real measure of the capability of a kitchen. In a small restaurant outside Lucca, a chef cut a porterhouse of Chiara beef the size of a dictionary and threw it on a charcoal grill just for her: She had never looked so happy. The beef was served with a mound of tender cannellini beans that had been cooked in a richly flavored stock. After that unforgettable steak, it was imperative to us that Campanile provide a steak of that caliber.

Red Wine Sauce

1 tablespoon unsalted butter
2 shallots, peeled, trimmed and chopped
    (2 tablespoons)
1 teaspoon freshly cracked black pepper
½ cup dry red wine
½ cup ruby port
2 cups Brown Veal Stock (see page 190)
Kosher salt

Prime Rib

Four 10- to 12-ounce prime ribeye steaks
    1½ inches thick
4 tablespoons freshly cracked black pepper
2 teaspoons kosher salt
Cannellini Beans (see page 246)
8 ounces bitter greens, such as mustard greens,
    arugula, or kale
Tapenade (see page 215)

Have ready

The Brown Veal Stock, warm, in a small
    saucepan over low heat
The cooked Cannellini Beans (see Marinated
    Bean Salad, page 65)
The Tapenade

To prepare the sauce: In a medium sauté pan, over medium heat, melt the butter. Sauté the shallots and the black pepper until the shallots become lightly colored, about 3 to 4 minutes. Add the red wine and the port and reduce by three quarters, about 10 minutes. Add the stock and reduce until the sauce thinly coats the back of a spoon, about 15 minutes. Strain through a fine-mesh, stainless-steel strainer into a clean, medium saucepan and season to taste with kosher salt. Keep warm over very low heat.

Start a fire in the grill and allow it to burn to medium-high temperature.

To prepare the prime rib: Sprinkle one side of the steaks with half the black pepper and kosher salt and press firmly to adhere the seasoning to the meat. Turn the steaks and repeat with the remaining seasoning.

On the grill, cook the steaks about 3 minutes on each side for medium rare, about 4 minutes for medium. Allow the steaks to rest in a warm spot for 5 to 10 minutes.

In a medium saucepan, over medium heat, heat the beans through, about 10 minutes, and then add the bitter greens, stirring briefly until the greens just wilt, about 5 minutes longer.

Spoon about ½ cup of the cannellini beans with a few greens onto the center of each of 4 large, warm plates. Spread a very thin layer (about 1 teaspoon) of Tapenade over each cooked steak and, using a very sharp knife, cut the steaks into slices of no more than ½ inch in thickness. Place the sliced steak next to the beans. Spoon about ¼ cup of sauce around each portion of steak, and serve immediately.

Stocks

Chapter 8

WITH good stock, you're halfway to a good meal. Investing a little time in stock preparation will save you much frustration later, as it is impossible to make a good sauce or soup if your stock is lacking depth or full flavor. Good stock is one of the advantages that quality restaurants have that make it possible for them to attain results that are difficult to duplicate at home. A good-quality stock can be the basis for an unlimited variety of dishes: soups, sauces, pastas, stews, even vegetables. Almost anything that comes out of the kitchen, except for desserts, is based on or enhanced by the flavor of good stock.

While making stock does take some time, it requires little skill or attention, and it can be prepared in large batches and frozen in small quantities, to be used as required. Stock is one of the few ingredients that can weather the freezing process without any change in quality. With a little forethought, high-quality homemade stock can be almost as convenient as canned, and the cost difference is minimal, especially when you consider the superior flavor of a homemade stock.

The use of carefully made, well-reduced stock cannot be emphasized too strongly, but we acknowledge that it isn't always convenient for the home chef. When that is the case, good quality, low-salt canned broth can be substituted without completely altering the flavor and character of your food; it is usually better than water. One should avoid bouillion cubes, as they have such a distinctive and undesirable flavor of salt, chicken fat, and MSG. Some butchers and specialty markets sell frozen premade stock, and that is an acceptable option if you are short on time.

An important ingredient in flavorful stock is a bouquet garni. This is the French name for a bundle of herbs and spices added to stocks, soups, and braising liquids to enhance their flavor. To aid in removing the sprigs before serving the dish, the herbs and spices are usually wrapped in cheesecloth and tied with kitchen string. Some good basic ingredients for a bouquet garni include bay leaves, parsley, and thyme. Of course, other herbs and spices can be included to suit your taste, the dish, or the season. The intent of a good bouquet garni is to add freshness and subtle flavors, not to overwhelm or dominate a dish with additional flavors. A certain level of care should be taken not to include too much of the stronger flavored herbs such as marjoram, rosemary, sage, and tarragon.

Chicken Stock

At Campanile it seems there is always chicken stock on the stoves—giant pots of new stock being made and smaller pots simmering and ready for use. Page through this book and you will see that chicken stock is listed with almost the same frequency as kosher salt and cracked black pepper. As excessive as this may seem initially, once you learn to rely on full-bodied stock, it will become almost as necessary as basic seasoning, and you will want it on hand whenever you cook.

Good chicken stock will become gelatinous when refrigerated. It should not be cloudy, nor should it be absolutely clear, but rather a pale golden hue. To achieve this, the stock should be strained through a colander lined with a double layer of cheesecloth to remove any minute solid particles that may cause discoloration. Make this stock in large quantities so you will always have some on hand.

6 to 8 pounds chicken bones, including necks, feet, backs, and wings
1 medium carrot, peeled, trimmed of root end, and cut into 1-inch pieces (¾ cup)
2 medium onions, peeled and quartered (1 cup)
1 celery stalk, cut into 1-inch pieces (½ cup)
1 small leek, trimmed, cut into 1-inch pieces, and well washed (1 cup)
1 head of garlic, cut in half horizontally
2 bay leaves
2 sprigs fresh thyme
4 sprigs fresh parsley
½ teaspoon freshly cracked black pepper

Put the chicken bones in a large stockpot and add cold water to cover by 2 inches (roughly 1½ to 2 gallons). Over high heat, bring the water to a vigorous boil, and skim off any fat or foam that collects on the top.

Add the carrot, onions, celery, leek, garlic, bay leaves, thyme, parsley, and black pepper, reduce the heat, and simmer gently, uncovered, for about 4 hours, skimming the fat and foam off the top as it accumulates. The stock is ready to be strained, and the bones removed, when all the cartilage has dissolved from the bones. Chicken stock has a delicate flavor that can be lost if it is reduced the way a stock made from veal or lamb would be.

Using a colander, strain the stock into a large, clean container. Press as much of the liquid out as possible, discard the vegetables and bones, and allow the stock to stand until the fat rises to the top, about 20 to 30 minutes. Skim off and discard any fat.

For a beautifully clear stock, strain the stock through a colander lined with a double layer of cheesecloth before cooling. The stock can be refrigerated, covered, for up to 3 days, or freeze the stock in small containers to use as needed.

Duck Stock

DUCK stock is richer, more concentrated, darker in color, and deeper in flavor than chicken stock. Compared to veal stock, it is gamier, more complex, and slightly sweeter. Duck stock isn't just for use with duck; it can be used almost interchangeably with brown veal stock. For example, replacing half the veal stock with duck stock would add a more complex flavor to the Braised Lamb Shanks (page 170). Purists might disagree and scold you for using duck stock in a veal or beef dish, but the flavor combination works quite well.

A good source for duck bones is usually an Asian market, as they sell far more duck than the local supermarket. Some butchers can be persuaded to order duck bones, but you may need to ask nicely.

6 to 8 pounds duck bones, including heads and feet if possible
1 head of garlic, cut in half horizontally
2 medium onions, peeled and quartered (2 cups)
2 medium carrots, peeled, trimmed of the root ends, and cut into 1-inch pieces (½ cup)
1 large celery stalk, cut into 1-inch pieces (½ cup)
1 medium leek, trimmed, cut into 1-inch pieces, and well washed (1 cup)
1 teaspoon freshly cracked black pepper
2 bay leaves
2 sprigs fresh thyme
4 sprigs fresh parsley

PREHEAT the oven to 350 degrees.

Put the bones in a large roasting pan and roast until well browned, turning halfway through to brown all sides, about 1½ hours. Take care not to allow the bones to burn, and be sure to remove any pieces that are blackened; otherwise your stock will be bitter.

After 1 hour, add the garlic, onions, carrots, celery, and leek to the roasting pan, and continue to roast until the vegetables are evenly browned, about 30 minutes.

Remove the roasting pan from the oven and transfer the bones and vegetables to a large stockpot. Add the black pepper, bay leaves, thyme, and parsley to the stockpot.

Pour off and discard the fat from the roasting pan. Add 2 cups of water to the pan and, over medium heat, deglaze the pan, scraping up any browned particles that stick to the pan. If any of the pan glaze is burned, do not deglaze it, as the liquid will be bitter and will ruin the stock.

Pour the deglazed liquid into the stockpot with additional water to cover the ingredients (about 1½ to 2 gallons), and bring to a boil. It is not a problem if some of the duck bones protrude from the water initially, as they will soften and collapse into the water after about 30 minutes of simmering. Reduce the heat and simmer gently, uncovered, 6 to 8 hours, skimming the fat and foam off the top as it accumulates.

Using a colander, strain the stock into a large, clean container. Press as much of the liquid out as possible, discard the vegetables and bones, and allow the stock to stand until the fat rises to the top, about 20 to 30 minutes. Remove and discard any fat. Strain the stock through a colander lined with a double layer of cheesecloth. Return the stock to the large stockpot and boil gently, uncovered, over medium heat, until reduced by half. Skim the stock frequently as it boils to remove any fat or foam that rises to the top.

Very gentle simmering and occasional skimming to remove the fat from the stock are very important in making a superior duck stock. If the stock boils too vigorously, some of the fat and small particles of the vegetables will become emulsified, or suspended, in the stock. If this happens, the stock will be greasy in flavor and cloudy in appearance.

Remove the stock from the heat, allow it to cool, and discard any fat that collects on top. For a beautifully clear stock, strain the stock again through a colander lined with a double layer of cheesecloth before cooling. The stock can be refrigerated, covered, for up to 3 days, or frozen in small containers for use as needed.

Brown Veal Stock

Makes 2 quarts

Brown veal stock is one of the cornerstones
of French cooking; a whole mythology of
incredibly rich and complex sauces is based on
it. If you have some brown veal stock in the
refrigerator or freezer you can quickly prepare a
meal with surprising depth of flavor.

Most butchers can order veal bones for you
with just a few days' notice. The bones may
arrive frozen, but it will make no discernible
difference in your final stock. You may be
required to order about 8 to 10 pounds; just
make sure they cut them up into pieces approximately 3 inches in size. You will not be able to
cut them yourself, unless you have a powerful
band saw.

To make demi-glace, reduce the stock by
three quarters after straining. Demi-glace is
very concentrated in flavor; it adds even more
richness to a soup or a stock, without increasing
the volume greatly.

10 pounds veal bones (neck or knuckle bones
    are best), cut into 3-inch pieces
1 head of garlic, cut in half horizontally
2 medium onions, peeled and quartered
    (2 cups)
2 medium carrots, peeled, trimmed of root
    end, and cut into 1-inch pieces (½ cup)
1 large celery stalk, cut into 1-inch pieces
    (½ cup)

1 medium leek, trimmed, cut into 1-inch
    pieces, and well washed (1 cup)
1 teaspoon freshly cracked black pepper
2 bay leaves
2 sprigs fresh thyme
4 sprigs fresh parsley

PREHEAT the oven to 350 degrees.

Distribute the bones in a large roasting pan
and roast until well browned, turning halfway
through to brown all sides, 1½ to 2 hours. Take
care not to allow the bones to burn, and be sure
to remove any pieces that are blackened; otherwise your stock will be bitter. After 1 hour, add
the garlic, onion, carrot, celery, and leek to the
roasting pan, and continue to roast until the vegetables are evenly browned, about 30 minutes.

Remove the roasting pan from the oven
and transfer the bones and vegetables to a large
stockpot. Take care not to pour the fat in the
roasting pan into the stockpot. Add the black
pepper, bay leaves, thyme, and parsley to the
stockpot.

Pour off and discard the fat from the roasting pan. Add 2 cups of water to the pan and,
over medium heat, deglaze the pan, scraping up
any browned particles that stick to the pan. If
any of the pan glaze is burned, do not deglaze
it, as the liquid will be bitter and will ruin the
stock.

Pour the deglazed liquid into the stockpot
with additional water to cover the ingredients
by 2 inches (roughly 1½ to 2 gallons), and bring

NANCY BUYING LEEKS: "WITH GOOD STOCK, YOU'RE HALFWAY
TO A GOOD MEAL."

to a boil. Reduce the heat and simmer gently, uncovered, 6 to 8 hours, skimming the fat and foam off the top as it accumulates and adding small amounts of water as needed to keep the bones and vegetables covered at all times.

Using a colander, strain the stock into a large, clean container. Press as much of the liquid out as possible, discard the vegetables and bones, and allow the stock to stand until the fat rises to the top, about 20 to 30 minutes. Remove and discard any fat. Strain the stock through a colander lined with a double layer of cheesecloth. Return the stock to the large stockpot and boil gently, uncovered, over medium heat, until reduced by half. Skim the stock frequently as it boils, to remove any fat or foam that rises to the top.

Very gentle simmering and occasional skimming to remove the fat from the stock are very important in making a superior veal stock. If the stock boils too vigorously, some of the fat and small particles of the vegetables will become emulsified, or suspended, in the stock. If this happens, the stock will be greasy in flavor and cloudy in appearance.

Remove the stock from the heat, allow it to cool, and skim off and discard any fat that collects on top. For a beautifully clear stock, strain the stock again through a colander lined with a double layer of cheesecloth before cooling. The stock can be refrigerated, covered, for up to 3 days. It can also be frozen in small containers, to be defrosted and used as needed.

Lamb Stock

Yields 2 quarts

LAMB stock is made like brown veal stock, except that we add extra garlic and sprigs of fresh rosemary to accentuate the flavor and aroma of the lamb. This is not a stock that you will make that often, as you can only use it for lamb dishes, or perhaps with lentils, but when you do have a good piece of lamb this will make a superior sauce.

8 pounds lamb bones (neck or knuckle bones are best), cut into 3-inch pieces
3 heads of garlic, cut in half horizontally
2 medium onions, peeled and quartered (2 cups)
2 medium carrots, peeled, trimmed of the root ends, and cut into 1-inch pieces (1½ cups)
1 large celery stalk, cut into 1-inch pieces (½ cup)
1 medium leek, trimmed, cut into 1-inch pieces, and well washed (1 cup)

1 teaspoon freshly cracked black pepper
2 bay leaves
2 sprigs fresh thyme
4 sprigs fresh parsley
2 sprigs fresh rosemary, 4 to 6 inches long

PREHEAT the oven to 350 degrees.

Put the bones in a large roasting pan and roast until well browned, turning halfway through to brown all sides, 1½ to 2 hours. Take care not to allow the bones to burn, and be sure to remove any pieces that are blackened; otherwise your stock will be bitter. After 1 hour, add the garlic, onions, carrots, celery, and leek to the roasting pan, and continue to roast until the vegetables are evenly browned.

Remove the roasting pan from the oven and transfer the bones and vegetables to a large stockpot. Add the black pepper, bay leaves, thyme, parsley, and rosemary to the stockpot.

Pour off and discard the fat from the roasting pan. Add 2 cups of water to the pan and, over medium heat, deglaze the pan, scraping up any browned particles that stick to the pan. If any of the pan glaze is burned, do not deglaze it, as the liquid will be bitter and will ruin the stock.

Pour the deglazed liquid into the stockpot with additional water to cover the ingredients by 2 inches (1½ to 2 gallons), and bring to a boil. Reduce the heat and simmer gently, uncovered, 6 to 8 hours, skimming the fat and foam off the top as it accumulates and adding water as needed to keep the bones and vegetables covered at all times.

Using a colander, strain the stock into a large, clean container. Press as much of the liquid out as possible, discard the vegetables and bones, and allow the stock to stand until the fat rises to the top, about 20 to 30 minutes. Remove and discard any fat. Strain the stock through a colander lined with a double layer of cheesecloth. Return the stock to the large stockpot and boil gently, uncovered, over medium heat, until reduced by half. Skim the stock frequently as it boils to remove any fat or foam that rises to the top.

Very gentle simmering and occasional skimming to remove the fat from the stock are very important in making a superior lamb stock. If the stock boils too vigorously, some of the fat and small particles of the vegetables will become emulsified, or suspended, in the stock. If this happens, the stock will be greasy in flavor and cloudy in appearance.

Remove the stock from the heat, allow it to cool, and discard any fat that collects on top. For a beautifully clear stock, strain the stock through a colander lined with a double layer of cheesecloth before cooling. The stock can be refrigerated, covered, for up to 3 days, or freeze the stock in small containers to use as needed.

Fish Stock

Makes about 2 quarts

I⊤ is vital that only the bones of lean, white-fleshed, saltwater fish—such as sole, halibut, sea bass, or John Dory—should be used for fish stock. The use of any oily or strongly flavored fish will result in an unpleasantly strong stock. Make certain that the bones are well cleaned under cold running water before using them. Discard the skin, gills, blood, and any organs of the fish. If some of these unwanted bits sneak into your stock it will take on an unpleasant color. It is important when preparing fish stock to avoid disturbing the stock as it cooks. It should not be stirred, and the cooking time should be limited to 30 minutes. This will make a clear, beautiful, and delicate stock. If you cook fish stock for too long, it will become murky, stale, and fishy.

With seafood, perhaps more than any other food, it is important that you use ingredients of the best possible quality. For making fish stock, either fresh or frozen fish bones may be used. On a consumer level, good fish and fish bones can be difficult to find; look for a trustworthy and busy fish market rather than a supermarket.

For a richer stock, substitute 2 cups of Chicken Stock (page 187) for 2 cups of the water.

3 pounds lean, white, saltwater fish bones
2 tablespoons vegetable oil
2 celery stalks, cut into 1-inch pieces (1 cup)
1 medium leek, trimmed, cut into 1-inch pieces, and well washed (1 cup)
1 medium white onion, peeled and quartered (1 cup)
5 garlic cloves, peeled and lightly crushed
4 sprigs Italian parsley
4 sprigs fresh thyme
1 bay leaf
1 teaspoon kosher salt
1 teaspoon freshly cracked pepper
1 cup dry white wine
¼ cup white wine vinegar

Have ready, if using

The Chicken Stock

Rınse the fish bones under cold, running water to remove any blood.

In a large saucepan, over medium heat, preheat the oil. Gently sweat the celery, leek, onion, garlic, parsley, thyme, bay leaf, salt, and black pepper for about 5 minutes. Do not let the vegetables color. Add the bones, white wine, and vinegar to the saucepan. Simmer, to steam the bones, for about 5 minutes.

Add 2 quarts of water and the Chicken Stock, if desired, and bring to a slow, gentle, simmer, with the bubbles just breaking the surface. Simmer for 30 minutes without stirring the bones or disturbing the ingredients in the saucepan.

While holding back the fish bones and vegetables with a large wooden spoon, carefully strain the stock through a colander lined with a double layer of cheesecloth into a large, clean container. For a beautifully clear stock, do not press the vegetables and bones to extract all the liquid; discard the vegetables and bones, and allow the stock to cool. The stock can be refrigerated, covered, for up to 3 days, or freeze the stock in small containers for use as needed.

Vegetable Stock

VEGETABLE stock is similar to Court Bouillon but has a stronger flavor because the vegetables are browned. Vegetable stock is also less acidic because it uses no vinegar. Vegetable stock can be used as a vegetarian replacement for fish or chicken stock. It isn't as flavorful as a meat stock, but sometimes that subtlety is desirable. It is an appropriate basis for a simple vegetable soup or a vegetarian pasta sauce. The delicate flavor and natural bouquet are easily overwhelmed, and thus most recipes in need of vegetable stock should be simply seasoned, relying on the quality of the natural ingredients to carry the flavor of the dish.

1 tablespoon vegetable oil
2 medium onions, peeled and quartered
2 large carrots, peeled and cut into 1-inch
    pieces
2 stalks celery, cut into 1-inch pieces
1 medium leek, trimmed, cut into 1-inch
    pieces, and well washed
8 ounces white button mushrooms, washed and
    quartered
1 head garlic, cut in half horizontally
1½ teaspoons freshly cracked black pepper
½ teaspoon freshly cracked allspice
1 teaspoon kosher salt
4 sprigs fresh parsley
4 sprigs fresh thyme
1 bay leaf

IN a large stockpot, over medium heat, preheat the vegetable oil. Add the onions, carrots, celery, leek, mushrooms, and garlic, and sauté until the vegetables are lightly browned, about 5 minutes. Take care not to allow the vegetables to burn, and be sure to remove any pieces that are blackened; otherwise your stock will be bitter.

Add the black pepper, allspice, salt, parsley, thyme, bay leaf, and 3 quarts of water, and bring to a boil. Reduce the heat to low, and simmer, uncovered, for about 1 hour, skimming as necessary to remove any foam that rises to the surface.

Using a colander lined with a double layer of cheesecloth, strain the stock into a large, clean container. Press the vegetables to extract most of the liquid, discard the vegetables, and allow the stock to cool. The stock can be refrigerated, covered, for up to 3 days, or freeze the stock in small containers to be used as needed.

Court Bouillon

Makes about 2 quarts

COURT bouillon is more delicate and slightly more acidic than vegetable stock. It is a simple vegetable-and-herb broth for steaming or poaching mildly flavored foods. It adds more flavor and aroma than plain water but is not used as the basis for a sauce the way vegetable stock would be. This recipe works well with delicate fish, shellfish, or vegetables. To poach salmon or other oily fish, add a few extra tablespoons of white wine vinegar. The only way to ruin this is to boil it too vigorously or too long. You don't need to keep vast quantities of this on hand, as it is very easy to make and requires only about 10 minutes of work and 30 minutes of simmering time.

NANCY AT THE FARMER'S MARKET: "ALMOST ANYTHING THAT COMES OUT OF THE KITCHEN IS ENHANCED BY THE FLAVOR OF GOOD STOCK."

1 tablespoon vegetable oil

1 medium white onion, peeled and quartered
(1 cup)

1 medium carrot, peeled, trimmed of root end,
and cut into 1-inch pieces (¾ cup)

1 celery stalk, cut into 1-inch pieces (½ cup)

1 medium leek, trimmed, cut into 1-inch
pieces, and well washed (1 cup)

1 sprig fresh thyme

1 bay leaf

1 teaspoon freshly cracked black pepper

¼ cup white wine vinegar

1 cup dry white wine

4 sprigs fresh parsley

In a large saucepan, over medium heat, preheat the oil. Sweat the onion, carrot, celery, leek, thyme, bay leaf, and black pepper about 5 minutes. Do not color the vegetables. Add the vinegar and the white wine and cook for about 3 minutes longer. Pour in 2½ quarts of cold water, add the parsley, and bring to a boil. Lower the heat and simmer for 20 minutes, skimming as necessary to remove any foam.

Using a colander lined with a double layer of cheesecloth, strain the court bouillon into a large, clean container. Press as much of the liquid out of the vegetables as possible, discard the vegetables, and allow the court bouillon to cool. Refrigerate, covered, for up to 3 days, or use as needed.

Sauces

Chapter 9

SAUCES are often thought to be one of the most intimidating aspects of cooking. This reputation comes from haute cuisine, where classic French cooking, with its complex geneaology of sauces, reigns supreme. In this very precise and structured system, everything must be done in a certain way, and in a certain order. Any deviation from the rules, and it's back to the beginning to start all over. This sort of precise and well-documented cuisine is all very admirable, and there are applications of it that do have a place in everyday cooking, but at Campanile, for the most part, we prefer to have a less rigid structure to the preparation of sauces.

Very often, cooks don't take the time to reduce a sauce enough to concentrate the flavor. To correctly reduce a sauce, you don't just boil it furiously until the majority of the liquid has evaporated. It must be simmered slowly and gently over moderate heat, and it must be diligently skimmed to remove any fat and foam. As the sauce reduces, you must taste it occasionally. For instance, a sauce may appear to be reduced properly, but it might taste fatty and weak. In this case, the stock may have been boiled too rapidly, or not enough care was taken in the initial skimming. At this point, the sauce can be saved, but it must be removed from the heat and allowed to cool, so the fat can rise to the surface to be skimmed. Taste is the most important determination in sauce making; if it isn't delicious, it isn't worth the effort.

Seasoning is the final aspect to sauce making. Salt is essential to flavor in cooking throughout the world. A well-seasoned sauce will not seem salty, but if it tastes right, there may be more salt than you might expect. Inadequate salting will produce sauce, and food in general, lacking in flavor, but most people will be unable to attribute the deficiency to the lack of salt.

Vinaigrettes

The best vinaigrettes are usually the simplest. There is rarely any point in
combining more than a few flavors in a vinaigrette. The sharpness of the vinegar is the dominant flavor, usually supported by mustard, shallot, or lemon,
the fruitiness of an extra-virgin olive oil, and the seasoning. Fresh seasonal
herbs, when used in moderation, are delicious in almost any vinaigrette. Many
delicate herbs, however, such as Italian parsley, chervil, tarragon, or basil, are
best when simply tossed with the salad.

Beurre Fondue

Yields ¾ cup

BEURRE Fondue is not a sauce in a strictly classical French sense, but it is used as one. It is similar to a beurre blanc, but it uses far less butter. Beurre Fondue goes well with many lighter dishes such as vegetables, fish, chicken, and even pork. The character of Beurre Fondue can be easily transformed by incorporating other ingredients. With delicately flavored fish, add some chopped tarragon, parsley, basil, or chervil just before serving. For monkfish, which has a meaty texture, we frequently use a Beurre Fondue with Roasted Garlic Puree and chopped Italian parsley. Grilled scallops can be served with Beurre Fondue flavored with a little saffron, instead of the traditional drawn butter. Beurre Fondue with a little chopped sage or thyme is excellent with roasted chicken.

Beurre Fondue, if kept warm in a double boiler to prevent separation, can be prepared up to 1 or 2 hours before needed. A properly made Beurre Fondue should have a viscosity similar to heavy cream. If the fondue becomes too thick, add warm chicken stock, 1 tablespoon at a time, to thin it.

1 stick (4 ounces) unsalted butter, cut into
    8 pieces
2 large shallots, peeled, trimmed, and chopped
    (2 tablespoons)
¼ cup dry white wine
2 tablespoons white wine vinegar
½ cup Chicken Stock or Vegetable Stock
    (see page 187 or 196)
Kosher salt
½ medium lemon

Have ready

The Chicken Stock or Vegetable Stock, warm,
    in a small saucepan over low heat

IN a medium sauté pan, over low heat, melt 1 tablespoon of the butter. Gently sauté the shallots until translucent, but not browned, about 3 minutes. Add the wine and the vinegar. Raise the heat to medium, and reduce until about 2 tablespoons remain, about 5 minutes. Add the Chicken Stock and reduce by half, about 10 minutes.

Reduce the heat to low, and whisk in the remaining butter, a piece at a time, whisking until it emulsifies into the Chicken Stock before adding additional butter. Correct the seasoning to taste with kosher salt and fresh lemon juice, and keep warm in a double boiler until needed. Whisk in any additional flavoring elements as desired just before serving.

Scallion Sauce

THIS is one of our favorite variations on Beurre Fondue. It goes well with most fish and poultry. At the restaurant we serve this sauce with sautéed halibut and horseradish potatoes. The Beurre Fondue can be made 1 or 2 hours before needed and kept warm over simmering water in a double boiler. The scallions, chives, and parsley should be cut and stirred in just before serving. If the sauce is too thick, add warm Chicken Stock, 1 tablespoon at a time, to thin it.

2 scallions (2 ounces), trimmed
1 recipe Beurre Fondue (see page 203)
2 tablespoons fresh lemon juice
Kosher salt
¼ bunch chives, cut into 1-inch slices
1 tablespoon chopped Italian parsley

Have ready

The Beurre Fondue, warm, in a double boiler
over simmering water

SLICE the scallions very thinly, on the bias. Remove the double boiler of Beurre Fondue from the heat; adjust the seasoning to taste with lemon juice and kosher salt. Stir the sliced scallions, chives, and parsley into the Beurre Fondue just before serving.

Brown Butter Sauce

Makes 2 cups

Brown Butter Sauce is similar to Beurre Fondue and is just as versatile. Browning the butter gives it a rich, nutty flavor that complements many seafood and poultry dishes. You can even use it with roast turkey as a substitute for Thanksgiving gravy.

The browning of the butter and the way the Chicken Stock is incorporated results in a sauce that will break, or separate, much more quickly than a sauce made with unbrowned butter such as Beurre Fondue, so this sauce must be made just before serving. As it can be prepared in under 15 minutes, this is usually not a problem.

2 sticks (8 ounces) unsalted butter, cut into
    small pieces
¼ cup dry white wine
1 large garlic clove, peeled and minced
    (1 teaspoon)
½ cup Chicken Stock (see page 187)
2 teaspoons fresh lemon juice
Kosher salt

Have ready

The Chicken Stock, warm, in a small saucepan
    over low heat

In a medium sauté pan, over medium heat, melt and cook the butter until it begins to brown and has a nutty, toasty aroma, about 5 to 7 minutes. The butter must be constantly stirred or swirled to promote even browning. Remove the pan from the heat. Carefully add the white wine to avoid spattering and return the pan to the heat. Add the garlic and simmer about 1 minute. Gradually add the Chicken Stock, whisking vigorously to emulsify it into the butter. Remove the pan from the heat. Add the lemon juice, stir, and correct the seasoning to taste with kosher salt. Serve immediately.

Brown Butter Sauce with Black-eyed Peas

Makes 2 cups

WE make this variation of basic brown butter sauce to accompany the Sweet Potato, Prosciutto, and Kale Ravioli (see page 108). The earthy qualities of the sweet potato, black-eyed peas, and the sage complement one another perfectly. This sauce also works well with grilled shrimp or tuna or any other hearty, flavorful fish. While not a delicate sauce, the brown butter does have a subtle undertone beneath the bold flavor of the sage.

The browning of the butter and the way the Chicken Stock is incorporated results in a sauce that will break, or separate, much more quickly than a sauce made with unbrowned butter such as Beurre Fondue, so this sauce must be made just before serving. As it can be prepared in under 15 minutes, this is usually not a problem. The black-eyed peas can be cooked in a manner similar to the recipe for Cannellini Beans (see page 246).

2 sticks (8 ounces) unsalted butter, cut into
    small pieces
1 cup black-eyed peas, cooked and rinsed
12 large sage leaves, finely chopped
1 large garlic clove, peeled and minced
    (1 teaspoon)
½ cup dry white wine
½ cup Chicken Stock (see page 187)
2 teaspoons fresh lemon juice
Kosher salt

Have ready

The black-eyed peas, cooked and rinsed
The Chicken Stock, warm, in a small saucepan
    over low heat

IN a medium sauté pan, over medium heat, melt and cook the butter until it begins to brown and has a nutty, toasty aroma, about 10 minutes. Remove the pan from the heat. Carefully add the cooked black-eyed peas, chopped sage, and minced garlic. Return the pan to the heat and sauté about 1 minute.

Add the white wine and simmer about 1 minute, taking care not to burn the garlic. Gradually add the Chicken Stock, whisking vigorously to emulsify it into the butter. Remove the pan from the heat. Add the lemon juice, stir, and adjust the seasoning to taste with kosher salt. Serve immediately.

Rouille

ROUILLE is quite often confused with aioli. Both sauces are variations on mayonnaise; the main difference is that Rouille has saffron and, sometimes, roasted sweet red pepper, and aioli doesn't. Some recipes call for Rouille, or aioli, to be bound and thickened with cooked potato, but we use bread, because it is lighter and adds a chunkier texture. Rouille originates in the south of France, where it is essential to bouillabaisse. We serve Rouille with our fish soup, but it also makes a wonderful accompaniment for steamed mussels or clams or simple crudité. It goes especially well with cold roast chicken.

For use with seafood, Fish Stock is preferred, but Chicken Stock will be perfectly adequate. In making Rouille, a mortar and pestle is superior to a food processor. A food processor heats up the mixture and whips in air, which oxidizes the garlic, resulting in a bitter Rouille. The Rouille also comes out too fluffy and pale because of the extra air. Rouille can be prepared in advance and kept covered in the refrigerator for up to 1 day.

1 slice sourdough bread (1 ounce), without
    crust
1 tablespoon champagne vinegar
2 large garlic cloves, peeled
1/2 cup vegetable oil
Kosher salt
1/4 teaspoon saffron threads
1/4 teaspoon cayenne pepper
1 extra-large egg yolk, at room temperature
Fresh lemon juice
1/2 cup extra-virgin olive oil
3 tablespoons Fish Stock or Chicken Stock
    (see page 194 or 187)

Have ready

The Fish Stock or Chicken Stock, at room
    temperature

MOISTEN the bread with the vinegar. Using a mortar and pestle, grind together the bread, garlic, 1 teaspoon of the vegetable oil, and 1/4 teaspoon kosher salt, forming a paste. Continue to grind, adding the saffron threads and cayenne pepper. Add the egg yolk and 1 tablespoon fresh lemon juice, grinding all the ingredients into a paste.

Slowly, adding a small amount at a time, whisk in first the remaining vegetable oil and then the olive oil, making a smooth, emulsified mixture, similar to mayonnaise with a few small pieces of coarsely ground bread and garlic. Whisk in the stock, a tablespoon at a time, to produce a consistency slightly more liquid than mayonnaise. Adjust the seasoning to taste with kosher salt and fresh lemon juice if necessary. Refrigerate, covered, up to 1 day.

Roasted Garlic Tartar Sauce

Yields 1½ cups

A variation on traditional tartar sauce, this garlic-infused condiment is more complex and sophisticated in flavor than its simple namesake. Mustard, garlic, fresh parsley, and cornichons or gherkins (tiny French pickles) are added to yield a sharp but rich sauce. Preparing tartar sauce from fresh ingredients makes all the difference in the world. It adds to the flavor of almost any grilled, poached, or fried fish. Used in place of traditional mayonnaise in a tuna fish sandwich, it adds a whole new taste to an old American standard. Mayonnaise variations such as this that are made with roasted garlic can be kept longer than those made with raw garlic before the flavor becomes bitter. The sauce can be refrigerated, covered, for up to 2 days.

1 extra-large egg yolk, at room temperature
1 tablespoon good-quality Dijon mustard
2 tablespoons Roasted Garlic Puree
  (see page 245)
2 teaspoons white wine vinegar
1 tablespoon fresh lemon juice
1¼ cups light vegetable oil (almond, safflower,
  canola)
½ small red onion, peeled and finely diced
  (⅓ cup)
4 cornichons or gherkins, finely diced
1½ tablespoons drained capers, finely chopped
2 tablespoons chopped fresh Italian parsley
  leaves
Kosher salt

Have ready

The Roasted Garlic Puree

In a medium mixing bowl, whisk together the egg yolk, mustard, Roasted Garlic Puree, vinegar, and lemon juice. Slowly add the oil a little at a time, whisking it in to make a thick emulsion.

Rinse the diced onion in a small mixing bowl filled with water. Drain and dry thoroughly with a clean kitchen towel. Stir the onion into the sauce with the diced cornichons, capers, and parsley. Correct the seasoning to taste with kosher salt. The capers and mustard are salty, so it might not be necessary to add much salt. Refrigerate, covered, until needed.

Mustard for Gravlax

Yields ¾ cup

THIS traditional accompaniment for Gravlax
(see page 38) should be prepared the day before
it is needed so that the flavors will blend and
meld with one another. The dry mustard will
enhance the Dijon, intensifying the flavor and
complexity of the mustard. The hint of sweetness from the brown sugar balances the saltiness
of the Gravlax. Be sure to use dried mustard
that is not more than three months old. If older
than that it will be stale and flat in flavor. This
will keep, covered and refrigerated, for up to
one week if the dill is added just before serving.

½ cup good-quality Dijon mustard
1 teaspoon dry mustard
2 teaspoons dark brown sugar
1 tablespoon chopped fresh dill

IN a small mixing bowl, whisk together the
Dijon mustard, dry mustard, and brown sugar.
Just before serving add the chopped dill, and stir
until well combined. Refrigerate, covered,
until needed.

Dill Cream

Makes about 1¼ cups

THIS condiment is primarily intended for
Gravlax (see page 38), but you can toss a little
with thinly sliced cucumbers and red onions for
a delicious quick summer salad. Dill cream also
makes a great accompaniment for any cold leftovers of fish or poultry.

Crème fraîche is preferred for the more
subtle flavor, but sour cream will do if crème
fraîche is unavailable. Dill cream can be made in
advance, as it will keep, refrigerated and covered, for up to 3 days if the dill is added just
before serving.

1 cup crème fraîche or sour cream
2 large shallots, peeled, trimmed, and minced
    (2 tablespoons)
2 teaspoons fresh lemon juice
Kosher salt
1 teaspoon freshly cracked black pepper
2 bunches fresh dill, chopped to make ¼ cup

IN a medium mixing bowl, combine the crème
fraîche, shallots, fresh lemon juice, and mix
well. Correct the seasoning to taste with kosher
salt and black pepper. Just before serving stir in
the dill. Refrigerate, covered, until needed.

Tomato and Red Pepper Sauce

Yields 1½ cups

THIS sauce should be made only between late
June and October, when tomatoes and bell
peppers are at their most flavorful and the
weather is perfect for cooking outdoors. Winter tomatoes don't have the flavor to make this
sauce stand out. The tomatoes and peppers are
grilled on sprigs of thyme, which blacken and
crumble, adding bits of charred herb and a
wonderful smokey flavor. This is delicious
served with Shrimp and Crab Cakes (see
page 46) or just about any grilled fish. It is also
great served over pasta like a marinara sauce.

For use with seafood, the Fish Stock is preferred, but Chicken Stock will be perfectly adequate. The tomatoes and peppers can be
charred in the broiler if grilling is inconvenient.
Soak the thyme in cold water for at least 1 hour
prior to broiling, leave the broiler door open,
and be ready for some smoke in your kitchen.
The sauce can be made in advance and reheated
over low heat just before serving.

3 tablespoons olive oil
3 medium tomatoes (1 pound)
Freshly ground black pepper
2 bunches fresh thyme (2 ounces), whole sprigs
1 large red bell pepper (8 ounces)
1 large shallot peeled, trimmed, and minced
　　(1 tablespoon)
2 large garlic cloves, peeled and minced
　　(2 teaspoons)

½ cup Fish Stock or Chicken Stock
　　(see page 194 or 187)
1 tablespoon chopped fresh basil
1 tablespoon chopped fresh parsley
Kosher salt

Have ready

The Chicken Stock or the Fish Stock, warm, in
　　a small saucepan over low heat.

START a fire in the grill and allow it to burn to
medium temperature.

In a medium mixing bowl, combine
2 tablespoons of the olive oil with the tomatoes
and a little black pepper, and toss gently to coat.

Make a bed of thyme sprigs on the grill,
just large enough to fit the tomatoes and red
bell pepper on top. Arrange the tomatoes and
the red bell pepper on the sprigs of thyme.
Cover with a large stainless-steel bowl, and
grill, turning as necessary, until the skins of
both vegetables are charred on all sides and the
tomatoes are soft, about 10 minutes for the pepper and 15 minutes for the tomatoes. Remove
the tomatoes and pepper from the grill and
allow them to cool. When they have cooled,
remove the stem and core from each tomato;
peel, core, and seed the pepper.

In a food mill, puree the tomatoes and red
pepper together. The yield should be about 1 to
1½ cups. Reserve the puree in a small mixing
bowl.

In a medium sauté pan, over medium heat, preheat the remaining 1 tablespoon of olive oil. Sweat the shallot and garlic, about 2 to 3 minutes. Add the stock, bring to a simmer, and reduce by two thirds, about 10 minutes. Add the reserved puree and continue to simmer for about 5 minutes. Just before serving, stir in the chopped basil and parsley. Correct the seasoning to taste with kosher salt and black pepper. Keep warm over low heat until needed.

Salsa Verde

Yields ¾ cup

THIS Salsa Verde is of Italian, not Mexican, origin. The flavor is a balance of garlic, anchovy, tart lemon, capers, and fresh herbs. Salsa Verde is perfect for serving with roasted meats. It fills the same taste niche as steak sauce, but because it's freshly made, the flavors are more vibrant. The lemon juice and the vinegar from the capers give it a cutting quality, and the anchovy adds a bite to the richness of roasted meats. It's a small flavor twist that works especially well on a roast beef sandwich. Salsa Verde is perfect with the Braised Lamb Shanks (see page 170) or roast chicken. It is important that Salsa Verde be prepared fresh no more than an hour before serving to catch all the flavors at their peak.

3 anchovy fillets, coarsely chopped
1 tablespoon plus 1 teaspoon capers, drained
   well
3 large garlic cloves, peeled
Kosher salt
½ cup extra-virgin olive oil
3 tablespoons coarsely chopped Italian parsley
2 tablespoons coarsely chopped fresh marjoram
2 tablespoons coarsely chopped fresh mint
2 teaspoons fresh lemon juice
Freshly cracked black pepper

USING a mortar and pestle, grind to a paste the anchovy fillets, capers, garlic, ¼ teaspoon kosher salt, and 1 tablespoon of the olive oil. Continue to grind, adding the herbs and 1 more tablespoon of olive oil. When the herbs have been ground to a coarse paste, slowly add the remaining olive oil, stirring to incorporate it into the paste.

When ready to serve, stir in up to 2 teaspoons fresh lemon juice to taste. Season to taste with kosher salt and black pepper, and serve immediately.

Grilled Corn and Tomato Sauce

Serves 6

IN midsummer, when sweet corn, tomatoes, and red peppers are at their peak, we serve this sauce with Shrimp and Crab Cakes (page 46) or grilled scallops. Grilling in the husk is the best way to cook fresh summer corn. The fire burns the husk in spots and browns the odd kernel of corn here and there, resulting in a powerful, fresh corn flavor with a smokey edge. The bacon also contributes to the smokey flavor of the sauce. What makes this sauce stand out is using ingredients at their peak of flavor; don't make this in February.

If you want to just grill the corn and eat it, spread a little herb butter over the kernels and wrap the husks back up, tie them with kitchen string, and grill over a medium fire.

3 ears fresh sweet corn, in the husks
3 thick slices bacon (3 ounces)
¾ stick (3 ounces) unsalted butter
1 large tomato, cored, seeded, and cut into
    ¼-inch dice (¾ cup)
1 small red bell pepper, cored, seeded, and cut
    into ¼-inch dice (⅓ cup)
⅔ cup Chicken Stock (see page 187)
1 tablespoon chopped fresh marjoram
1 tablespoon chopped fresh Italian parsley
Kosher salt
Freshly cracked black pepper
Fresh lemon juice

Have ready

The Chicken Stock, warm, in a small saucepan
    over low heat

START a fire in the grill, and allow it to burn to medium temperature.

Carefully peel back the husks of each ear of corn, ensuring that the husks remain attached at the base, and remove the silk. Close the husks over the corn and tie with butcher's string to hold in place. Place the corn on the grill and cook, turning to cook on all sides, about 15 minutes. The husks and a few kernels will char and blacken, but the corn will be cooked properly inside the husks. Remove from the grill and allow to cool.

Remove and discard the husks. Using a sharp knife, cut the kernels from the cob and discard the cob, reserving the kernels.

In a medium sauté pan, over medium heat, cook the bacon until chewy, not crisp. Drain it on absorbent paper and allow to cool. When the bacon is cool, using a sharp knife, slice it on the bias into julienne and reserve.

In a medium sauté pan, over medium-high heat, melt 2 tablespoons of the butter. Sauté the corn, tomato, red bell pepper, and bacon for 1 to 2 minutes to bring out the flavor. Add the stock, reduce the heat to medium low, and reduce until the sauce slightly thickens, about 5 to 10 minutes. Whisk in the remaining 4 tablespoons of butter; add the marjoram and parsley. Season with kosher salt, black pepper, and a squeeze of fresh lemon juice to taste.

Serve immediately, or keep warm in a double boiler for up to 30 minutes.

G r e m o l a t a

Yields ⅓ cup

THIS is a condiment similar in principle to Salsa Verde, but the flavor is quite different. Gremolata relies on the combination of the light bitterness of the parsley and the sharp sweetness of the lemon zest to produce a pronounced flavor. It is necessary to use it sparingly to avoid overwhelming the flavor of the food it accompanies. As a condiment it is a wonderful accent to roasted meats and poultry.

Zest of 1 small lemon
1 large garlic clove, peeled
Kosher salt
½ cup fresh Italian parsley leaves, coarsely chopped
Freshly cracked black pepper
Fresh lemon juice

USING a mortar and pestle, grind to a paste the lemon zest, garlic, and a pinch of kosher salt. Continue to grind, adding the parsley. Correct the seasoning to taste with kosher salt and black pepper, and a few drops of lemon juice. The Gremolata will not retain its fresh quality for more than 1 hour.

Pesto

A superior pesto is almost as much an accomplishment of technique as of ingredients. The mixture should be ground to the point that the flavor of each ingredient is still distinct, and the composition holds together like a proper emulsification. The finished result should be similar in texture to whole grain mustard. A good mortar and pestle is the best way to produce the desired results. Any electric appliance will pulverize the mixture and incorporate too much air into the pesto, causing it to become pale, frothy, and bitter.

Basil is pretty much out of season in the fall and winter, but parsley and marjoram are readily available all year round. To make a pesto of parsley or marjoram is simply a matter of a few variations from traditional basil pesto. With parsley pesto, you can have the perception of summer in the dead of winter. We frequently serve parsley pesto on fish, usually escolar or scallops, so the traditional Parmesan cheese is not used. Pesto should be eaten within six hours of being made if the color and vibrant flavors are to be at their fullest.

2 tablespoons pine nuts
3 large garlic cloves, peeled
Kosher salt
½ cup extra-virgin olive oil
¾ cup fresh Italian parsley, coarsely chopped
¼ cup fresh mint, coarsely chopped

In a small sauté pan, over medium heat, toast the pine nuts to a pale golden color, watching carefully and stirring to prevent burning, about 3 to 5 minutes. Remove the pine nuts from the pan and allow to cool.

Using a mortar and pestle, grind to a coarse paste the pine nuts, garlic, and ½ teaspoon of kosher salt, adding about a tablespoon of olive oil as you grind. When the desired consistency is reached, add the parsley and mint, continuing to grind, and adding small amounts of olive oil until the mixture is smooth. Slowly add enough of the remaining oil to make a thick sauce with the consistency of whole grain mustard. Correct the seasoning to taste with kosher salt. Refrigerate, covered, or use as needed.

To prepare Parsley-Lemon Pesto, add the zest of 1 medium lemon with the pine nuts and garlic, and 1½ teaspoons fresh lemon juice, added last, just before correcting the seasoning. Make this lemon variation no more than 1 hour before use. The pesto will turn brown within 1 hour because of the high level of acidity.

To prepare Basil Pesto, use ¾ cup of fresh basil and ¼ cup of fresh Italian parsley. Omit the mint, and whisk in ¼ cup of freshly grated Parmesan as the last step.

To prepare Marjoram Pesto, use ⅓ cup of fresh marjoram and ⅔ cup of fresh Italian parsley, and add a few sprigs of fresh mint. The ratio favors parsley because marjoram is so much stronger in flavor.

Tapenade (Black Olive Puree)

Yields about 1 cup

TAPENADE is a strongly flavored puree of black olives, garlic, lemon zest, and other pungent ingredients. It can be used as a garnish or condiment for grilled steak (see Grilled Prime Rib Steak with Red Wine Sauce, page 180). It is also delicious with grilled tuna or as a simple appetizer, spread on pieces of grilled bread. The puree will keep in the refrigerator for up to three to four weeks.

A food processor heats up the Tapenade, whips in air, and can quickly overpuree it. Preparing this by hand with a mortar and pestle produces a Tapenade of coarser texture. Each ingredient retains its identity but subtly blends with the others.

2 anchovy fillets, drained
1 teaspoon lemon zest
½ teaspoon orange zest
1 garlic clove, peeled
1 cup pitted black Kalamata or Niçoise olives
¼ cup extra-virgin olive oil
1 teaspoon fresh lemon juice
4 large leaves (1 tablespoon) chopped basil
Freshly cracked black pepper

USING a mortar and pestle, grind into a paste the anchovy fillets, lemon zest, orange zest, and garlic. Add the olives, and grind into a paste. Fold in the extra-virgin olive oil, lemon juice, and basil, and correct the seasoning to taste with black pepper. Transfer to a clean container with a tightly fitting lid, and refrigerate until needed.

Green Peppercorn Tapenade

Makes ¾ cup

GREEN peppercorns and green olives are a variation on the traditional black olive tapenade condiment. It is piquant and strong, wonderful with pork or veal chops. Even something as prosaic as a salami sandwich, with Green Peppercorn Tapenade instead of mustard, is truly scrumptious. The peppercorns come packed in brine or vinegar; drain them well before using. We sauté them to bring out and intensify the flavor. If used straight from the bottle, the peppercorns' flavor will be dominated by the brine or vinegar.

1½ tablespoons green peppercorns, drained
2 anchovy fillets
1 teaspoon drained capers
½ teaspoon minced lemon zest
1 large garlic clove, peeled
20 green Kalamata olives, pitted (½ cup)
1 teaspoon fresh Italian parsley, chopped
2 mint leaves, chopped
2 basil leaves, chopped
3 tablespoons extra-virgin olive oil
1 teaspoon fresh lemon juice
Freshly cracked black pepper

IN a small sauté pan, over low heat, sauté the green peppercorns until dry, about 5 minutes. When dry, the peppercorns will begin to pop. Remove the peppercorns from the pan and allow to cool.

Using a mortar and pestle, grind to a paste the anchovy fillets, green peppercorns, capers, lemon zest, and garlic. Add the green olives, and grind to a paste. Fold in the parsley, mint, basil, olive oil, and lemon juice. Correct the seasoning to taste with black pepper. Transfer to a clean container with a tightly fitting lid, and refrigerate until needed.

Lamb Sauce with Rosemary

Yields 1 cup

THIS sauce is good with almost any sort of lamb preparation you can possibly think of—chops, saddles, shanks, or legs. Any cut is perfect. If you have some lamb sausages on the grill, whisk a tablespoon of whole grain mustard into the sauce just before serving. Another variation is to add a little freshly chopped mint instead of the rosemary.

Lamb Stock is the kind of thing to keep a little of in the freezer. You may not need it often, but when you do, it makes a big difference. This sauce can be made as much as 2 hours ahead of time and kept warm in a double boiler until needed. If it becomes too thick, thin it with a little Chicken Stock (see page 187), 1 tablespoon at a time.

2 tablespoons (1 ounce) unsalted butter
2 large shallots, peeled, trimmed, and minced
  (2 tablespoons)
½ cup dry red wine
2 tablespoons red wine vinegar
1 cup Lamb Stock (see page 192)
1 sprig fresh rosemary, 4 to 6 inches long
Kosher salt
Freshly cracked black pepper

Have ready

The Lamb Stock, warm, in a small saucepan
  over low heat

IN a medium sauté pan, over medium heat, melt 1 tablespoon of the butter. Add the shallots and sauté until golden, about 4 minutes. Pour in the wine and the vinegar and reduce by three fourths, about 10 minutes.

Add the stock, reduce the heat to medium-low, and simmer until the sauce thickens slightly, about 10 minutes. Skim the sauce as necessary to remove any fat or foam. Turn off the heat and steep the rosemary sprig in the sauce for about 5 minutes.

Using a fine-mesh, stainless-steel strainer lined with a double layer of cheesecloth, strain the sauce into a clean pan, pressing down on the shallots to extract as much flavor as possible. Whisk in the remaining 1 tablespoon of butter. Adjust the seasoning to taste with kosher salt and black pepper. Keep warm, covered, in a double boiler until needed.

Shiitake Mushroom Sauce

THE rich, earthy flavor of the shiitake mushroom works well with Mediterranean cuisine even though the fungus is of Far Eastern origin. Shiitake Mushroom Sauce is ideal for grilled veal or pork chops, especially with a little of the Green Peppercorn Tapenade (see page 216). Crimini or other mushrooms may be substituted, but the flavor and texture of the shiitake mushroom is unique, and the use of other mushrooms will alter the character of this sauce. The severe browning over high heat gives them a smokey flavor, and a chewiness that survives the simmering in the sauce. The quantity of black pepper in the sauce does not seem like much, but because it is toasted by the high-heat sauté, the peppery flavor is very pronounced. The sauce can be prepared as much as 2 hours ahead of time and kept warm, covered, in a double boiler.

6 ounces fresh shiitake mushrooms
2 tablespoons vegetable oil
Kosher salt
Freshly cracked black pepper
2 shallots peeled, trimmed, and thinly sliced
(2 tablespoons)
1 large garlic clove, peeled and minced
(1 teaspoon)
1 cup dry white wine
2 cups Brown Veal Stock (see page 190)

Bouquet garni (1 sprig Italian parsley, 1 basil leaf, 1 bay leaf, 1 sprig oregano)
1 tablespoon cognac
1 tablespoon (½ ounce) unsalted butter
Freshly cracked black pepper

Have ready

The Brown Veal Stock, warm, in a small saucepan over low heat

USING a damp kitchen towel, wipe the shiitake mushrooms clean. Using a sharp knife, remove and discard the stems from the shiitake mushrooms, then slice the mushrooms very thinly.

In a medium sauté pan, over medium-high heat, preheat the 2 tablespoons of vegetable oil to just smoking. Sauté the sliced mushrooms without stirring until almost charred, about 1 to 2 minutes. Continue to sauté, stirring occasionally, about 3 more minutes, until evenly browned. As the shiitakes brown, season them lightly with ½ teaspoon each of kosher salt and black pepper.

Reduce the heat to medium, add the shallots and garlic, and sauté for about 1 minute. Deglaze the pan with the wine and reduce by three fourths, about 5 minutes. Add the stock and the bouquet garni, reduce the heat to medium low, and simmer gently until the sauce thickens slightly, about 10 to 15 minutes. Skim off any foam or fat that rises to the surface.

Remove the pan from the heat. Remove and discard the bouquet garni, stir in the cognac and the butter, and correct the season-ing to taste with kosher salt. Keep warm in a double boiler, or use as needed.

Lemon Oil

Yields about 1 quart

LEMON Oil, with its infusion of citrus, is lighter in flavor than olive oil. It can be used to add a tart, summery character to salads or almost anything else that you would drizzle a little extra-virgin olive over. It will keep well if treated like extra-virgin olive oil, and sealed tightly and stored in a cool, dry place. Don't use olive oil to make this; the wonderful flavor of an extra-virgin olive oil should stand on its own and should not interfere with the fresh citrus flavor of Lemon Oil. This is an oil for vinai-grettes and seasoning, not cooking, as the deli-cate lemon flavor disappears when this oil is subjected to the high heat of sautéing.

1 quart vegetable oil (almond or safflower)
2 lemons, cut in half
1 bay leaf
¼ teaspoon whole black peppercorns
1 small dried red chile pepper

IN a medium saucepan, over medium heat, combine the vegetable oil, lemon halves, bay leaf, peppercorns, and the chile, and heat just until the lemons begin to produce small bubbles in the oil. It is important that the oil does not become too hot—never above a very low simmer—as the lemons will produce a bitter flavor in the oil. Remove the pan from the heat and allow the oil and lemon mixture to cool, about 1 hour. Refrigerate, covered, for at least 12 hours.

Then, using a fine-mesh, stainless-steel strainer, strain the oil into a clean container with a tightly fitting lid. Discard the lemon halves and herbs, reserving the lemon-infused oil. Store the oil in a tightly sealed container for up to 1 month, and use as needed.

Lemon Oil Vinaigrette

Yields 1¼ cups

IF you have the Lemon Oil, this is so simple to prepare that it is almost embarrassing to include as a recipe, but it's so delicious we couldn't leave it out. Lemon Oil Vinaigrette is not as sweet and rich as balsamic vinaigrette; rather it is sharper, and more lively. It is delicious as a quick, simple dressing for grilled chicken or fish, grilled vegetables, and, of course, on simple salads.

1 cup Lemon Oil (see page 219)
3 tablespoons fresh lemon juice
3 tablespoons champagne vinegar or white
    wine vinegar

Kosher salt
Freshly cracked black pepper

Have ready

The Lemon Oil

IN a medium mixing bowl, whisk together the Lemon Oil, lemon juice, and vinegar. Correct the seasoning to taste with kosher salt and black pepper. To taste for correct seasoning, spoon a little of the dressing over a few greens. Taste the greens and adjust the seasoning as necessary. Refrigerate, covered, until needed, up to 2 days.

Lemon Oil Vinaigrette with Red and Yellow Peppers

Yields 2 cups

THIS lemon oil vinaigrette is very brightly flavored with a sharp onion and vibrant sweet peppers. A simple salad of whole romaine leaves with some of this vinaigrette spooned over is the perfect summer salad. The vinaigrette will keep, refrigerated, in a covered container for up to 2 days. After the second day the peppers will begin to get mushy.

1 small red bell pepper (8 ounces), cored,
    seeded, and cut into ¼-inch dice
1 small yellow bell pepper (8 ounces), cored,
    seeded, and cut into ¼-inch dice
½ red onion (4 ounces), peeled, trimmed, and
    cut into ¼-inch dice
1 cup Lemon Oil (see page 219)
2 tablespoons plus 1 teaspoon champagne
    vinegar or white wine vinegar
2 tablespoons fresh lemon juice

Kosher salt
Freshly cracked black pepper

Have ready

The Lemon Oil

IN a medium mixing bowl, whisk together the red bell pepper, yellow bell pepper, onion, Lemon Oil, vinegar, and the lemon juice. Correct the seasoning to taste with kosher salt and black pepper. To taste for correct seasoning, spoon a little of the dressing over a few greens. Taste the greens and adjust the seasoning as necessary. Refrigerate, covered, until needed.

Aromatic Spice Rub

Makes about ¼ cup

THIS mixture goes on the Sautéed Salmon with Red Onion Vinaigrette (see page 154), as a variation on blackened redfish. It can also add a spicy flavor to the Crisp Flattened Chicken with Wilted Parsley Salad (see page 157) or other milder meat, fish, or poultry recipes. The toasting brings out the flavor and pungency, but it must be used within a few days or it will lose the majority of its flavor.

2 tablespoons black peppercorns
1 tablespoon whole cumin
1 tablespoon whole anise seed
3 dried red chile peppers, stems removed
1 teaspoon (12 whole) allspice

IN a small sauté pan, over low heat, combine the peppercorns, cumin, anise, chiles, and allspice. Toast, stirring constantly, until the mixture becomes aromatic and the ingredients begin to turn slightly brown, about 8 to 10 minutes. Take care not to burn any of the spices. Immediately remove the spices from the pan and allow to cool.

Grind the cooled mixture in a spice grinder or with a mortar and pestle. Transfer to a small, tightly covered container, and use as desired.

Preserved Lemon Peel

Yields ⅓ cup

Preserved Lemon Peel is a condiment from the North African shores of the Mediterranean. The salt and sugar cure that is used to preserve the lemon peel also greatly concentrates the lemon flavor. Preserved Lemon Peel allows you to add lemon flavor to a dish without adding a lot of juice or acidity. The flavor is very intense, so it should be used sparingly. At the restaurant, we sprinkle a little over roasted chicken or braised lamb shanks.

Preserved Lemon Peel should not be cooked, so it is important to add it only just before serving. You will never use all this Preserved Lemon Peel at one time, but it keeps so well that you should make a large batch; it can add a last-minute spark to so many dishes. And if you're going to make Preserved Lemon Peel, you may as well make lemonade. There will be a lot of fresh lemon juice to use.

10 medium lemons, well washed
⅓ cup granulated sugar
2 tablespoons kosher salt
2 teaspoons fresh thyme leaves, washed

In a medium saucepan, bring approximately 2 quarts of water to a boil. Using a small, sharp knife, carefully peel the lemons. Then, using the same knife, scrap away all the white pith, leaving only the outside peel. Blanch the peel in the boiling water for 10 to 15 seconds. Drain the peel and allow it to cool to room temperature.

In a small mixing bowl, combine the sugar and kosher salt. Add the blanched lemon peel and toss to coat well. Stir in the thyme leaves and gently toss again.

Refrigerate, well covered, for at least 1 day before using. It will keep, well covered, for up to 3 months in the refrigerator. Before using, scrape off the sticky curing mixture, cut the peel into julienne, and use sparingly.

Lemon and Garlic Confit

Yields 2 ½ cups

THIS is similar to onion compote, or soubise, in that it is neither a sauce nor a vegetable, but somewhere in between. It works especially well with heartily flavored poultry, like grilled chicken with a potent spice rub. A low temperature is important to prevent the garlic from deep-frying in the oil. The garlic mustn't brown during cooking, or the essence of the lemon oil will be gone, and the confit will be left with a bitter and unpleasant flavor.

12 ounces peeled whole garlic cloves
   (6 whole heads)
1½ cups Lemon Oil (see page 219)
Bouquet garni (3 small sprigs each thyme and
   savory)
Zest of 2 lemons
1 cup Chicken Stock (see page 187)
1 teaspoon kosher salt
1 tablespoon fresh lemon juice
½ cup chopped fresh Italian parsley

Have ready

The Lemon Oil
The Chicken Stock

IN a medium saucepan, over medium heat, combine the whole garlic cloves, Lemon Oil, bouquet garni, and the lemon zest, and bring to a simmer. Reduce the heat to very low and simmer until the garlic is very tender, about 25 minutes. (If the oil begins to boil, remove the pan from the heat for 1 or 2 minutes, reduce the heat, then return the pan to the heat. You will find that the oil will continue to simmer, even when removed from the heat.) Remove the pan from the heat, discard the bouquet garni, and reserve the confit. At this point, the confit can be refrigerated in a clean container with a tightly fitting lid for up to 3 days.

In a medium saucepan, combine the Chicken Stock, kosher salt, and reserved confit and bring to a boil over high heat. When the mixture has just come to a full boil, remove it from the heat. Add the fresh lemon juice and the parsley, stir briefly, and serve immediately.

Balsamic or Sherry Wine Vinaigrette

Yields about 1 1/2 cups

THIS vinaigrette can be prepared with balsamic or sherry wine vinegar. At Campanile, we rely on these two vinaigrettes to grace an immense variety of greens, especially bitter greens. Our conviction is that the best vinaigrettes are the simplest vinaigrettes, the ones that enhance the flavor of the greens and coax out that essence of freshness. The two most important hints here are a healthy respect for the intensity of walnut oil and the adjustment of strength and seasoning only after tasting the vinaigrette on the greens.

Always use a larger bowl than you think you will need so you won't make a mess when whisking vigorously. Minced shallots will oxidize and become bitter when stored, so if they are not added until just before serving, this vinaigrette will keep for up to a week, refrigerated.

⅔ cup vegetable oil (almond, safflower, or canola)
⅓ cup walnut oil
⅓ cup sherry wine vinegar or balsamic vinegar
1 large shallot, peeled, trimmed, and minced (1 tablespoon)
Kosher salt
Freshly cracked black pepper

IN a medium mixing bowl, whisk together the vegetable oil, walnut oil, vinegar, and shallot. Correct the seasoning to taste with kosher salt and black pepper. To taste for the correct seasoning, spoon a little of the dressing over a few greens. Taste the greens and adjust the seasoning as necessary. Refrigerate, covered, and use as needed.

Mustard Vinaigrette

THIS is more forceful than a basic red wine vinaigrette. The mustard and the garlic give it extra vibrancy, and the lemon adds a clean, fruity element that contrasts with the zest of the mustard. At Campanile we use both extra-virgin olive oil and simple vegetable oil, such as almond or safflower oil, to produce a lighter flavor than if we were to use olive oil exclusively. For some reason that has never been fully clear to us, plain vegetable oil emulsifies better than extra-virgin olive oil. Incorporating the vegetable oil before the olive oil will reduce the likelihood that this, and all emulsified vinaigrettes, will separate. Vinaigrettes such as this are better suited to salads made of greens with a hearty structure, such as romaine, or a sharp flavor, such as arugula. Delicate greens, like mâche or mesclun, would be overwhelmed by this dressing. The vinaigrette will keep, refrigerated, for up to 2 days.

1 extra-large egg yolk at room temperature
1 large garlic clove, peeled and minced
    (1 teaspoon)
¼ cup whole grain mustard
Juice from 1 lemon (4 tablespoons)
⅓ cup red wine vinegar
½ cup vegetable oil
½ cup extra-virgin olive oil
Kosher salt
Freshly cracked black pepper

IN a medium mixing bowl, whisk together the egg yolk, garlic, mustard, lemon juice, and red wine vinegar. Add the vegetable oil in a slow trickle, whisking continuously until all the oil is incorporated. Repeat the procedure with the olive oil. Correct the seasoning to taste. To taste for the correct seasoning, spoon a little of the dressing over a few greens. Taste the greens and adjust the seasoning as necessary, with kosher salt and black pepper. Refrigerate, covered, and use as needed.

Garlic Croutons or Bread Crumbs

Yields 1–2 cups

WE often use Kalamata olive bread in the restaurant, but any good sourdough bread will do. These bread crumbs can be used to top all sorts of pastas or vegetables. With just some Garlic Bread Crumbs, a little pasta, and a few Slow-roasted Tomatoes (see page 241), you have a simple but very satisfying and full-flavored meal. As a topping for creamy winter soups, these add a zesty garlic crunch that cuts through the richness. For the best flavor, bread crumbs should be prepared and used on the same day.

2 cups soft inside of sourdough bread, torn into
    1-inch pieces
2 tablespoons extra-virgin olive oil
1 large garlic clove, peeled and minced
    (1 teaspoon)
Kosher salt
Freshly cracked black pepper

PREHEAT the oven to 325 degrees.

In a medium mixing bowl, toss the bread pieces with the olive oil and minced garlic. Season lightly with kosher salt and black pepper and spread out on a baking pan. Bake until golden on all sides, about 7 or 8 minutes, turning or tossing after 3 or 4 minutes. Remove the pan from the oven, and allow to cool. The croutons can be used as is, or crushed fine using the bottom of a clean, dry pan.

Store the croutons or crumbs at room temperature in a sealed container for up to 1 day.

Vegetables

Chapter 10

Anyone with a home vegetable garden knows the difference between freshly picked vegetables and what we often find available at the supermarket. Vegetables, through the wonders of modern transportation, are often available at the supermarket when they are not necessarily at their best. January sweet corn is almost an oxymoron. Following the seasons is still the best guide to vegetables; it should enhance your cooking with flavor and vitality.

The rise of farmer's markets has given people the opportunity to purchase produce that is fresher and more seasonal than is available at the supermarket. It is also inevitably more expensive. Usually the expense is justified; sometimes it is not. In picking fresh vegetables, there is no substitute for your own experience and judgment.

Much of the produce available at farmer's markets is grown organically. For the most part, organic vegetables are not nutritionally different from those grown with chemical fertilizers and pesticides. The trace amounts of these chemicals that are found on supermarket produce are harmless to most people. The real and long-term benefit of organic farming is that it causes far less damage to the environment. With organic farming practices, the soil and the water table, along with the rivers and oceans, are not subjected to the long-term devastating effects of chemical pesticides and fertilizers.

Meat, fish, or poultry isn't necessary for every meal. Current dietary guidelines are emphasizing fruits, vegetables, and starches as the staples of our diet, rather than the animal proteins and fats of generations past. This is the classic diet of Mediterranean climates, relying on the bountiful goodness of the sun and earth for sustenance, pleasure, and healthy longevity. Pasta with a few vegetable side dishes can make a delicious and satisfying meal.

Vegetable dishes are usually less complex than main courses, but that doesn't mean that they should be simply boiled and buttered. They should be prepared with the same attention and care as any other part of a meal. Sautéed kale is good all by itself, but with a little crisped garlic on top, it is truly delicious. The pairing of vegetables with other dishes requires some thought. You should match strength with strength and delicacy with delicacy. Sautéed kale and crisped garlic is too powerful to accompany something so delicate as sautéed halibut but would be delicious with braised lamb shanks.

At Campanile, we spend as much time and care on purchasing and preparing fresh seasonal vegetables as we do on meat, fish, and poultry. It seems like we are always eagerly anticipating the arrival of the vegetables of each new season.

Campfire Roasted Potatoes

Serves 4

ROASTING the potatoes in the mesquite coals of the grill at the restaurant adds a charred and smokey flavor to them, and it works just as well at home in a backyard grill. The potatoes come out unevenly browned and look and taste quite rustic. This is not a fancy preparation in any way, but almost everyone, from fine chefs to toddlers, is charmed by the process and the result. If you want roasted potatoes without the trouble of firing up the grill, these can be done in the oven, but they won't have quite the same flavor.

¼ cup extra-virgin olive oil
12 small new potatoes (1¼ pounds), well
    washed and unpeeled
2 teaspoons chopped fresh rosemary
Kosher salt
Freshly cracked black pepper
1 slice bacon (1 ounce), thick cut

PREHEAT the oven to 450 degrees, or start a fire in the grill and allow it to burn to medium temperature.

Combine the oil and the potatoes in a large mixing bowl, and toss well to coat the potatoes. Sprinkle the potatoes with rosemary and season generously with kosher salt and black pepper. Line another large mixing bowl with 2 sheets of aluminum foil placed in a cross, 1 sheet perpendicular to the other, with lots of excess on top, enough to fold over and seal around the potatoes.

Place the potatoes in the foil-lined bowl. Place the slice of bacon on the potatoes and fold the foil over, enclosing the potatoes completely. Carefully remove the package from the mixing bowl, and wrap with at least 5 more layers of aluminum foil. Take care to ensure that the package is well sealed, with no openings or leaks. Place the packet on the side of a mound of hot, gray coals in a grill, or in the oven.

Roast until the potatoes are tender, about 45 minutes. If roasting on coals, gently turn the package, using long steel tongs, about every 10 minutes. In the oven, the packet need only be turned upside down once, after about 25 minutes. Remove the packet from the heat and let it rest for at least 5 minutes. Using a knife, cut the packet open, taking care not to allow any foil or ash particles to fall into the potatoes. If desired, the bacon can be diced and tossed with the potatoes just before serving. Serve immediately, or allow to cool, and warm for 10 minutes in a 450-degree oven for 10 minutes before needed.

Sautéed Potatoes with Oregano and Lemon

Serves 4 to 8

THIS lemon-infused side dish provides a delicious contrast to roasted or grilled meats and poultry, or almost any rich main course. At Campanile we use Yukon Gold potatoes because they have a firm, waxy texture that holds up to the thorough browning the potatoes experience. This is a quick but flavorful dish that can be thrown together at the last minute. It is important to toss the cooked potatoes with the marinade while the potatoes are still quite hot in order to temper the flavor of the garlic.

Marinade

¼ cup extra-virgin olive oil
Juice of 1 lemon
2 large garlic cloves, peeled and chopped
    (2 teaspoons)
Pinch of dried red chile pepper flakes

Potatoes

5 medium Yukon Gold potatoes (2 pounds),
    washed, and unpeeled
½ cup vegetable oil
Leaves from 5 sprigs fresh oregano, coarsely
    chopped
Kosher salt
Freshly cracked black pepper

TO prepare the marinade: In a medium mixing bowl, combine the olive oil, lemon juice, garlic, and chile pepper flakes. Mix well and reserve.

To prepare the potatoes: Cut away the ends of the potatoes and cut each potato into ¼-inch-thick round slices.

In a large cast-iron skillet, over high heat, preheat the vegetable oil until it just begins to smoke. Arrange the potatoes in a single layer in the skillet and brown on 1 side, about 1 to 2 minutes. With a stainless-steel spatula, carefully turn each slice over. Brown the other side about 2 more minutes, or until the potato slices are cooked through.

After the potato slices are cooked, remove them from the pan using a stainless-steel spatula. Put the potatoes in a medium mixing bowl, drizzle the marinade over, sprinkle the oregano over, and toss the potatoes gently to coat well. Season to taste with kosher salt and black pepper, and serve immediately.

Garlic Mashed Potatoes

Serves 4 to 6

GARLIC seems to give many people emotional fits; either it's love or loathing—there doesn't seem to be any middle ground. This recipe includes a surprising amount of garlic, but it is cooked down to be quite mild, more of a rich flavor accent than a pungent assault. Of course, the cream and butter help smooth it out as well. The result is exceptional mashed potatoes, mild but deeply flavorful and filling: a perfect companion for grilled meat. Chances are slim that even the most strident garlic hater will dislike these potatoes. Like the Celery Root Puree (see page 236), these potatoes can also be used as a ravioli filling, or as a base for potato pancakes. This can be made in advance and kept warm in a double boiler.

4 large russet potatoes (3 pounds), peeled and
    quartered
4 heads of garlic, cloves separated and peeled
1 cup heavy cream
2 sticks (8 ounces) unsalted butter, cut into
    small pieces
Kosher salt

IN a large saucepan, bring approximately 1 quart of water to a boil. Using a vegetable steamer, steam the potatoes and garlic over medium-high heat until very tender, about 20 minutes. In a medium saucepan, over high heat, scald the cream, about 2 minutes. Add the butter, remove the pan from the heat, and stir the butter in as it melts, about 1 minute. Using a food mill, electric mixer, or a potato masher (but not a food processor), puree the potato and garlic. Fold in the melted butter and cream to give the puree a smooth texture. Season to taste with kosher salt. Serve immediately, or keep warm in a double boiler until needed.

Potato Galette

Serves 4

PEOPLE get very enthusiastic about potatoes, so it's hard not to like this galette of overlapping rounds of browned, buttery potato, all crispy edged and savory. With a little practice one can produce a very pretty galette with evenly spaced overlaps and a beautiful, uniform appearance. When the galette comes out of the oven, it should be removed from the skillet in one piece, and sliced like a pie for serving. The starchiness of the potatoes and the amount of overlap will determine how well the galette holds up. It is important to use only russet potatoes for this dish; white or red rose potatoes just don't have enough starch to bind the galette. At Campanile, we serve this galette with Herbed Baby Chicken with Lemon-Thyme Butter (see page 160).

The galette can be prepared in advance and warmed in the oven when needed. This recipe can be made in one 12-inch-diameter cast-iron skillet, or two 8-inch-diameter skillets.

2 large russet potatoes (1½ pounds), peeled
Kosher salt
Freshly cracked black pepper
1½ sticks (6 ounces) unsalted butter, clarified, to yield 4 ounces, kept warm

PREHEAT the oven to 400 degrees.

Using a mandolin or a very sharp, thin-bladed knife, slice the potatoes into very thin rounds. Toss with 1 teaspoon of kosher salt, ⅓ teaspoon pepper, and 2 tablespoons of clarified butter.

Warm 1 large or 2 small ovenproof cast-iron skillets over medium heat for about 30 seconds. Completely coat the inside of the skillet using 4 tablespoons of melted, clarified butter. Arrange the potatoes in a circle in the skillet, 1 slice overlapping another. First make the circle around the perimeter of the pan, then work in, forming a smaller circle for each row, spiraling in to fill the entire pan. Drizzle the remaining clarified butter over the potatoes.

Over medium heat, cook the potatoes until the edges begin to turn brown, about 8 to 10 minutes. Transfer to the oven and bake until the top of the potatoes begins to brown and the potatoes are tender, 10 to 15 minutes.

Using a thin spatula, hold the galette in the skillet and pour off most of the excess butter. Then, using the same spatula, loosen the galette, carefully working around the perimeter, and into the center. Cover the skillet with a large platter and invert the skillet, turning out the galette. Keep warm or serve immediately.

"WITH A LITTLE PRACTICE ONE CAN PRODUCE A VERY PRETTY GALETTE WITH EVENLY SPACED OVERLAPS AND A BEAUTIFUL, UNIFORM APPEARANCE."

Celery Root Puree

Serves 4 to 6

THIS dish is like mashed potatoes—a traditional, creamy, rich puree—except that the celery root brings a more pronounced character to the flavor. At the restaurant, we steam the celery root and potatoes rather than boil them, as this preserves better taste and texture.

Used cold, this puree can be an element in a wide range of other dishes. Adding some sautéed leeks and garlic could make it into a stuffing for ravioli, or with a little flour and egg, you could make outstanding potato pancakes. For a variation on shepherd's pie, it could be used to cover some leftover stew, topped with grated Parmesan cheese, and baked in a 400-degree oven, just until the top browns, and the wonderful aroma of crispy Parmesan cheese has filled your kitchen.

3 large celery roots (1½ pounds), trimmed,
   peeled and quartered
2 large russet potatoes (1½ pounds), peeled and
   quartered
1 cup heavy cream
2 sticks (8 ounces) unsalted butter, cut into
   small pieces
Kosher salt

IN a large saucepan, bring approximately 1 quart of water to a boil. Using a vegetable steamer, steam the celery roots and potatoes over medium-high heat until very tender, about 20 minutes. In a medium saucepan, over high heat, scald the cream, about 2 minutes. Add the butter, remove the pan from the heat, and stir the butter in as it melts, about 1 minute. Using a food mill, electric mixer, or a potato masher (but not a food processor), puree the celery roots and potatoes. Fold in the melted butter and cream to give the puree a smooth texture. Season to taste with kosher salt. Serve immediately, or keep warm in a double boiler until needed.

Potato-Parsnip Puree

Serves 6 to 8

In this dish, the poor, unappreciated, under-rated parsnip gets a chance to shine. Similar to Celery Root Puree (see page 236), this is a variation on mashed potatoes, but the flavor is sweet and earthy with the essence of parsnips and a real suggestion of autumn. Served with Crisp Flattened Chicken (see page 157) at Campanile, this dish could also accompany roast beef to add a little something new to a delicious traditional cold weather dinner. This can be prepared earlier in the day and warmed in a double boiler when needed.

2 large russet potatoes (1½ pounds), peeled and quartered
4 large parsnips (1½ pounds), peeled and quartered
8 large garlic cloves, peeled
1 cup heavy cream
2 sticks (8 ounces) unsalted butter, cut into small pieces
Kosher salt

In a large stockpot, bring approximately 2 quarts of water to a boil. Using a vegetable steamer, steam the potatoes, parsnips, and garlic over medium-high heat until very tender, about 20 minutes. In a medium saucepan, over high heat, scald the cream, about 2 minutes. Add the butter, remove the pan from the heat, and stir the butter in as it melts, about 1 minute. Using a food mill, electric mixer, or a potato masher (but not a food processor), puree the potatoes, parsnips, and garlic into a large mixing bowl. Fold in the melted butter and cream to give the puree a smooth texture. Season to taste with kosher salt. Keep warm in a double boiler until needed.

Yam Puree

Serves 4 to 6

THIS is a recipe that is as easy to prepare as mashed potatoes. It can be used almost interchangeably with them as well, except that it is sweeter and a bit more dense. It is particularly appropriate as a complement to lamb. Yams are similar in flavor and appearance to sweet potatoes, but they are different plants. For this recipe, we use yams for the sweeter, richer flavor, and the less fibrous texture. At Campanile we use a little Roasted Garlic Puree to round out the flavor and add complexity to the dish.

4 large yams (2 pounds)
1 cup heavy cream
1 stick (4 ounces) unsalted butter, cut into
    pieces
2 tablespoons Roasted Garlic Puree
    (see page 245)
Kosher salt
Fresh lemon juice

PREHEAT the oven to 325 degrees.

Using a fork, poke a number of small holes around the outside of each yam. In a large roasting pan, bake the yams until soft and brown-skinned, about 1 hour. Remove the pan from the oven and allow the yams to cool until they can be handled comfortably, about 10 to 15 minutes.

In a medium saucepan, over medium heat, bring the cream to a gentle boil, about 5 minutes. Add the butter, and remove the pan from the heat.

Cut each yam in half lengthwise. Using a spoon, scoop out the soft insides of the yams, taking care not to scrape up any of the skin. In a large mixing bowl, using a large whisk, mash together the yams and Roasted Garlic Puree. Then fold in the cream-and-butter mixture.

Stir in 1 teaspoon of kosher salt and 1 teaspoon of fresh lemon juice, then correct the seasoning to taste with additional kosher salt and fresh lemon juice, as necessary.

Serve immediately, or keep warm in a double boiler until needed.

Creamed Corn

Yields about 2²⁄₃ cups

As a child, I hated creamed corn, but that was canned, and this dish is an entirely different experience. Making creamed corn from fresh sweet corn will yield a wonderful taste of summer. This dish should only be made during the height of the corn season, which runs from June through September, and the corn should be as fresh as possible.

Serve this creamed corn with almost any grilled or roasted meat such as sausages, steaks, chicken, or even scallops. Grilling the corn improves the flavor; it's both sweet and a little smokey. Buy the corn with the husks on, as you need them to grill it.

10 large very fresh ears sweet corn, with husks
1 stick (4 ounces) unsalted butter
1 large garlic clove, peeled and minced
　　(1 teaspoon)
½ teaspoon chopped fresh thyme
½ teaspoon chopped fresh rosemary
Kosher salt
Freshly cracked white pepper
¼ cup Chicken Stock (see page 187)
¼ cup heavy cream

Have ready

The Chicken Stock, warm, in a small saucepan
　　over low heat

START a fire in the grill, and allow it to burn to medium temperature.

Carefully peel back the husks of each ear of corn, ensuring that the husks remain attached at the base, and remove the silk. In a small saucepan, over low heat, melt the butter. Add the garlic, thyme, rosemary, ¼ teaspoon kosher salt, and ¼ teaspoon white pepper to the butter and stir well. Brush the herb butter over the corn. Close the husks over the corn and tie with butcher's string to hold in place.

Place the corn on the grill and cook, turning to cook on all sides, about 15 minutes. The husks and a few kernels will char and blacken, but the corn will be cooked properly inside the husks. Remove the ears from the grill and allow them to cool.

Remove and discard the husks. Using a small, sharp knife, cut a slit down the middle of each row of corn kernels. Then, holding the corn by the stalk, scrape the knife down the ear, removing the creamy inside of the kernels. Repeat the procedure with each ear of corn, discarding the cob.

Transfer the creamy insides of the kernels to a medium saucepan. Add the stock and cream. Over medium heat, warm the creamed corn through, about 5 to 10 minutes. Correct the seasoning to taste with kosher salt and white pepper. Serve immediately, or keep warm in a double boiler until needed.

Caramelized Root Vegetables

Serves 6

As a garnish for roasted meats, as a vegetable course, or even as an addition to a soup, this dish is sweet and flavorful. Just because it is based on root vegetables doesn't mean this dish should be served only in the fall. The brief cooking time makes it great for summer as well. The natural sugar in the root vegetables caramelizes and produces a rich, earthy flavor. Just toss them with a vinaigrette and add to a salad. This can also become a new variation on tried and true meat and potatoes when served in the winter with braised veal shanks.

The dicing of the vegetables is the main time investment for this recipe. The vegetables can be prepared early in the day, cooked, and then spread out on a baking sheet to cool. Just before needed, warm them in a 350-degree oven for 10 minutes. If preparing this in advance, do not add the thyme and parsley until just before serving.

¼ cup vegetable oil
1 tablespoon (½ ounce) unsalted butter
½ pound carrots, peeled, trimmed, and cut into ½-inch dice (1 cup)
½ pound rutabaga, peeled, trimmed, and cut into ½-inch dice (1 cup)
¼ pound parsnip, peeled, trimmed, and cut into ½-inch dice (½ cup)
¼ pound turnip, peeled, trimmed, and cut into ½-inch dice (½ cup)
Kosher salt
Freshly cracked black pepper
1 tablespoon fresh lemon thyme leaves, chopped
1 tablespoon fresh Italian parsley, chopped

In a large sauté pan, over high heat, preheat the oil and the butter. As the butter begins to brown, add the carrots, rutabaga, and parsnip, and brown without stirring, about 1 minute. Add the turnip and continue to brown, without stirring, for 1 to 2 more minutes. While the vegetables are browning, season them lightly with kosher salt and black pepper.

Reduce the heat to medium, and stir the vegetables. Continue cooking until the vegetables are tender, about 5 more minutes, stirring occasionally. Sprinkle with the lemon thyme and chopped parsley. Correct the seasoning to taste with kosher salt and black pepper, and serve immediately.

Slow-roasted Tomatoes

Yields 4 cups

At Campanile, we use these in almost anything that calls for cooked tomatoes. The flavor of the tomatoes concentrates and improves during the roasting as moisture evaporates, and the garlic, thyme, and pepper contribute their essence. Slow-roasted Tomatoes can be coarsely chopped and used over pasta, as a delicious sauce on sandwiches, or just to top toasted bread as a simple appetizer. If you have less-than-perfect tomatoes, say between November and April, and you want to improve the flavor, this is a great technique. Anything in which you might use a 28-ounce can of cooked roma tomatoes, roasted tomatoes will make it better.

¼ cup extra-virgin olive oil
10 medium tomatoes (3½ pounds)
15 large garlic cloves, peeled and thinly sliced
2 tablespoons kosher salt
2 teaspoons freshly cracked black pepper
Leaves from 5 sprigs fresh thyme, chopped

Preheat the oven to 225 degrees.

Spread a little of the olive oil over a large baking pan.

Remove and discard the cores of the tomatoes, then cut each tomato in half horizontally. Put the tomato halves on the baking pan, cut side up. Insert about 10 slices of garlic halfway down into the seeds of each cut tomato. Season the tomatoes with the kosher salt, black pepper, and thyme, then drizzle with the remaining olive oil.

Roast the tomatoes for about 3 hours, until they are very soft. Remove the pan from the oven, and allow the tomatoes to cool for 30 minutes before removing them from the pan. Refrigerate in a clean container with a tightly fitting lid for up to 3 days, or use as needed.

Onion Compote (Soubise)

Serves 6

Halfway between a condiment and a vegetable, Onion Compote adds a sharpness that pairs well with grilled meats or seafood such as salmon, tuna, or scallops. As the onions cook down and become more concentrated, the flavor increases dramatically in sweetness and intensity. This is similar to the Onion Soubise with Red Wine (see page 244), but more subtle. The term *compote* generally refers to a mixture that has been cooked long enough to soften all the ingredients to the consistency of preserves. Soubise is pureed compote that has the uniform texture of a sauce.

Onion Compote can be prepared in advance and warmed over low heat when needed, adding a little Chicken Stock (see page 187) or water if it becomes too thick. Obviously, Chicken Stock will make the compote richer and more flavorful than water will. To make a compote with the proper pale consistency, white onions are preferred; yellow will do, but red onions are not acceptable. Vegetable stock or any stock made with roasted vegetables will cause the compote to come out too dark.

2 tablespoons vegetable oil
4 large white onions (3 pounds), peeled, trimmed, and cut into ½-inch dice
¾ cup dry white wine
½ cup white wine vinegar
1 sprig lemon thyme
1 bay leaf
Kosher salt
2 cups Chicken Stock (see page 187), or water, as necessary
1 stick (4 ounces) unsalted butter, cut into pieces

Have ready

The Chicken Stock, warm, in a medium saucepan over low heat

In a medium saucepan, over medium heat, add the oil and the onions and sweat, stirring often, about 5 minutes, taking care not to brown. Pour in the wine and vinegar. Add the thyme, bay leaf, and ½ teaspoon of kosher salt, and bring to a simmer.

Reduce the heat to low, cover the pan with a tightly fitting lid or foil, and gently simmer until the onions are very soft, adding liquid (stock or water) as necessary, about 4 hours. Check every half hour to see that there is plenty of liquid slowly simmering with the onions. The soubise should not dry out during this long cooking; if it appears to have too little moisture, add a little more wine.

When the onions are quite soft, increase the heat to high and bring the compote to a rapid boil. Boil the compote about 10 minutes to thicken, stirring regularly to prevent it from burning.

Remove the sprig of lemon thyme and the bay leaf.

"YOU MAY FIND YOURSELF TRYING ONION SOUBISE WITH
EVERYTHING THAT COMES OFF THE GRILL."

Stir in the butter and correct the seasoning to taste with kosher salt. To make the compote into soubise it must be pureed through a food mill with a medium sieve.

Keep warm in a double boiler until needed, or refrigerate in a clean container with a tightly fitting lid for up to 1 week. Warm in a saucepan over low heat when needed.

Onion Soubise with Red Wine

Yields 1 1/2 cups

THIS is a red wine version of traditional onion soubise. The reduced wine and the concentrated onions combine to produce a very intense flavor that is succulent and rich, but at the same time tart, so that it is not cloying or overwhelming. A little soubise has a lot of flavor; take care not to serve too much. It is such a perfect counterpoint to grilled meat that you may find yourself trying it with everything that comes off the grill.

1/4 cup red wine vinegar
3 cups red wine
4 large red onions (3 pounds), peeled, trimmed, and cut into 1/2-inch dice
Bouquet garni (1 sprig each of thyme, bay leaf, and Italian parsley)
Kosher salt
1/2 stick (2 ounces) unsalted butter, cut into pieces
Freshly cracked black pepper

IN a large saucepan, over medium-high heat, combine the vinegar and wine and reduce by half, about 15 minutes.

Add the onion pieces, the bouquet garni, and 1/2 teaspoon of kosher salt.

Cover the saucepan with a tightly fitting lid, or with aluminum foil, and continue to cook over medium-high heat for about 3 to 5 minutes. Reduce the heat to very low and cook for about 4 hours. Check every half hour to see that there is plenty of liquid slowly simmering with the onions. The soubise should not dry out during this long cooking; if it appears to have too little moisture, add a little more wine.

When the onions are quite soft, increase the heat to high and bring the compote to a rapid boil. Boil the compote about 10 minutes to thicken, stirring regularly to prevent it from burning.

Remove the pan from the heat. Remove the bouquet garni, stir in the butter, and correct the seasoning to taste with kosher salt and black pepper. At this point you have red onion compote that may be served as is or pureed through a food mill into soubise.

Keep warm in a double boiler until needed, or refrigerate in a clean container with a tightly fitting lid for up to 1 week. Warm in a saucepan over low heat when needed.

Roasted Garlic Puree

Yields about 1 1/4 cups

ROASTED garlic is simply wonderful used as a condiment or as a flavor-enhancing ingredient. It has so many uses, you almost can't make too much. Just about any soup, vinaigrette, or meat dish will blossom with a small spoonful of this savory puree. Sweet and flavorful, it can be spread on grilled bread in place of butter. For a more boldly flavored variation, roasted garlic can be blended into mashed potatoes or any other pureed root vegetable. Used in place of mustard on grilled sausages, it adds wonderful complexity to the smokey taste of the meat.

If you are looking for the ultimate in extra-rich flavor, roast the garlic heads in duck fat. Reserve the garlic-infused oil (or duck fat) for sautéing at a later time. Even a little bit will add flavor to just about anything that could be sautéed—poultry, vegetables, or even risotto cakes.

12 large garlic heads (2 pounds), whole
2 cups light vegetable oil (almond, olive, canola, safflower)

PREHEAT the oven to 325 degrees.

Arrange the heads of garlic in a small roasting or baking pan. Pour the vegetable oil over the heads of garlic. Toss the garlic briefly to coat well with the oil. In the pan, the oil should reach about 1/3 of the way up the sides of the garlic. Add additional oil if necessary. Roast the garlic until it is very tender, about 1 hour. Turn the heads of garlic every 20 minutes to ensure that the tops do not burn. Remove the pan from the oven and allow the garlic and oil to cool.

Remove the garlic from the roasting pan and drain it on absorbant paper. Using a serrated knife, cut the garlic heads in half horizontally. Squeeze out the garlic puree into a small dish, discarding the skins. Transfer the garlic to a container with a tightly fitting lid, and add a small amount of the oil. Use as needed, or refrigerate, covered, for up to 1 week. Reserve the remaining oil for sautéing, using in a vinaigrette, or to roast more garlic at a later time.

Roasted Onions or Shallots

Serves 4 to 6

In spring, when the onions are sweet and tender, this dish will be at its best, but in any season it is worth making. One of the easiest dishes to prepare, it's versatile and delicious; drizzled with a little vinaigrette, it's great as an appetizer, or straight from the oven as an accompaniment to roasted meats.

At the start of the season, any small onion—not just white boiling onions—can be roasted this way. Shallots, which have a distinct and slightly sharper flavor, can be roasted this way as well. The onions should be prepared in advance, and at serving time returned to a 400-degree oven for about 5 minutes, just to heat through. Try to buy onions of uniform size for even cooking.

¼ cup extra-virgin olive oil
24 small white boiling onions or shallots, root
    ends trimmed off
2 teaspoons chopped fresh rosemary
2 teaspoons kosher salt
1 teaspoon freshly cracked black pepper

Preheat the oven to 400 degrees.

In a large mixing bowl, combine the olive oil, onions, rosemary, kosher salt, and black pepper, and toss to coat well. Distribute the onions in 1 layer on a large baking pan and roast until they're soft but still holding their shape, about 30 to 35 minutes. Serve immediately, or allow to cool and warm before serving.

Cannellini Beans

Yields 4 to 5 cups

Cannellini beans are almost a meal all by themselves. Just add a drizzle of olive oil, a shaving of Parmesan, and a sprinkle of freshly cracked black pepper; with a good piece of bread and a glass of wine, you can eat your way to blissful satisfaction. To take a slightly more bourgeois approach, these beans make a perfect companion for grilled steak with black olive tapenade. A drizzle of truffle oil adds an air of true elegance to what most people would consider crude peasant food. Nancy especially likes to eat these beans cold with a fork, standing at the open refrigerator door.

If cannellini beans are not available, great

northern beans, although a little smaller and not quite as flavorful, can be used. This cooking method can also be used for a wide variety of beans—borlotti, scarlet runners, small navy, cranberry—just about any kind of dried bean.

2 tablespoons extra-virgin olive oil
½ large onion, peeled, trimmed, and diced (½ cup)
6 garlic cloves, peeled and lightly crushed
1 teaspoon chopped fresh rosemary
1½ teaspoons chopped fresh thyme
1 bay leaf
1 smoked ham hock, or ¼ pound bacon, in 1 piece
3 tablespoons balsamic vinegar
8 to 9 cups Chicken Stock (see page 187), or a mixture of half stock and half water
2 cups dry cannellini beans (1 pound), rinsed
Kosher salt
Freshly cracked black pepper

Have ready

The Chicken Stock, warm, in a large saucepan over low heat

In a large, heavy-bottomed stockpot, over low heat, preheat the olive oil. Sweat the onion with the garlic, rosemary, thyme, and bay leaf until the onion is translucent, about 5 minutes.

Add the ham hock or slab of bacon, vinegar, 5 cups of the stock, and the dry beans. Increase the heat and bring to a boil. Reduce the heat to low, and simmer very gently, just barely bubbling, until the beans are tender, about 1½ to 2 hours, adding stock as needed to keep the beans covered. Periodically skim any foam that rises to the top. This keeps the broth clear. If the heat setting is low enough, the beans should not stick to the bottom of the pot. Using a rubber spatula, gently stir the beans only once every 30 minutes; if stirred more often, they might break apart. Season with kosher salt and black pepper to taste.

Remove the ham hock or bacon and bay leaf. Discard the bay leaf. Allow the ham hock or bacon to cool. Using your fingers, separate the meat of the ham hock from the fat and the bone, shred the meat, and add it to the beans. Or, using a sharp knife, cut the bacon into ¼-inch dice, and add it to the beans. Use as desired, or refrigerate, covered, up to 1 week.

Green Lentils

Serves 4 to 6

Of the many types of lentils grown throughout the world, lentiles vertes du Puy from France are the best lentils for this dish. A salad of green lentils and goat cheese enjoyed some years ago at Chez Panisse demonstrated that these green lentils are best for their texture and superior flavor. They remain firm when cooked, rather than dissolving as most other lentils do. At Campanile we usually serve warm lentils as a side dish for lamb or hearty fish, such as swordfish or monkfish.

We use good-quality, bulk-produced balsamic vinegar in this recipe. Top-quality, long-aged balsamic is too expensive to use this way as its fine qualities would be lost during the cooking process.

1 cup green lentils (½ pound)
1 tablespoon vegetable oil
1 small carrot, cut into ¼-inch dice (¼ cup)
1 small onion, cut into ¼-inch dice (¼ cup)
1 stalk celery, cut into ¼-inch dice (¼ cup)
1 large garlic clove, peeled and minced
	(1 teaspoon)
⅓ cup balsamic vinegar
3 cups Chicken Stock or Vegetable Stock
	(see page 187 or 196)
Kosher salt
Bouquet garni (1 sprig each of rosemary,
	thyme, parsley, sage, and bay leaf)

1 whole dried red chile pepper
Freshly cracked black pepper

Have ready

The Chicken Stock or the Vegetable Stock,
	warm, in a medium saucepan over low heat

Rinse the lentils in a colander under cold running water.

In a medium saucepan, over medium-high heat, preheat the vegetable oil. Stir in the carrot, onion, celery, and garlic and sweat about 2 to 3 minutes. Stir in the lentils, balsamic vinegar, stock, and 1 teaspoon of kosher salt, and bring to a simmer. Reduce the heat to low, add the bouquet garni and the red chile, and continue to simmer, adding small amounts of stock as necessary. Simmer until the lentils are tender, about 30 minutes, stirring occasionally. Remove and discard the bouquet garni and the red chile pepper and correct the seasoning to taste with kosher salt and black pepper. Serve immediately, or keep warm until needed.

For a warm salad, the lentils can be drained and tossed with a vinaigrette. For a cold salad, the lentils can be chilled, drained in a colander, and briefly rinsed with cold water to remove excessive starch. The lentils can then be incorporated into all sorts of cold salads. When served warm, the natural starch contributes to the thick, hearty texture of the lentils.

Kale with Crisp Garlic

Serves 6

THIS is a wonderful side dish for a large autumn meal. We have served it with great success a number of times at Thanksgiving. The sharp, clean flavor of kale goes wonderfully with roasted poultry or almost any hearty fare. It is easy to prepare, healthy, and delicious. Kale is readily available throughout most of the year.

Kosher salt
2 bunches kale (1½ pounds), well washed
¼ cup vegetable oil
6 large garlic cloves, peeled and thinly sliced
    (about ¹⁄₁₆-inch thick)
Fresh lemon juice from ½ lemon

IN a large stockpot, bring approximately 4 quarts of water to a boil and add 1 tablespoon of kosher salt. Fill a large mixing bowl with ice water.

Using a sharp knife, remove and discard the stems and any large ribs from each leaf of the kale. Tear the remaining leaves into pieces of manageable size. Blanch the torn kale in the large stockpot of boiling water about 4 to 5 minutes. Remove the kale from the boiling water and plunge it into the ice water for about 2 minutes. Remove the kale from the ice water, press it dry, and reserve.

In a large sauté pan, over a medium-low flame, heat the vegetable oil to hot, not smoking. Sauté the sliced garlic until it is pale golden, about 5 to 7 minutes. Take care not to brown the garlic, or it will be bitter. Using a slotted spoon, remove the garlic from the pan and drain on absorbent paper. When it cools it should be crisp.

Add the kale to the vegetable oil in the large sauté pan. Lightly season with kosher salt and sauté over medium heat until tender, about 6 to 8 minutes. Remove the pan from the heat and correct the seasoning to taste with kosher salt and fresh lemon juice. Transfer the kale to a large platter, sprinkle the crisp garlic over the top, and serve immediately.

The kale can be kept warm for up to 30 minutes if the crisp garlic and lemon juice are not added until just before serving.

Stuffed Artichokes

THESE artichokes, stuffed with onion, garlic, tomato, and bread crumbs, make a great appetizer, side dish, or even quick lunch. The peak of artichoke season runs from March through May. It is best to make this dish during that period, when they are the firmest, freshest, and most flavorful. Buy larger artichokes because they are easier to stuff. As a substantial first course before a quick pasta, these artichokes are exceptional, with a complex combination of flavors and a dramatic appearance.

1 large lemon, cut in half
½ teaspoon freshly cracked black pepper
1 bay leaf
1 dried chile pepper
Kosher salt
6 medium or 4 large artichokes

Stuffing

¼ cup extra-virgin olive oil
¼ pound good-quality whole wheat bread, sliced
3 garlic cloves, peeled
1 medium zucchini (6 ounces), cut into ¼-inch dice (1 cup)
1 medium onion (8 ounces), cut into ¼-inch dice (1 cup)
1 medium tomato, seeded and cut into ¼-inch dice (½ cup)
½ cup freshly grated Parmesan cheese
2 tablespoons chopped fresh Italian parsley
2 tablespoons chopped fresh basil leaves
1 teaspoon kosher salt
½ teaspoon freshly cracked black pepper

½ cup Chicken Stock or Vegetable Stock (see page 187 or 196)
6 tablespoons Lemon Oil Vinaigrette with Red and Yellow Peppers (see page 220)

Have ready

The Chicken Stock or Vegetable Stock
The Lemon Oil Vinaigrette with Red and Yellow Peppers

In a large saucepan, bring approximately 2 quarts of cold water to a boil with the lemon halves, black pepper, bay leaf, chile pepper, and 1 tablespoon of kosher salt.

Using a serrated knife, cut away the stems so the artichokes will stand upright, then cut one inch off the top. To do this, place each artichoke on its side and slice off the top. Put the artichokes in the saucepan, stem down, and cover the pan with a lid. Reduce the heat to medium, and cook until the artichokes are tender, about 25 to 30 minutes.

To prepare the stuffing: While the artichokes are cooking, brush a little olive oil on both sides of the bread slices and place them under the broiler to toast both sides. Remove them from the oven and rub a garlic clove over the toasted bread. Allow to cool. Cut away the crusts, break into pieces, and transfer to a food processor fitted with a steel blade. Pulse the food processor until the bread has been reduced to coarse crumbs, and set aside.

Fill a large mixing bowl with ice water. To test the artichokes for doneness, poke the point of a sharp knife into the base of the artichoke, or try pulling out a leaf. The artichoke should be tender, but not mushy. Remove the artichokes and refresh them in the ice water, about 5 minutes. When they are cool, remove them from the water and gently squeeze out the water that has seeped into the artichokes.

Gently pull back the first 4 layers of outer leaves and remove the soft inner leaves. With a small spoon, scrape out the fuzzy inner part, which is the choke, keeping the heart and outer leaves intact.

Mince the remaining 2 cloves of garlic. In a medium sauté pan, over medium-high heat, preheat the remaining 2 tablespoons of olive oil. Gently sauté the zucchini, onion, and garlic without browning, about 2 to 3 minutes. Transfer to a medium mixing bowl to cool. When cool, stir in the tomato, ¼ cup of the grated Parmesan cheese, parsley, basil, and the bread crumbs; reserve the remaining ¼ cup of Parmesan cheese. Correct the seasoning to taste with kosher salt and black pepper.

Preheat the oven to 400 degrees.

Gently spread the artichoke leaves open. Season the inside of the artichokes lightly with kosher salt and black pepper. Spoon equal amounts of the stuffing into the center of each artichoke. The artichokes should be loosely stuffed.

Pour the stock and ½ cup of water into a large baking pan. Place the artichokes upright in the baking pan. Spoon the Lemon Oil with Red and Yellow Peppers over the artichokes, then sprinkle the remaining ¼ cup Parmesan cheese over the tops.

Bake until the artichokes are heated through and the tops are lightly browned, about 20 to 25 minutes.

Remove the artichokes from the baking pan and place 1 artichoke in the center of each plate. Spoon some of the pan juices over each artichoke, and serve immediately.

Ragout of Mushrooms

Serves 4 to 6

Mushroom ragout is somewhere between a sauce and a vegetable side dish. It can be served over risotto cakes, sautéed penne, or polenta, either soft or crisped. If made with Vegetable Stock, just top any of those dishes with a little julienne of radicchio, and you have a robust and flavorful vegetarian meal.

You can use a variety of just about any three kinds of mushrooms; the choice is up to you and seasonal availability. Only woodear mushrooms are too tough for this particular recipe. Wild mushrooms have a lot of flavor; using a higher percentage of them will make the flavor more intense. This is a fall dish; September through December is when the best mushrooms are readily available. With familiarity and practice, you can fine-tune the proportions of the various mushrooms to your taste and personalize this recipe.

½ ounce dried porcini mushrooms
½ pound fresh white button mushrooms
½ pound assorted fresh mushrooms (morel, shiitake, chanterelle, oyster, cèpe)
¼ cup vegetable oil
Kosher salt
Freshly cracked black pepper
2 shallots, peeled, trimmed, and cut into thin slices
3 large garlic cloves, peeled and minced (1 tablespoon)
1 large leek, white part only, washed well and cut into thin slices
½ cup tawny port
¼ cup Chicken Stock or Vegetable Stock (see page 187 or 196)
2 tablespoons balsamic vinegar

Have ready

The Chicken Stock or Vegetable Stock, warm, in a small saucepan over low heat

In a small mixing bowl, combine the dried porcini mushrooms with ½ cup of warm water. Allow about 30 minutes for the mushrooms to reconstitute adequately.

Wash the button mushrooms and, using a damp cloth, wipe the other mushrooms clean and remove the stems (reserve for soups or stocks). Cut any large mushroom caps into halves or quarters. In a medium sauté pan, over medium-high heat, preheat 3 tablespoons of the vegetable oil. Sauté the mushrooms until the button mushrooms are deeply browned, turning to brown evenly, about 7 to 10 minutes. Add the reconstituted porcini mushrooms to the sautéed mushrooms after about 5 minutes, reserving the soaking water. While sautéing, season the mushrooms lightly with kosher salt and black pepper. Remove the pan from the heat, transfer the mushrooms to a medium mixing bowl, and keep warm.

Wipe the sauté pan clean. Over medium heat, preheat the remaining vegetable oil. Wilt the shallots, garlic, and leek, about 2 to 3 minutes. Season the vegetables lightly with kosher salt and black pepper, and add the port. Deglaze the pan and reduce by one fourth, about 10 minutes. Pour in the stock and balsamic vinegar and reduce by half, about 10 minutes. Add the porcini soaking water, taking care not to pour into the pan any of the grit from the porcinis that will have collected on the bottom of the bowl. Add the sautéed mushrooms and stir to combine. Reduce the heat to low and gently simmer about 15 minutes. Remove the pan from the heat, correct the seasoning to taste with kosher salt and black pepper, and keep warm, or serve immediately.

Grilled Portobello Mushrooms with Spinach and Polenta

Serves 4

PORTOBELLO mushrooms are big and meaty, so they can be grilled individually. Portobello mushrooms have a mild flavor and a dense texture that is quite satisfying to vegetarians, and of course, for carnivores, they also are a perfect accompaniment for grilled meat. The polenta is a soft, creamy contrast to the chewy texture of the mushrooms, and the spinach adds a fresh, slightly tannic counterpoint. If you make the polenta with Vegetable Stock, this can be served as a purely vegetarian main course. In smaller portions it also serves well as an appetizer.

8 large, fresh portobello mushroom caps
  (1 pound)
11 large garlic cloves, peeled
¼ cup extra-virgin olive oil
1 teaspoon chopped fresh mint
1 teaspoon chopped fresh thyme
Freshly cracked black pepper
¼ cup vegetable oil
½ pound fresh spinach leaves, cleaned and
  stemmed
Kosher salt
Polenta (see page 138)

Have ready

The soft polenta, warm, in a double boiler over
  low heat

Gently wipe the mushrooms with a damp kitchen towel to clean them. Remove the stems. Mince 1 clove of garlic, and slice the remaining 10 very thinly lengthwise. Reserve the sliced garlic in a small bowl. Place the mushrooms in a medium mixing bowl, drizzle with the ¼ cup of olive oil, and season with the herbs, minced garlic, and 1 teaspoon black pepper, tossing gently to combine. Marinate, refrigerated, for at least 1 hour.

Start a fire in the grill, and allow it to burn to medium temperature.

In a large sauté pan, over medium-low heat, preheat the vegetable oil. Sauté the sliced garlic until it is pale golden, about 5 to 7 minutes. Take care not to brown the garlic, or it will be bitter. Using a slotted spoon, remove the garlic from the pan and drain on absorbent paper. When it cools it should be crisp. Discard all but about 2 tablespoons of the vegetable oil from the sauté pan and set aside.

Grill the mushrooms with the top side down about 4 minutes. Turn the mushrooms over and grill 3 to 4 minutes longer on the other side. The mushrooms should be cooked through, but take care not to char them. Remove them from the grill and keep warm.

In the large sauté pan, over medium heat, preheat the vegetable oil. Put the spinach in the pan, and season lightly with kosher salt. Sauté the spinach until it is just wilted, about 3 minutes. Remove the pan from the heat.

To serve, spoon about ½ cup of soft Polenta into each of 4 large, warm soup plates. Place 2 mushroom caps on each serving of polenta, surround with sautéed spinach, sprinkle with crisp garlic, and serve immediately. A little flavorful extra-virgin olive oil or pesto is delicious drizzled over each portion just before serving.

Roasted Squash

SQUASH is available in an incredible array of flavors and textures. Some have a great deal of flavor—kabocha, acorn, spaghetti (also very fun to eat)—but many of the more decorative varieties, such as some of the miniature pumpkins, are almost flavorless. The best squash is available in the fall, but you can find decent varieties year round, if you learn to choose carefully. You can season the squash with a variety of fresh herbs when you roast it, but be judicious, as too much can overpower the subtle flavor. We use a 3-pound squash as an average size. If you can find only 2-pound squash, don't ransack the market; adjust the recipe or buy a few more of the smaller varieties.

1 stick (4 ounces) unsalted butter
1 squash, about 3 pounds
3 large garlic cloves, peeled and minced
    (1 tablespoon)
½ teaspoon chopped fresh rosemary
½ teaspoon chopped fresh thyme
Kosher salt
Freshly cracked black pepper

PREHEAT the oven to 375 degrees.

In a small saucepan, over medium heat, melt the butter, about 2 minutes. Using a sharp knife, remove the stem of the squash, then cut the squash in half lengthwise, and remove the seeds and strings with a spoon. Cut each half into 6 or 8 slices lengthwise, each about 2 inches wide. Place the squash slices skin side down in a large baking pan. Brush the melted butter over the squash and season each slice with the minced garlic, rosemary, thyme, about ½ teaspoon kosher salt, and a little black pepper.

Roast until tender, about 1 hour. Remove the squash from the oven and serve immediately, or keep warm in a low-temperature oven until needed.

Desserts

Chapter 11

HIGH-QUALITY, seasonal ingredients at the peak of flavor are the basis of the desserts at Campanile. As in all of the food we prepare, the priority is on flavor, before appearance or presentation. Even the most beautiful dessert is a disappointment if there isn't real flavor. The inspiration at Campanile comes from tasting an ingredient and allowing the imagination to build from that.

A great dessert is comforting and immediately familiar without being ordinary. In the fall, when the quality of the available apples is good enough to really have flavor, we serve Mom's Apple Pie. It looks like a scaled-down traditional apple pie and, more important, tastes like apples, but it isn't just crust and filling. Served warm with Scotch Caramel Ice Cream, it is a balance of soft filling complementing tender, flaky crust, and warm, tartly flavorful apples contrasting dense, sweet, ice cream. It is beautiful in that it is an honest representation of what Mom might have made, and it also tastes wonderful.

Here there are no complicated techniques, no serious molds, folding, or cutting, no precision piping, no fancy equipment—there isn't anything in these desserts that requires years of practice. All you need is good ingredients and a little forethought. At Campanile we let Mother Nature do the hardest work, and step in to finish it off.

Dried Fruit

PROPERLY dried fruit is so beautiful and has such outstanding flavor that it is the perfect garnish for many different desserts. Garnishes that are purely visual, flavorless, and add nothing to the dish are not found in the food of Campanile. A garnish should not only be edible, but delicious in and of itself. Dried fruit is a perfect answer. It is wonderful eaten straight from the oven, or adding a touch of elegance to a rustic dessert.

This isn't the dried fruit from the health food store, tough, leathery, and lacking vibrant color. Our dried fruit is moist, delicate, and beautifully colorful. What makes the difference is just a little added sugar. The reason we add it is that the natural sugar content in fruit is not high enough to yield the flavor and texture we desire. As the fruit dries, natural fruit juice is released, and it mixes with the extra sugar and reduces, creating a beautiful, shiny glaze on the side of the fruit that is touching the plastic wrap. For presentation, the fruit should be served shiny side up.

We use two different methods of adding sugar, depending on the fruit. Some types, like apples and pears, come out best simmered in a simple sugar syrup. Other fruits—like strawberries, bananas, and pineapple—need only be sprinkled with sugar before drying.

Different fruits have different requirements for drying as well. Apples, pears, and bananas can be dried in a low-temperature oven. Juicy fruit, such as strawberries, nectarines, and peaches, need a convection oven or a fruit dehydrator to dry properly. The moisture from the fruit must be evaporated with the help of the fan.

Dried fruit can be stored in an airtight container at room temperature for up to 3 days, but you probably won't need to store it at all, it disappears so quickly.

Dried Apples or Pears

2 cups granulated sugar
Juice of ½ lemon
2 large apples, Granny Smith or Golden
    Delicious, or 2 large pears, Yellow Bartlett
    or Red Anjou, ripe but not too soft

In a medium saucepan, over medium-high heat, whisk together the sugar and 1½ cups of water, and bring to a boil. Add the lemon juice, and turn off the heat while you slice the fruit.

Using a mandolin, slice the apples or pears vertically, as thinly as possible, about ⅟16 inch thick. The fruit should be just thick enough to hold its shape, with no holes or tears. The cores, stems, and seeds should not be removed, because they make the most beautiful slices.

Return the sugar syrup to a simmer. Add the slices of fruit, one at a time, to the sugar syrup. Continue to gently simmer until the slices become translucent, about 20 to 30 minutes. It is important that the syrup not simmer too vigorously, or the thin fruit may tear.

Remove the pan from the heat and allow it to sit, at room temperature, covered, until completely cool, at least 4 hours. I prefer to let the fruit sit in the syrup at room temperature overnight before drying; it just seems to come out better that way.

Preheat the oven to 200 degrees; or preheat the convection oven to 200 degrees and set the convection fan to high; or adjust the fruit dehydrator according to the manufacturer's instructions.

If drying the fruit in a conventional or convection oven, line a baking pan with plastic wrap, folding it around the sides of the pan to secure it firmly. If you are using a fruit dehydrator, the fruit will be placed directly on the screens and plastic wrap is not necessary.

Carefully remove the fruit slices from the sugar syrup and, using your fingers, wipe off the excess syrup. Arrange the fruit slices on the plastic, or on the screens, so that they do not touch each other.

Dry the fruit until it appears lightly amber colored and translucent, feels firm and dry to the touch, peels away from the plastic wrap easily, and holds its shape.

The drying time in a conventional oven is about 2 to 3 hours, in a convection oven, about 2 to 3 hours, and in a fruit dehydrator, about 4 to 5 hours. Check the fruit a few times during the drying process. If it appears to be coloring too much, reduce the oven heat to 150 degrees.

Dried Bananas, Strawberries, Peaches, Nectarines, and Pineapple

BANANAS can be dried in a conventional oven, but strawberries, peaches, nectarines, and pineapple can be properly dried only in a convection oven or a fruit dehydrator.

For the Bananas

2 large bananas, ripe but not mushy, peeled
¾ cup granulated sugar

THINLY slice the bananas about ⅛ inch thick, diagonally on an angle of about 45 degrees.

For the Strawberries

15 large strawberries, ripe but not too soft
¾ cup granulated sugar

REMOVE the tops from the strawberries and thinly slice them, vertically, about ⅛ inch thick.

For the Peaches or Nectarines

2 large peaches, or nectarines, ripe but not too soft
¾ cup granulated sugar

CUT the peaches or nectarines in half, and remove the stone. Thinly slice the peaches or nectarines, vertically, about ⅛ inch thick.

For the Pineapple

1 pineapple
¾ cup granulated sugar

CUT away the rind from the pineapple. Cut the pineapple in half horizontally. Reserve one half for other uses (Pineapple Upside-down Cake, see page 281). Then, using a paring knife, remove all the eyes.

Cut the half pineapple vertically, away from the core, into 4 pieces. Place each piece flat side down and cut into thin cross-sectional slices about ⅛ inch thick.

To Dry the Fruit

PREHEAT the convection oven to 200 degrees, and set the convection fan to high, or set the fruit dehydrator according to the manufacturer's instructions.

Line a baking pan with plastic wrap, folding it around the sides of the pan to secure it firmly. If you are using a fruit dehydrator, the baking pan and plastic are not necessary.

Arrange the slices on the plastic wrap or screen. They must overlap each other by at least ¼ inch because this prevents the small slices from shriveling up or drying too much. There will be small gaps between the pieces of fruit, but there should be no spaces larger than about

¼ inch in the layer of fruit. Generously sprinkle the slices with the granulated sugar. Once dried, the fruit can be removed from the plastic wrap in individual pieces, or in small sections to create a decorative pattern.

Dry the fruit in the convection oven for 2 to 4 hours, or 8 to 10 hours in the fruit dehy-drator. Check the fruit a few times during the drying process; if it appears to be coloring, reduce the oven heat to 150 degrees. When the fruit is done, it will no longer be watery; it will be slightly sticky, and it should peel away in a solid layer from the plastic or screen.

Chess Pie

Yields twelve 4-inch pies or one 10-inch pie

IF we could get away with serving warm apple-sauce and chilled cream as a dessert at the restaurant, we would. You can't really find a more harmonious combination than apples and cream. But most customers expect a more elab-orate presentation. We felt we needed some-thing to serve the applesauce and cream with. This variation on Chess Pie is the perfect match. When served warm, it is a luscious, tex-tural, and seductive dessert.

At the restaurant we serve this in large soup plates. First we ladle in a small puddle of apple-sauce, then surround it with ice-cold cream, and then place the warm Chess Pie on top.

Nonstick pie molds are available at most kitchenware shops. Disposable aluminum molds are usually available at the supermarket.

Cream Cheese Dough (see page 267)
1½ sticks (6 ounces) unsalted butter
¾ cup insides of sourdough bread, torn in
    1-inch pieces
4½ tablespoons apple cider vinegar
1 cup plus 2 tablespoons granulated sugar
6 extra-large egg yolks
1½ teaspoons pure vanilla extract
1½ tablespoons unbleached all-purpose flour,
    plus extra for dusting
2 cups heavy cream
1 cup Applesauce (see page 266)

Chess Pie *(cont.)*

Have ready

The Cream Cheese Dough, chilled
The Applesauce

Line 1 or 2 baking sheets with parchment paper.

Lightly dust a work surface with flour. Turn the Cream Cheese Dough out onto the work surface. Lightly dust a rolling pin with flour, and roll the dough out to about ⅛ inch thick. Cut the dough into twelve 5-inch circles, or one 12-inch circle. It may be necessary to gather the scraps together and roll the dough out again to cut all 12 circles. Place the dough circles on the parchment-lined baking sheet, and chill in the refrigerator at least 30 minutes.

Line twelve 4-inch pie molds, or one 10-inch pie mold, with the dough. Do not trim the top edge. To make a decorative edge around the pie, pinch together your index finger and thumb of one hand, then, using your index finger of the other hand, work around the perimeter of each pie, crimping the dough between the fingers of both hands, to form a fluted edge. The crust should extend above the rim of the pie mold about ⅛ inch. Chill the lined pie molds in the refrigerator for at least 30 minutes.

In a large saucepan, over medium-high heat, melt the butter. Cook the butter until it browns and becomes foamy, about 2 to 3 minutes. It will bubble somewhat vigorously as it browns. Then it will produce a nutty aroma and begin to smoke. Remove the pan from the heat, and pour the butter into a heatproof measuring cup. If the melted browned butter measures less than half a cup, add additional butter as necessary to make half a cup. It is not necessary to brown the additional butter. Chill the butter in the refrigerator until firm, about 30 minutes.

Preheat the oven to 350 degrees, and space the racks in the top and bottom thirds of the oven for optimum air circulation.

In a food processor fitted with a steel blade, grind the pieces of bread into crumbs, pulsing the machine briefly until finely ground, taking care not to overprocess the bread. In a stainless steel mixing bowl, combine the bread crumbs and the vinegar, and set aside.

Fill the bowl of the electric mixer with warm water, and let stand for 2 to 3 minutes. Empty the warm water from the mixing bowl and wipe it dry with a kitchen towel.

Remove the chilled browned butter from the refrigerator. Transfer the chilled browned butter from the measuring cup to the bowl of the electric mixer.

Using the paddle attachment, starting on low speed, begin to mix the butter. As it starts to soften, increase the speed to medium. Mix the butter until smooth, about 1 to 2 minutes, scraping the sides of the bowl down as needed.

Add the granulated sugar and mix until the butter lightens in color, about 2 minutes. Add the egg yolks, one at a time, scraping down the sides of the mixing bowl with a rubber spatula after each yolk is added. Add the reserved bread crumbs and mix until combined, about 30 seconds.

Remove the bowl from the electric mixer and, using a rubber spatula, scrape the bottom of the bowl to ensure that the batter is well combined. Return the bowl to the electric mixer.

In a small, stainless-steel mixing bowl, combine ¾ cup of water and the vanilla extract, and slowly add half of the mixture to the mixer, running on medium-low speed. Add the flour, and then slowly add the remaining half of the water and vanilla mixture and mix just to combine, about 1 minute. The batter will slightly separate and appear to be curdled as the last of the water and vanilla mixture is added. The more slowly the liquid is added, the less severe will be the appearance of curdling, and the eventual separation. The batter should be used immediately, as it will continue to separate as it sits.

Remove the lined pie molds from the refrigerator. Ladle about ⅓ cup of filling into each mold, stirring between each ladling. Bake the pies in the bottom third of the oven. If using two baking sheets, place one on each of the racks, and rotate halfway through the cooking period. Bake the pies until the filling is browned on top and set, but still soft, and the crust is lightly browned, about 20 to 25 minutes.

While the pies are baking, chill the cream, and if necessary, warm the applesauce.

To thoroughly chill the cream it is necessary to use an ice bath. Pour the heavy cream into a medium stainless-steel bowl, fill a large stainless-steel bowl with ice and water, and place the bowl containing the cream in it, and place in the refrigerator to chill for about 30 minutes.

Remove the pies from the oven, and allow to cool for about 15 minutes. The filling will fall slightly as the pies cool.

Just before serving, spoon 2 tablespoons of warm applesauce into each of 8 large soup plates. Then ladle ¼ cup of chilled cream around the applesauce in each plate. Unmold each individual pie, or slice the large pie, and place each portion halfway on the applesauce and cream. Serve immediately.

Applesauce

APPLESAUCE is something that just about
everyone likes. We prefer to make applesauce
rather than buy it, because we like to embellish
the flavor with butter, sugar, and vanilla beans.
Of course, you don't have to include all those
ingredients if you have dietary concerns; a simple puree of the most flavorful apples will yield
a delicious homemade applesauce. We have
found that Granny Smith apples are perfect
because they yield an applesauce that is full in
apple flavor and neither watery nor mealy.

6 large, tart green apples (2¾ pounds)
½ stick (2 ounces) unsalted butter, cut into
    pieces
2 teaspoons fresh lemon juice
¾ cup granulated sugar
2 vanilla beans

PEEL the apples and cut around the core, then
cut the large pieces into 1-inch chunks. In a
large saucepan, combine the apples, butter,
lemon juice, ⅓ cup of water, and ½ cup of the
sugar, reserving ¼ cup to correct the sweetness
after cooking.

Using a small paring knife, split the vanilla
beans lengthwise. Use the back of the knife to
scrape out the pulp and the seeds of the vanilla
beans. Add the scrapings from the vanilla beans
plus the vanilla bean pods themselves to the
apple mixture.

Cover the saucepan tightly with aluminum
foil, crimping the edges to seal the pan, so no
steam escapes.

Bring to a boil and cook no more than 3 to
5 minutes, or until the foil has puffed. When
the foil has puffed up from the top of the
saucepan, turn off the heat, and allow the pan
to sit, covered, for about 20 to 25 minutes.

Remove the foil. Test the apples by pierc-
ing with a knife to determine if they are completely cooked. If not tender enough, re-cover
the saucepan with foil, bring back to a boil,
turn off the heat, and allow it to sit for 15 to 20
additional minutes.

Remove and discard the vanilla beans.
Transfer the cooked apples and any liquid to a
food mill or food processor fitted with a steel
blade. Put the applesauce through the food mill,
or pulse the food processor, just until the apples
are pureed. In a food processor it may be necessary to process the applesauce in batches. Take
care not to process too long, as this will incorporate air into the applesauce. Taste the applesauce. If it is not sweet enough, add the
remaining sugar, up to ¼ cup, and stir to combine completely. This must be done while the
applesauce is still hot, so the sugar will melt.

Serve warm, or allow to cool and refrigerate until needed. The refrigerated applesauce
can be warmed as needed in a double boiler.
Applesauce will keep, covered, in the refrigerator for up to 2 weeks.

Cream Cheese Dough

Yields 1 pound, 5 ounces,
enough for twelve 5-inch
circles or one 12-inch circle

A tart shell made from Cream Cheese Dough has a similar flakiness to one made from puff pastry. However, Cream Cheese Dough is a lot easier to make, as there is no folding or turning. We use this dough as the crust for Chess Pie (see page 263).

Scraps of the dough can be used for small jam-filled cookies: Cut the dough into 2-inch circles, place a spoonful of good jam in the center, and fold the dough over to make half-moon shapes. Press the edges to seal. Bake in a 350-degree oven until lightly browned, about 15 to 20 minutes.

2 sticks (8 ounces) unsalted butter, chilled, cut
    into small pieces
6 ounces cream cheese, chilled, cut into small
    pieces
2 cups unbleached all-purpose flour, plus
    additional for dusting

FILL the bowl of the electric mixer with warm water, and let stand for 2 to 3 minutes. Empty the warm water from the mixing bowl and wipe it dry with a kitchen towel.

Using the paddle attachment, starting on low speed, cream the butter. As it starts to soften, increase the speed to medium. Cream the butter until smooth, about 1 to 2 minutes, scraping the sides of the bowl down as needed.

With the machine still running, add the cream cheese pieces a few at a time, and continue to mix until well blended, about 2 minutes. Reduce the speed to low, add the flour, and mix just until the mixture forms a soft, sticky dough.

Lightly dust your hands and work surface with flour. Turn the dough out onto the work surface, knead the dough a few times, form it into a ball, flatten it slightly into a disk, and wrap it in plastic wrap. Refrigerate until firm, about 2 to 4 hours, before rolling to the desired shape. The dough can be kept in the refrigerator for up to 2 days, or it will keep in the freezer for several weeks.

Mom's Apple Pie

DURING the holidays, many a tense family gathering has been salvaged and soothed by the perfume of apple pie baking in the oven. The aroma blossoms when you first break the crust and the steam escapes, carrying the essence of fall and the promise of blissful fulfillment.

During apple season, late summer to early fall, apples from local farmer's markets make the best apple pies. Some of the less common varieties that we use on the West Coast include Gravenstein, Northern Spy, and Primrose, but even good-quality, flavorful examples of the old standards—Granny Smith, Golden Delicious, and Gala—will make a good pie.

Nonstick pie molds are available at most kitchenware shops. Disposable aluminum molds are usually available at the supermarket.

Mom's Apple Pie Dough (see page 270)

Pie Filling

¾ cup light brown sugar
¼ cup granulated sugar
1 tablespoon ground cinnamon
8 large (3½ pounds), tart apples, peeled, cored, and cut into ⅜-inch dice
½ cup cornstarch
2 teaspoons pure vanilla extract
1 cup sour cream or crème fraîche
½ stick (2 ounces) unsalted butter

Glaze

2 tablespoons granulated sugar
½ teaspoon cinnamon
¼ cup milk

Have ready

1 recipe Mom's Apple Pie Dough
1 recipe Scotch Caramel Ice Cream (optional)

LINE 2 baking sheets with parchment paper.

Lightly dust a work surface with flour. Turn the Mom's Apple Pie Dough out on the work surface.

Divide the pie dough into 2 pieces. Lightly dust a rolling pin with flour, and working with 1 piece of dough at a time, roll the dough out about ⅛ inch thick. Using a template, such as the lid of a jar, cut out sixteen 5-inch circles or two 12-inch circles. It may be necessary to gather the scraps together and roll the dough out again to cut all the circles. Place the dough circles on the parchment-lined baking sheets, and chill in the refrigerator at least 30 minutes.

Remove half the dough circles from the refrigerator. Line eight 4-inch-diameter individual pie molds with half of the dough circles. If preparing 1 large pie, line a 10-inch mold with one of the 12-inch circles. Reserve the remaining eight as top crusts for covering the pies. Do not trim off the excess dough that extends beyond the edges of the pie molds. Return the pie shells to the refrigerator and chill for 30 to 60 minutes.

To make the pie filling: In a large mixing bowl, combine the light brown sugar, granulated sugar, and cinnamon. Add the pieces of apple and toss to coat well. Set aside for 30 minutes. In a small mixing bowl, whisk the cornstarch, vanilla extract, and sour cream together until smooth and completely incorporated, with no cornstarch lumps remaining. If it is necessary to remove any cornstarch lumps, the mixture may be pushed through a fine-mesh, stainless-steel strainer with a rubber spatula. Add the sour cream mixture to the apples, mix well to coat completely, and reserve.

Remove the pie shells and top crusts from the refrigerator. Spoon 1 heaping cup of apple mixture into the center of each individually lined pie mold, or all of the mixture into one 10-inch mold. Do not spread the mixture out to the edges of the shell, but form it into a mound in the center. Divide the butter into 8 equal portions, and place 1 portion on top of each of the individual uncovered mounds of apple filling, or distribute it evenly over the surface of the filling of the 10-inch pie.

Cover the filling of each pie with a reserved top crust, gently pressing the top crust down to conform to the mound of filling. Using your thumb and index finger, pinch the edges of the 2 crusts together.

To make a decorative rim, using two fingers of one hand fold a section of the pinched edge of the dough up toward the filling, and gently press down to seal. Working around the perimeter of the pie, continue to fold up sections of the pinched edge while gently holding the previously folded section with the index finger and thumb of your other hand. Press down where the two edges overlap to ensure that the dough holds the folded shape.

Return the pies to the refrigerator and chill for about 30 minutes, or at this point the pies can be wrapped in plastic and frozen.

Preheat the oven to 400 degrees and place a rack in the bottom third of the oven.

Remove the pies from the refrigerator.

To make the glaze: In a small mixing bowl, combine the granulated sugar and cinnamon. Using a pastry brush, coat the top of each pie lightly with milk, and sprinkle with the granulated sugar and cinnamon mixture.

Using the tip of a knife, pierce the top of each pie and rotate the knife slightly to widen the steam vent hole. Distribute the pies on a baking sheet.

Bake the pies on the bottom rack for 40 minutes at 400 degrees. Reduce the oven to 350 degrees and bake 35 additional minutes, until the crust is well browned, bubbly, and flaky. To promote even baking, rotate the sheet halfway when the temperature is reduced.

Remove the baking sheet from the oven and allow to cool until the pies can be handled comfortably. Carefully invert each pie into 1 hand to unmold it. Place each pie on a large plate, and top with a scoop of Scotch Caramel Ice Cream, and serve immediately.

Mom's Apple Pie Dough

Yields 3 pounds, 12 ounces, enough for sixteen 6-inch circles or two 12-inch circles

MANY pie and pastry doughs seem to come out better when made by hand, and there is generally some merit to the notion that all the extra work and the gentle touch produce special results. This dough, however, actually comes out better made in a machine. We're not quite sure why this reverse method works so well, but it always produces exceptional results. Of course this dough can be made by hand, but you would need to follow a more traditional process; see Rustic Pie Dough (see page 274).

3 sticks (12 ounces) unsalted butter, chilled and cut in pieces
2⅓ cups vegetable shortening, chilled and broken up
7¾ cups unbleached pastry or unbleached all-purpose flour, plus extra for dusting
1½ tablespoons kosher salt
½ cup water plus ice to measure ¾ cup

FILL the bowl of the electric mixer with warm water, and let stand for 2 to 3 minutes. Empty the warm water from the mixing bowl and wipe it dry with a kitchen towel. Using the paddle attachment, starting on low speed, cream the butter and shortening. As it starts to soften, increase the speed to medium. Cream the butter and shortening until smooth, about 1 to 2 minutes, scraping the sides of the bowl down as needed. Reduce the speed to low, add the flour and salt, and mix just until the dough attains the consistency of coarse cornmeal. After the ice in the water has melted, add the water, mixing just until the dough comes together. If the flour is not completely incorporated, an additional tablespoon of water may be necessary. The amount of water required to produce a completely combined dough will depend on the moisture in the flour and the humidity of the working environment.

Lightly dust a smooth work surface and your hands with flour. Turn the dough out onto the work surface, knead the dough a few times, and form it into a ball. Flatten it slightly into a disk, and wrap it in plastic wrap. Refrigerate until firm, about 2 to 4 hours, before rolling it into the desired shape. The dough can be kept in the refrigerator for up to 2 days, or it will keep in the freezer for several weeks.

Rustic Cherry Pie

Yields 8 individual pies
or 1 large pie

TRADITIONAL double-crust cherry pie is usually one of those unreachable ideals of baking. You can order cherry pie at almost any lunch counter, but it never quite meets the high expectations. Rustic Cherry Pie is our free-form interpretation of the lunch counter cherry pie ideal.

Most commercial fillings are made from fresh sour cherries. However, unless you have a good connection at the local farmer's market, they can be quite difficult to find. This recipe produces a filling with all the good sweet-sour and sticky character of a perfect commercial filling, but using readily available Jubilee, Brooks, Bing, or Black Garnet cherries for proper color, and a little balsamic vinegar and sour dried cherries to achieve that penetrating depth of flavor.

The recipe for Streusel yields more than is necessary for topping the pies. The excess can be frozen for later use. The individual pies can also be assembled in advance and baked straight from the freezer. No defrosting is necessary before baking.

Dried sour cherries are usually available at specialty food shops.

Streusel (yields 1 1/2 cups)

½ cup unbleached all-purpose flour
½ cup granulated sugar
1 stick (4 ounces) unsalted butter, chilled and cut into small pieces

Cherry Compote

1½ cups granulated sugar
1 vanilla bean
2¼ pounds fresh cherries, stemmed and pitted (6 cups)
¼ cup brandy
1 cinnamon stick
12 ounces dried sour cherries (1½ cups)
1 to 2 tablespoons cornstarch
3 tablespoons balsamic vinegar

1 recipe Rustic Pie Dough (see page 274)
About ¾ cup Streusel (see above)
2 cups plain yogurt
⅔ cup balsamic vinegar

Have ready

1 recipe Rustic Pie Dough

TO prepare the Streusel: In an electric mixer fitted with the paddle attachment, on medium-low speed, mix the flour, sugar, and butter until the texture is coarse and crumbly. Streusel can also be made in a food processor fitted with a steel blade.

Reserve in the refrigerator or freezer until needed.

To prepare the compote: In a large saucepan, over medium-high heat, combine the sugar and ½ cup cold water. Using a small paring knife, split the vanilla bean lengthwise. Use the back of the knife to scrape out the pulp and the seeds of the vanilla bean. Add both the vanilla bean scrapings and pod to the saucepan. Bring the mixture to a boil without stirring.

When the water boils, it will throw sugar onto the sides of the pan. At this point wash down the sides of the pan with a pastry brush dipped in water.

When the sugar starts to color, after about 3 to 4 minutes, begin gently stirring the mixture with a wooden spoon while swirling the pan, to ensure even coloring. Continue to cook the mixture until it turns a translucent caramel color, just before it begins to smoke. If the mixture becomes opaque and slightly grainy, continue to cook, gently stirring while swirling the pan, until the sugar completely melts and the mixture becomes clear. If the mixture seizes completely and becomes solid and white, it must be discarded.

As soon as the sugar is lightly caramel colored, remove the pan from the heat and add the fresh cherries. The mixture will spatter, and part of it may seize and harden.

Carefully add the brandy, cinnamon stick, and the dried sour cherries; return the pan to medium-high heat and cook the mixture, stirring, until the sugar melts again, and the cherries soften, about 5 minutes.

Remove the pan from the heat and strain the cherry compote through a colander into a medium mixing bowl. Remove and discard the cinnamon stick and the vanilla bean pod. Allow the cherries in the colander to drain into the mixing bowl for a few minutes.

Return the cherry liquid to the large saucepan, and reserve the cherries in the mixing bowl. Bring the liquid to a boil over medium-high heat.

While the liquid is heating, in a small mixing bowl combine the cornstarch and 1 tablespoon of cold water.

When the cherry liquid begins to boil, remove the saucepan from the heat. Add the cornstarch mixture, whisk to combine, return the pan to the heat, and continue to boil for 1 minute.

Remove the saucepan from the heat, add the balsamic vinegar, and mix well. Pour the cherry liquid over the reserved cooked cherries in the mixing bowl, mix well, and allow to cool for at least 15 minutes. Refrigerate until cold, at least 1 hour. When chilled, the compote should be thick and sticky, with almost no liquid remaining.

If the compote is runny, strain it through a colander and repeat the steps in the previous five paragraphs.

While the compote is cooling, roll out the dough.

Line 1 or 2 baking sheets with parchment paper.

Lightly dust a work surface with flour. Turn the Rustic Pie Dough out on the work surface. Lightly dust a rolling pin with flour, and roll the dough out to about ⅛-inch thickness. Cut the dough into eight 5-inch circles or one 12-inch circle. It may be necessary to gather the scraps together and roll the dough out again to cut all the circles.

Arrange the circles of dough on the baking sheets, with a margin of about 2 inches between each circle.

Spoon about ⅓ cup of cherry compote in the center of each circle of dough. Do not spread the compote out on the shell, but form it into a mound in the center.

The filling is partially enclosed by folding up the perimeter of the dough circle in 6 sections, to form a shape similar to a stop sign.

Fold a 1-inch-deep section of the edge of the dough up toward the filling. Gently hold the folded section with the index finger and thumb of 1 hand as you use 2 fingers of the other hand to fold another 1-inch flap of dough up toward the filling. Press down where the two edges overlap to ensure that the dough holds the folded shape. Continue to work around the pie, making 6 folds. Gently cup your hand over the entire tart and press down the pleats to ensure that they seal well and will not unfold and open during the baking process.

Repeat the procedure with the remaining

RUSTIC CHERRY PIE: "THIS IS OUR FREE-FORM INTERPRETATION OF THE LUNCH COUNTER IDEAL."

dough circles. Refrigerate the formed pies for at least 30 minutes, or freeze for longer periods.

Preheat the oven to 375 degrees, and adjust the oven racks to the top and bottom positions.

Remove the formed pies from the refrigerator. If necessary adjust the placement of the pies on the baking sheets to ensure that the pies are at least 2 inches apart.

Spoon a heaping 2 tablespoons Streusel on top of the exposed cherries of each pie.

Rustic Cherry Pie *(cont.)*

Bake the pies until the crust is golden brown, about 30 minutes, rotating the baking pans on the racks halfway through the baking period to ensure even baking.

Remove the pies from the oven and allow to cool slightly, about 10 minutes. Remove the pies from the baking sheets with a wide spatula. Use care as the pies are somewhat fragile.

Place each pie in the center of a large dinner plate. Mix the yogurt a little with a spoon to thin it, so it is a bit runny, then artfully swirl a thick layer of about 2 to 3 tablespoons of yogurt around each pie. Using the back of the spoon, make two or three shallow indentations in the yogurt. Pour a little balsamic vinegar in each indentation. Top each pie with a small scoop of good-quality vanilla ice cream, and serve immediately.

Rustic Pie Dough

Yields 1 pound, 5 ounces;
eight 5-inch circles,
or one 12-inch circle

At Campanile, what we call a Rustic Pie is actually an individual free-form tart. We make a few different versions; cherry, apple, and pear. Rustic Pie is a good dessert for people who are nervous about the idea of lining a tart shell and striving for that perfect presentation.

We make this dough by hand because we eagerly accept any excuse to get our hands a little dirty.

2 cups unbleached pastry or unbleached
    all-purpose flour, plus extra for dusting
¼ cup granulated sugar
2 sticks (8 ounces) unsalted butter, chilled, cut
    into small pieces
1 tablespoon pure vanilla extract

Put the flour on a smooth work surface, add the sugar, and mix to combine. Add the pieces of butter to the flour, and toss to coat. Then, using the tips of your fingers, crumble the butter to a coarse cornmeal-like consistency, keeping the butter pieces well coated with the flour mixture to prevent it from becoming greasy.

In a small mixing bowl, combine 2 tablespoons cold water and the vanilla, and then sprinkle it over the flour, sugar, and butter mixture. Gather the dough together into a loose ball. The mixture will not be completely incorporated, and it will be very sticky.

Clean and completely dry your hands.

Lightly dust your work surface and one hand with flour. Using the heel of your hand, begin to smear small portions of the dough away from you. The smearing process is messy and sticky, but it blends the ingredients together with the least working of the dough. It may be necessary to dust your hand with flour a number of times. When all the dough is smeared out, use a dough scraper or metal spatula to collect all the dough and reincorporate it into one mass. Scrape the work surface clean.

Clean and completely dry your hands.

Lightly dust your hands and the work surface again with flour. Knead the dough a few times, form it into a smooth ball, flatten it slightly into a disk, and wrap in plastic wrap. Refrigerate until firm, about 2 to 4 hours, before rolling to the desired shape. The dough can be kept in the refrigerator for up to 2 days, or it will keep in the freezer for several weeks.

Alternately, the dough can be made in an electric mixer fitted with the paddle attachment, or if absolutely necessary, a food processor using the metal blade. In either machine, combine the flour and the sugar, and mix completely. Add the small pieces of butter, and mix just to a coarse cornmeal-like consistency.

In a small mixing bowl, whisk together the water and vanilla extract, and pour into the flour mixture. Mix just until the liquid brings the dough together into a rough ball. Lightly dust your hands and a smooth work surface with flour. Knead the dough a few times, form it into a ball and flatten it slightly into a disk, and wrap in plastic wrap.

Lemon Meringue Tart with Champagne Vinegar Sauce

Yields one 10-inch tart

THIS is certainly not to be confused with the standard mile-high lemon meringue tart with the cornstarch-thickened lemon filling. Our meringue tart is thin, elegant, sleek, and compact.

If you are lucky enough to find Meyer lemons, use them; they have a slightly more refined and gentle flavor than other lemons.

The meringue wedges may be made up to 2 days in advance. It is best to store them in an airtight container with the parchment paper (see directions below) still attached.

Meringue

1 cup lightly packed powdered sugar
2 extra-large egg whites
¼ cup unbleached all-purpose flour

Filling

1½ cups fresh lemon juice (from 10 large lemons)
¾ cup granulated sugar
6 extra-large eggs
¾ cup heavy cream

Have ready

1 Pâte Sucré tart shell (10-inch), prebaked (see page 278)
The Champagne Vinegar Sauce (see page 279), at room temperature

To prepare the meringue: Preheat the oven to 350 degrees.

Cut a circle of parchment paper 10-inches in diameter. Fold the circle into eighths, cut into 8 individual wedges, and set aside.

In a large mixing bowl over a saucepan of simmering water, combine the powdered sugar and egg whites. Whisk until smooth and warm to the touch, about 1 to 2 minutes. Remove the mixing bowl from the heat, push the flour through a fine-mesh, stainless-steel strainer into the egg white mixture, and whisk to combine completely.

Distribute the wedges of parchment paper on a smooth work surface. Using an offset spatula, spread the meringue in an ⅛-inch-thick layer over each wedge of parchment paper, taking care to completely cover the parchment, so that when the paper is lifted from the work surface, a perfect wedge shape of meringue will be formed.

Distribute the wedges on a baking sheet about 1 inch apart and bake until the meringue rises and the top is smooth, shiny, and lightly brown, about 10 minutes.

To test for doneness, peel the paper away from the meringue. The paper should separate cleanly. When the meringue wedges are done, allow them to cool, peel off and discard the paper, and reserve the meringue wedges.

To prepare the filling: Preheat the oven to 275 degrees, and adjust the rack to the middle position.

In a medium saucepan, over medium heat, whisk together the lemon juice and the sugar, and cook until the sugar dissolves, about 1 to 2 minutes. In a large, stainless-steel mixing bowl, whisk the eggs and cream, just to combine.

Remove the lemon juice and sugar mixture from the heat. Slowly add it to the mixing bowl containing the egg-and-cream mixture, and whisk to incorporate completely. Using a fine-mesh, stainless-steel strainer, strain the custard into a second large mixing bowl.

Pour the custard into the prebaked tart shell and bake until the center still jiggles a bit when gently shaken, about 30 to 40 minutes. Remove the tart from the oven, and allow to cool about 15 to 20 minutes.

Remove the tart ring. Using a sharp knife, cut the tart in wedges that are the same size as the pieces of meringue. Place each piece of tart on a dessert plate and top with a meringue wedge. Spoon a few tablespoons of Champagne Vinegar Sauce next to each portion and serve immediately.

Pâte Sucré (Sweet Pastry Dough)

Yields 1 1/2 pounds, enough
for two 10-inch tart shells

THIS lightly sweetened dough recipe comes from Nancy's first book, *Desserts*. It is perfect; there is no need to ever have another. This pastry dough is tender and cookielike, yet it holds its shape well, so it's perfect for lining tart shells that need to be prebaked. Any leftover scraps could be cut into small shapes, such as animal cookies, and baked just like a tart shell.

2¾ cups unbleached pastry or all-purpose flour, plus additional for dusting
½ cup granulated sugar
2 sticks (8 ounces) unsalted butter, chilled and cut in small pieces
2 extra-large egg yolks
¼ cup heavy cream, plus extra as needed

PUT the flour on a smooth work surface, add the sugar, and mix to combine. Add the pieces of butter to the flour, and toss to coat. Then, using the tips of your fingers, crumble the butter to a coarse cornmeal-like consistency, keeping the butter pieces well coated with the flour mixture to prevent it from becoming greasy.

Form the mixture into a mound, and make a large well in the center. Into the well, add the egg yolks and the heavy cream. Using the fingers of one hand, briefly stir the eggs and cream together, then begin to draw in the butter and flour mixture. When it is completely incorpo-rated, the dough should be very sticky. If not, add 1 to 2 tablespoons of extra cream. Gather the dough together into a loose ball.

Lightly dust your work surface and one hand with flour. Using the heel of your hand, begin to smear small portions of the dough away from you. The smearing process is messy and sticky, but it blends the ingredients together with the least working of the dough. It may be necessary to dust your hand with flour a number of times. When all the dough is smeared out, use a dough scraper or metal spatula to collect all the dough, and reincorporate it into one mass. Scrape the work surface clean.

Clean and completely dry your hands.

Lightly dust your hands and the work surface again with flour. Knead the dough a few times, form it into a smooth ball, flatten it slightly into a disk, and wrap in plastic wrap. Refrigerate until firm, about 2 to 4 hours, before rolling to the desired shape. The dough can be kept in the refrigerator for up to 2 days, or it will keep in the freezer for several weeks.

Alternately, the dough can be made in an electric mixer fitted with a paddle attachment, or if absolutely necessary, a food processor using a metal blade. In either machine, combine the flour and the sugar, and mix completely. Add the small pieces of butter, and mix just to a coarse cornmeal-like consistency.

In a small mixing bowl, whisk together the egg yolks and the heavy cream, and pour into the flour mixture. It may be necessary to add as much as 2 tablespoons of extra cream to make the dough moist enough to form a ball. Mix just until the cream and eggs bring the dough together into a rough ball. Lightly dust your hands and a smooth work surface with flour.

Turn the dough on to the work surface, knead the dough a few times, form it into a smooth ball, and flatten it slightly into a disk. Wrap it in plastic wrap.

Champagne Vinegar Sauce

Yields 2 cups

THIS is much more straightforward than it sounds, and not just an attempt to use new and different ingredients. Balsamic vinegar is sometimes used in desserts to emphasize tartness, such as on marinated strawberries, or to enhance less than ripe cherries. This is basically an acidic caramel sauce, in the way a lemon is acidic, but with a different flavor. We serve this with the Lemon Meringue Tart (see page 276), but it is also good with just about any sort of fruit-flavored tart.

2 cups granulated sugar
1 vanilla bean
1 cup champagne vinegar
½ stick (2 ounces) unsalted butter, cut into pieces

IN a large saucepan, over medium-high heat, combine the sugar and ½ cup of water, and bring the mixture to a boil without stirring. Using a small paring knife, split the vanilla bean lengthwise. Use the back of the knife to scrape out the pulp and the seeds of the vanilla bean, and add the pod and the scrapings to the sugar and water mixture.

When the mixture boils, it will throw sugar onto the sides of the pan. At this point wash down the sides of the pan with a pastry brush dipped in water.

When the sugar starts to color, after about 4 to 5 minutes, begin gently stirring the mixture with a wooden spoon while swirling the pan, to ensure even coloring. Continue to cook the mixture until it turns a translucent caramel color, just before it begins to smoke.

If the mixture becomes opaque and slightly grainy, continue to cook, gently stirring while swirling the pan, until the sugar completely melts and the mixture becomes clear. If the mixture seizes completely and becomes solid and white, it must be discarded.

As soon as the sugar is lightly caramel colored, remove the pan from the heat and add the champagne vinegar. The mixture will spatter, and part of it may seize and harden.

Return the pan to medium-high heat and cook the mixture, stirring, until the sugar melts again, and the mixture reduces slightly, about 3 to 4 minutes.

Remove the pan from the heat, and stir the butter into the mixture. The mixture will foam up and become cloudy. Continue to cook to reduce the mixture about 3 to 4 minutes.

To test for doneness, spoon out a few drops, sprinkle them on a smooth surface, allow the drops to cool slightly, and sample them for texture and flavor. The thickness of the sauce should be such that the drops hold their shape and are slightly sticky to the touch. If the sauce is too runny, return the pan to medium-high heat and continue to reduce for about 1 minute longer. The flavor should be tart but not so sour as to be unpleasant. If it isn't quite tart enough, add a little extra vinegar, return the pan to medium-high heat, and continue to reduce for about 1 minute longer.

Fill a large mixing bowl with ice water.

Using a fine-mesh, stainless-steel strainer, strain the sauce into a medium mixing bowl; place the bowl in the ice-water bath to cool the sauce. Discard the vanilla bean. The sauce must be whisked occasionally to prevent the butter from separating and hardening on the sides of the bowl. As soon as it is slightly thickened, about 5 minutes, remove it from the ice bath. The sauce should have the appearance and texture of a thin, emulsified caramel sauce.

The sauce should be served at room temperature. It can be refrigerated for several weeks. To reheat the sauce, scrape it out of the bowl and warm in a saucepan over low heat, and then cool in the same manner as described above.

Pineapple Upside-down Cake

THIS recipe is not an attempt to re-create some long-lost childhood memory. Traditional pineapple upside-down cake, made from canned pineapple, maraschino cherries, and a standard birthday cake mix, is not one of my favorite desserts. We wanted to pursue the hidden potential of the theme a little further into what could be considered an extreme of Polynesian Delight: fresh pineapple, long-shred coconut, toasted macadamia nuts, and a truly delicious cake base.

Nonstick pie molds are available at most kitchenware shops. Disposable aluminum molds are usually available at the supermarket.

1¼ cups unsalted macadamia nuts
2 sticks minus 2 tablespoons (7 ounces) unsalted butter
1 vanilla bean
1 pineapple
8 tablespoons light brown sugar (½ cup, firmly packed)
¾ cup unsweetened, long-shred coconut

Cake Batter

2½ teaspoons baking powder
½ teaspoon kosher salt
¾ cup plus 1 tablespoon unbleached pastry or unbleached all-purpose flour
¾ cup plus 1 tablespoon and 1 teaspoon cornmeal
1 stick minus 1 tablespoon (3½ ounces) unsalted butter, chilled and cut in small pieces
1 cup granulated sugar
3 extra-large eggs
6 extra-large egg yolks
¼ cup dried sour cherries

Sabayon (optional) (see page 284)
Unsweetened Whipped Cream (optional) (see page 287)
Dried Pineapple (optional) (see page 262)

PREHEAT the oven to 325 degrees, and adjust the oven racks to the top and bottom positions.

Spread the macadamia nuts on a baking sheet, and toast on the top rack in the oven until lightly browned, about 8 to 10 minutes. Remove the pan from the heat and allow the nuts to cool. Using a sharp knife, coarsely chop the macadamia nuts and set aside.

In a large saucepan, over medium-high heat, melt the butter. Using a small paring knife, split the vanilla bean lengthwise. Use the back of the knife to scrape out the pulp and the seeds of the vanilla bean. Add the scrapings from the vanilla bean plus the vanilla bean pod itself to the melted butter. Cook the butter until it begins to brown and has a nutty, toasty aroma, about 2 to 3 minutes. The butter must be stirred or swirled to promote even browning; take care that it does not burn. It will bubble somewhat vigorously as it browns. As soon as it subsides, remove the pan from the heat.

Use tongs to remove and discard the vanilla bean pod, and immediately distribute equal amounts of the butter into each 4-inch mold. Refrigerate until set, about 30 minutes.

Cut away all the rind from the pineapple. Cut the pineapple in half horizontally. Reserve one half for other uses (for example, Dried Pineapple, see page 262).

Slice ten ¼-inch-thick rounds from the pineapple. Using an apple corer or paring knife, remove and discard the core from the center of each round. Using a paring knife, or an appropriately sized circular cutter, trim the pineapple rounds to a size that is between ¼ and ½ inch smaller in diameter than the pie molds. Reserve the pineapple rounds.

Remove the molds from the refrigerator. Sprinkle about 2 teaspoons of brown sugar in a thin layer on top of the chilled brown butter in each mold to completely cover the brown butter. Then, sprinkle on about 1 tablespoon of shredded coconut. Place one of the reserved pineapple rounds on top of the coconut in each mold. Fill the center hole, and around the edges

of the pineapple, with about 2 tablespoons of the reserved macadamia nuts.

Increase the oven temperature to 350 degrees.

To prepare the cake batter: In a dry, large mixing bowl, stir together the baking powder, kosher salt, flour, and cornmeal to combine thoroughly, and set aside. Fill the bowl of the electric mixer with warm water, and let stand for 2 to 3 minutes. Empty the warm water from the mixing bowl and wipe it dry with a kitchen towel.

Using a paddle attachment, starting on low speed, cream the butter. As it starts to soften, increase the speed to medium. Cream the butter until smooth, about 1 to 2 minutes, scraping the sides of the bowl down as needed. Add the granulated sugar and mix until completely combined, about 1 minute.

In a small mixing bowl, whisk together the eggs and the egg yolks. Then add them to the butter mixture, in small increments, mixing briefly on medium-low speed to incorporate the eggs in between each portion. If the batter begins to separate, it may be necessary to add a few tablespoons of the reserved flour mixture before all the eggs have been added. The flour will help bind the mixture together.

Reduce the speed of the electric mixer to low. Add half the flour mixture to the butter mixture, mixing just to incorporate, then add the remaining half and mix until just combined, about 1 minute. Remove the mixing bowl from the machine, fold in the dried cherries using a rubber spatula, and set aside.

Put a scoop of cake batter over each slice of pineapple, dividing the batter equally among the 10 molds. Use a long-bladed spatula to spread the batter smoothly and evenly to the sides of the molds. The batter should be no more than ½ to ¾ inch thick. Take care not to disrupt the layers of nuts and pineapple.

If your molds are deeper than ¾ inch thick, spread the batter to the sides with the back of a spoon. There will not be enough batter to completely fill ten disposable molds.

Place the molds on 1 or 2 baking sheets and bake in the oven until lightly springy to the touch and just starting to color, about 15 to 18 minutes, rotating the baking pans on the racks halfway through the baking period to ensure even baking.

Remove the baking sheets from the oven, and allow the cakes to cool until they can be handled comfortably, about 5 to 10 minutes. To serve, carefully invert each cake onto a plate to remove it from the mold.

Serve immediately with Sabayon or Unsweetened Whipped Cream, and a few slices of Dried Pineapple on the side.

The cakes may be baked ahead of time, allowed to cool, and refrigerated overnight if desired. The cakes should be warmed, still in the mold, in a 400-degree oven for 2 to 3 minutes, as needed.

Sabayon

SABAYON is a whipped custard that resembles whipped cream in texture but has a fuller flavor. Because Sabayon has a more distinct flavor than whipped cream, it isn't suitable as a universal substitute, but for the right desserts, it adds just a touch more interest to the flavor.

5 extra-large egg yolks
¾ cup granulated sugar
1 vanilla bean
1½ cups dry white wine
1 cup whipping cream

IN a large mixing bowl, briefly whisk the egg yolks just to combine, and set aside.

In a large saucepan, over medium-high heat, combine the sugar and ¼ cup of water, and bring the mixture to a boil without stirring. Using a small paring knife, split the vanilla bean lengthwise. Use the back of the knife to scrape out the pulp and the seeds of the vanilla bean, and add the pod and the scrapings to the sugar-and-water mixture.

When the mixture boils, it will throw sugar onto the sides of the pan. At this point wash down the sides of the pan with a pastry brush dipped in water.

When the sugar starts to color, after about 4 to 5 minutes, begin gently stirring the mixture with a wooden spoon while swirling the pan to ensure even coloring. Continue to cook the mixture until it turns a translucent caramel color, just before it begins to smoke.

If the mixture becomes opaque and slightly grainy, continue to cook, gently stirring while swirling the pan, until the sugar completely melts and the mixture becomes clear. If the mixture seizes completely and becomes solid and white, it must be discarded.

As soon as the sugar is lightly caramel colored, remove the pan from the heat and add the white wine. The mixture will spatter, and part of it may seize and harden.

Return the pan to medium-high heat and cook the mixture, stirring, until the sugar melts again; then remove it from the heat and set it aside.

While the sugar is melting, bring about 2 cups of water to a boil in a large saucepan.

In a slow, steady stream, pour the hot white wine syrup into the egg yolks, whisking to combine completely.

Place the mixing bowl over the simmering water, ensuring that the bottom of the bowl does not touch the water, and cook the eggs, whisking vigorously until the mixture doubles in volume, no longer tastes raw, and is hot to the touch, about 5 to 10 minutes. It is important to rotate the bowl as you whisk to ensure that all the mixture is evenly cooked.

Transfer the custard to the bowl of an electric mixer fitted with a whisk attachment. On medium speed, whip until the bottom of the bowl is no longer warm to the touch, about 5 minutes. The mixture should be triple its original volume, quite fluffy, and pale yellow. Remove the mixing bowl from the electric mixer, and set aside. At this point the Sabayon can be stored in the refrigerator for up to 1 day, if desired.

Whip the cream according to the instructions on page 287.

Using a rubber spatula, fold one third of the whipped cream into the pale yellow Sabayon and stir to combine. Then fold in the remaining whipped cream, and stir to combine.

Serve immediately, or reserve in the refrigerator, covered, until needed.

Raspberry-Caramel Sauce

Yields 2 1/2 cups

At Campanile we usually serve this sauce with a raspberry custard tart, but it is great over ice cream or any dessert that calls for raspberry flavor. It is brilliant red, assertively raspberry flavored, and has more substantial body than traditional raspberry sauce. The caramelization of the sugar yields a sauce with more depth of flavor and subtle character than a fruit sauce simply sweetened with sugar. The small amount of added butter tempers the bitterness of the caramel, and it also adds a beautiful sheen to the finished sauce.

Although the raspberry seeds are strained out, I prefer that a small amount be added back into the sauce, as a visual clue to its origins. The seeds immediately inform you to expect raspberry flavor.

3½ cups fresh raspberries
2 cups granulated sugar
¼ stick (1 ounce) unsalted butter

In a food processor fitted with a steel blade, or in a blender, puree the raspberries. Take care not to overprocess. Set aside the pureed raspberries.

In a large saucepan, over medium-high heat, combine the sugar and ½ cup of water. Bring the mixture to a boil without stirring. When the water boils, it will throw sugar onto the sides of the pan. At this point wash down the sides of the pan with a pastry brush dipped in water.

When the sugar starts to color, after about 3 to 4 minutes, begin gently stirring the mixture with a wooden spoon while swirling the pan, to ensure even coloring. Continue to cook the mixture until it turns a translucent caramel color, just before it begins to smoke. If the mixture becomes opaque and slightly grainy, continue to cook, gently stirring while swirling the pan, until the sugar completely melts and the mixture becomes clear. If the mixture seizes completely and becomes solid and white, it must be discarded.

As soon as the sugar is lightly caramel colored, remove the pan from the heat and add the pureed raspberries. The mixture will spatter, and part of it may seize and harden.

Return the pan to medium heat, and cook the mixture, stirring, until the sugar melts again, about 1 to 2 minutes.

Using a fine-mesh, stainless-steel strainer, strain the sauce to remove the seeds. Reserve about 1 tablespoon of the seeds; discard the rest. While the mixture is still warm, add the butter and the reserved seeds and stir to combine.

Serve warm, at room temperature, or refrigerate, covered, for longer storage. To reheat the sauce, scrape it out of the bowl and warm in a saucepan over low heat for about 3 to 5 minutes.

Unsweetened Whipped Cream

Yields 2 cups

Aт first, making whipped cream to top a dessert would seem to be childishly simple; you just whisk it until it is light and fluffy. Yet quite often, when dining out, we're served a dessert smothered by rigid peaks of overwhipped cream. The only option is to scrape it off to the side of the plate.

Perfectly whipped cream has a smooth sheen like white, shiny frosting and will hold its shape, but not sharp peaks. Cream must be very cold to whip properly, and it is important to chill the bowl and the whisk as well. This is because whipped cream separates very easily and even a little heat enhances the problem.

Cream should be whipped no more than a few hours before use, because it absorbs flavor from all the pungent things that are in your refrigerator. If you must whip it in advance, underwhip it slightly, cover it well, and refrigerate until needed. Just before serving, remove it from the refrigerator and whisk it briefly before serving to bring out the full body.

The addition of a little sour cream or crème fraîche to every cup of whipping cream will ensure that beautiful sheen, extra smoothness, and fuller flavor.

1 cup whipping cream
4 tablespoons sour cream or crème fraîche, to
   taste

To whip cream by hand you need a very large bowl and a large, balloon-style whisk. The large bowl is necessary to be able to whip the cream vigorously without making a mess, and the style of whisk is very important: If your whisk is too small or has too few wires, it will take much more effort to whip the cream. Whisking vigorously, it should take about 3 to 5 minutes to bring the liquid cream to the proper consistency.

By machine, start on a low speed until the cream thickens enough not to spatter. Increase the speed to medium high and continue to whip, stopping the machine before the cream will hold soft peaks. Remove the bowl from the electric mixer and finish whipping the cream by hand with a whisk.

Note: Salvaging extremely overwhipped cream can be done. You must add up to ¼ cup of cold whipping cream and work it in, stirring with a rubber spatula to restore the proper consistency.

Chocolate Chip Cookies

MOST chocolate chip cookie recipes are simply variations using the trusted and true ingredients—just slightly different quantities, yielding similar results, some a little cakier, some a little too bready, and some as hard as rocks. This recipe is also a variation on tradition, but the results are outstanding.

Freshly baked cookies are a moderate amount of work, but they are so delicious that it's worth the effort. Three-day-old baked cookies, however, are not nearly so pleasing. The solution to this is to bake only what you can use that day, reserving the unbaked dough in the refrigerator for up to two days, or it can be shaped and frozen for longer periods. Baking all the dough at once will, however, deprive the midnight dough thieves in your family of the opportunity to practice their art. Frozen shaped dough can go directly from the freezer to the oven. The baking time for frozen dough must be increased by about 1 minute.

6 ounces (1½ cups) walnut halves
8 ounces bittersweet chocolate
2¼ sticks (9 ounces) unsalted butter
1 cup granulated sugar
¾ cup light brown sugar, packed
1 extra-large egg
1 teaspoon pure vanilla extract
2½ cups unbleached pastry or all-purpose flour
½ teaspoon baking soda
½ teaspoon baking powder

PREHEAT the oven to 325 degrees.

Spread the walnuts on a baking sheet. Toast the nuts on the top rack for about 5 to 6 minutes. Shake the pan about halfway through to ensure that the nuts toast evenly. Take care not to overly color the nuts, as that will produce a bitter flavor. Remove the baking pans from the oven, remove the nuts from the baking pans, and allow to cool.

Using a sharp knife, chop the chocolate into rough ⅜-inch pieces and reserve in a cool place. Then chop the walnut halves coarsely.

Fill the bowl of the electric mixer with warm water, and let stand for 2 to 3 minutes. Empty the warm water from the mixing bowl and wipe it dry with a kitchen towel.

Using the paddle attachment, starting on low speed, cream the butter; as it starts to soften, increase the speed to medium. Cream the butter until smooth, about 1 to 2 minutes, scraping the sides of the bowl down as needed. Add the granulated sugar and the brown sugar, mixing until well blended, about 1 minute.

In a small mixing bowl, whisk together the egg and the vanilla extract. Then add the mixture, in 2 portions, to the butter mixture, mixing on medium speed between each addition.

In a dry, large mixing bowl, stir together the flour, baking soda, and baking powder to combine thoroughly. Add half the flour mixture to the creamed butter, and mix on medium speed for about 1 minute; then add the remaining half and mix until just combined, about 1 more minute.

Add the chopped walnuts and the chocolate pieces, and mix about 1 minute longer. Remove the dough from the electric mixer, gather into a ball, wrap in plastic, and refrigerate until firm, about 2 hours.

Preheat the oven to 350 degrees, and adjust the oven rack to the middle position.

Line 1 or 2 baking sheets with parchment paper.

Using your hands, form the dough into 1½-inch balls and place them about 2 inches apart from one another on the baking sheets. Using the palm of your hand, lightly press each ball of dough to flatten it slightly.

Bake the cookies until they have risen and deflated slightly, the center has cracked a little, and they have become golden brown, about 15 to 20 minutes. Halfway through the baking period, the baking sheets should be rotated, to promote even baking.

The degree of doneness is a matter of personal preference. The cookies can be removed from the oven as soon as the centers have cracked, and slightly deflated. At that point they will be soft and chewy, but if left in the oven for an additional 2 minutes they will be more deeply browned and firm. Of course they can be baked even longer, if you prefer them very darkly browned and crispy.

Remove the baking sheets from the oven and allow to cool.

Biscotti

THE literal translation of the Italian word *biscotti* is biscuit, in this case a
small, crisp, sweet composed of flour, sugar water, fat, eggs, and flavorings.
The common usage refers to the twice-baked, elegantly sliced oblong cookies
that accompany a coffee at the local café. In the tradition of the latter, here are
three variations on the theme.

These biscotti are baked twice, once in the form of a flat loaf, and then again
after slicing the loaf into individual cookies. The process yields a crumbly but
firmly textured cookie. The loaves can be baked and stored, uncut and
wrapped in plastic, for up to 1 week. For the freshest cookies, slice off and
bake the individual cookies as needed.

Brown Butter Semolina Biscotti

Yields 3 1/2 dozen

1 stick (4 ounces) unsalted butter, chilled and
    cut into pieces
1 vanilla bean
3 extra-large eggs
¾ cup granulated sugar
½ cup cornmeal
1 teaspoon baking powder
2¼ cups unbleached all-purpose or pastry flour,
    plus extra for dusting
¼ cup sesame seeds

PREHEAT the oven to 350 degrees, and adjust the oven rack to the middle position.

In a large saucepan, over medium-high heat, melt the butter. Using a small paring knife, split the vanilla bean lengthwise. Use the back of the knife to scrape out the pulp and the seeds of the vanilla bean. Add the scrapings from the vanilla bean plus the vanilla bean pod itself to the melted butter. Cook the butter until it begins to brown and has a nutty, toasty aroma, about 2 to 3 minutes. The butter must be stirred or swirled to promote even browning; take care that it does not burn. It will bubble somewhat vigorously as it browns; as soon as it subsides, remove the pan from the heat.

Use stainless-steel tongs to remove and discard the vanilla bean pod, and pour the butter into a heatproof measuring cup. If the melted, browned butter measures less than ½ cup, add additional butter as necessary to make ½ cup. It is not necessary to brown the additional butter.

Allow the brown butter to cool to room temperature, about 10 to 15 minutes.

Separate two of the eggs, reserving the yolks in the bowl of an electric mixer and the whites in a small mixing bowl.

In the electric mixer, fitted with a whisk attachment, on medium speed, whip the reserved egg yolks and all but 2 tablespoons of the sugar until the mixture is thick, pale yellow, and tripled in volume, about 1 to 2 minutes. Slowly add the browned butter and mix to incorporate, about 1 minute.

In a large mixing bowl, combine the cornmeal, baking powder, and flour. Change to the paddle attachment on the electric mixer, and on medium-low speed, add the flour to the whipped egg yolks; mix until the batter has the consistency of coarse meal, about 1 to 2 minutes.

Remove the dough from the electric mixer, reserve in a large mixing bowl, and thoroughly wash and dry the bowl of the electric mixer. Change to the whisk attachment on the electric mixer, and on medium-low speed, whip the two reserved egg whites to soft peaks, about 2 to 3 minutes. Increase the speed to high, and gradually add the remaining sugar, mixing until stiff, about 1 to 2 minutes.

Remove the egg whites from the electric mixer, and using a rubber spatula, add one-third of the egg whites to the batter, and quickly mix to combine. Fold the remaining egg whites into the batter.

Line a baking sheet with parchment paper. Lightly dust a smooth work surface and your hands with flour. Turn the dough out on the work surface, and divide it into 2 equal pieces. Working with 1 piece of dough at a time, roll it out into a log, about 1 inch in diameter and 9 inches long. It is important to work the dough firmly to ensure that there are no air pockets in the middle of the log. Transfer the log to the lined baking sheet.

Repeat with the remaining dough, placing the logs about 4 to 5 inches apart. Flatten each log slightly to form a loaf about 2 inches wide and 10 inches long.

Separate the remaining egg, reserving the white, and saving the yolk for other uses. Brush the top of the loaves lightly with the egg white and sprinkle the sesame seeds over the tops.

Bake the loaves on the middle rack until firm to the touch and lightly golden, about 25 minutes.

Remove the loaves from the oven and allow to cool completely, at least 6 hours.

Preheat the oven to 150 degrees.

Line 2 baking sheets with parchment paper.

Using a serrated knife, slice the loaves into individual cookies. Arrange the biscotti, closely spaced, on the baking sheets.

Bake the biscotti until firm and dry, about 20 to 30 minutes. Take care not to brown the cookies. Remove the biscotti from the oven and allow them to cool.

Chocolate-Hazelnut Biscotti

Yields 3 ½ dozen cookies

¾ cup whole hazelnuts

3 extra-large eggs, in all

1 stick plus 1 tablespoon (4½ ounces) unsalted butter

1 vanilla bean

1 cup granulated sugar

2¼ cups unbleached, all-purpose or pastry flour, plus additional for dusting

1 teaspoon baking powder

6 ounces bittersweet chocolate, chopped into ¼-inch chunks

PREHEAT the oven to 325 degrees, and adjust the oven rack to the middle position.

Spread the hazelnuts on a baking sheet and toast in the oven until lightly browned, about 8 to 10 minutes. Shake the pan about halfway through to ensure that the nuts toast evenly. Take care not to overly color the nuts, as this will produce a bitter flavor. Remove the baking sheet from the oven. Remove the nuts from the baking sheet and allow them to cool. Then gather the nuts in a kitchen towel and rub together to remove the skins. Using a sharp knife, coarsely chop the hazelnuts and set aside.

Increase the oven temperature to 350 degrees.

Separate 2 eggs, reserving the yolks in the bowl of the electric mixer and the whites in a small mixing bowl.

In a small saucepan, over low heat, melt the butter with the vanilla bean, about 1 to 2 minutes. Remove the pan from the heat. Remove and discard the vanilla bean.

In an electric mixer, fitted with the whisk attachment, on medium speed, whip the reserved egg yolks and ½ cup of the sugar until thick, pale yellow, and tripled in volume, about 1 to 2 minutes. Slowly add the melted butter and mix to incorporate, about 1 minute.

In a large mixing bowl, combine the flour and baking powder. Change to the paddle attachment on the electric mixer, and on medium-low speed, add the flour to the whipped egg yolks, mixing until the batter has the consistency of coarse meal, about 1 to 2 minutes. Remove the dough from the electric mixer. Reserve in a large mixing bowl, and thoroughly wash and dry the bowl of the electric mixer.

Change to the whisk attachment on the electric mixer, and on medium-low speed, whip the reserved egg whites to soft peaks, about 2 to 3 minutes. Increase the speed to high, and gradually add the remaining sugar, mixing until stiff, about 1 to 2 minutes.

Remove the egg whites from the electric mixer and, using a rubber spatula, add one-third of the egg whites to the batter, and quickly mix to combine. Fold the remaining whipped egg whites into the batter. Add the chocolate and the hazelnuts to the batter, and mix thoroughly.

Line a baking sheet with parchment paper.

Lightly dust a smooth work surface and your hands with flour. Turn the dough out onto the work surface, and divide it into 2 equal pieces. Working with 1 piece of dough at a time, roll it out into a log, about 1 inch in diameter and 9 inches long. It is important to work the dough firmly to ensure that there are no air pockets in the middle of the log. Transfer the log to the lined baking sheet. Repeat with the remaining dough, placing the logs about 4 to 5 inches apart. Flatten each log slightly, to form a loaf about 2 inches wide and 10 inches long. Separate the remaining egg, reserving the white, and saving the yolk for other uses. Brush the top of the loaves lightly with the egg white.

Bake the loaves until firm to the touch and lightly golden, about 30 minutes.

Remove the loaves from the oven and allow to cool completely, at least 6 hours.

Preheat the oven to 200 degrees.

Line 2 baking sheets with parchment paper. Using a serrated knife, slice the loaves into individual cookies. Arrange the biscotti, closely spaced, on the baking sheets.

Bake the biscotti until firm and dry, about 20 to 30 minutes. Remove the biscotti from the oven and allow them to cool.

Mary Kay's Pistachio and Currant Biscotti

Yields 4 dozen

¾ stick (3 ounces) unsalted butter, chilled and
    cut into small pieces
1 cup granulated sugar
2 extra-large eggs
2½ cups unbleached all-purpose or pastry flour,
    plus extra for dusting
½ teaspoon baking soda
½ teaspoon baking powder
⅛ teaspoon kosher salt
¾ cup (3 ounces) raw, unsalted, whole
    pistachios
½ cup (3 ounces) dried currants or raisins

PREHEAT the oven to 325 degrees, and adjust
the oven rack to the middle position.

Fill the bowl of the electric mixer with
warm water, and let stand for 2 to 3 minutes.
Empty the warm water from the mixing bowl
and wipe it dry with a kitchen towel. Using the
paddle attachment, starting on low speed,
cream the butter. As it starts to soften, increase
the speed to medium. Cream the butter until
smooth, about 1 to 2 minutes, scraping the sides
of the bowl down as needed. Add the sugar,
mixing until well blended, about 1 minute.

In a small mixing bowl, whisk together the
eggs. Add the eggs in 3 portions to the butter
mixture, mixing on medium speed between
each addition.

In a large mixing bowl, stir together the
flour, baking soda, baking powder, and kosher
salt, to combine thoroughly. Add half the flour
mixture to the creamed butter, and mix on
medium-low speed for about 1 minute; then
add the remaining half and mix until almost
combined, about 1 more minute.

Add the pistachios and the dried currants,
and mix until thoroughly combined, about
1 minute longer.

Line a baking sheet with parchment paper.

Lightly dust a smooth working surface and
your hands with flour. Turn the dough out on
the work surface, and divide it into 2 equal
pieces. Working with 1 piece of dough at a
time, roll it out into a log, about 1 inch in diameter and 10 inches long. It is important to work
the dough firmly to ensure that there are no air
pockets in the middle of the log. Transfer the
log to the lined baking sheet. Repeat with the
remaining dough, placing the logs about 4 to 5
inches apart. Flatten each log slightly, to form a
loaf about 3 inches wide and 11 inches long.
Separate the remaining egg, reserving the white
and saving the yolk for other uses. Brush the
top of the loaves lightly with the egg white.

Bake the loaves until they fall, expand in
width to about 4 inches wide, and are firm to
the touch and lightly golden, about 35 minutes.

Remove the loaves from the oven and
allow to cool completely, at least 6 hours.

Preheat the oven to 200 degrees.

Line 2 baking sheets with parchment paper.

Using a serrated knife, slice the loaves into individual cookies. Arrange the biscotti, closely spaced, on the baking sheets.

Bake the biscotti until firm and dry, about 20 to 30 minutes. Remove the biscotti from the oven and allow them to cool.

Macadamia Nut Shortbread

Yields 4 dozen

MACADAMIA nuts and butter is a good combination of rich but individually distinct flavors. Traditional shortbreads cook for a fairly long time at low temperature to bring out the flavor of the butter without coloring. This shortbread, however, uses brown butter, so the flavor is deep and fully developed within a shorter cooking time.

If you simply want to make plain shortbread, just omit the macadamia nuts from the recipe.

1½ sticks (6 ounces) unsalted butter, plus
    additional as needed
1 vanilla bean
1¼ cups unsalted macadamia nuts
½ cup granulated sugar
2 extra-large egg whites
3 tablespoons heavy cream
2 cups minus 2 tablespoons cake flour

PREHEAT the oven to 325 degrees.

In a large saucepan, over medium-high heat, melt the butter. Using a small paring knife, split the vanilla bean lengthwise. Use the back of the knife to scrape out the pulp and the seeds of the vanilla bean. Add the scrapings from the vanilla bean plus the vanilla bean pod itself to the melted butter. Cook the butter until it begins to brown and has a nutty, toasty aroma, about 2 to 3 minutes. The butter must be stirred or swirled to promote even browning; take care that it does not burn. It will bubble somewhat vigorously as it browns; as soon as it subsides, remove the pan from the heat.

Use stainless-steel tongs to remove and discard the vanilla bean pod, and pour the butter into a heatproof measuring cup. If the melted, browned butter measures less than ½ cup, add additional butter as necessary to make ½ cup. It is not necessary to brown the additional butter. Chill the butter in the refrigerator until firm, about 1 hour.

Spread the macadamia nuts on a baking

sheet and toast in the oven until lightly browned, about 8 minutes. Shake the pan about halfway through to ensure that the nuts toast evenly. Take care not to overly color the nuts, as this will produce a bitter flavor.

Remove the baking sheet from the oven and allow the nuts to cool. In a food processor, fitted with a steel blade, grind the toasted nuts with the granulated sugar until the mixture has the consistency of a very coarse meal. It is important to grind the nuts with a few short pulses of the food processor to prevent the mixture from becoming a paste.

When the butter is completely firm, proceed with the recipe.

Fill the bowl of the electric mixer with warm water, and let stand for 2 to 3 minutes. Empty the warm water from the mixing bowl and wipe it dry with a kitchen towel.

Using a spoon, remove the chilled browned butter from the measuring cup and transfer it to the warmed bowl of the electric mixer. Using the paddle attachment, starting on low speed, begin to mix the butter. As it starts to soften, increase the speed to medium. Mix the butter until smooth and softened, about 1 to 2 minutes. Browned butter does not cream in the same fashion as plain butter; it will appear to be grainier.

Add the sugar and nut mixture, decrease the mixer speed to low, and mix until just combined, about 1 minute. In a small mixing bowl, combine the egg whites and the cream. Add the cream mixture in 3 portions to the batter and mix until incorporated, about 1 minute, between each addition. Add the flour in 3 portions and mix until just incorporated, about 1 minute, between each addition.

Remove the dough from the electric mixer and gather it into a ball. Flatten it into a disk, wrap in plastic, and refrigerate until firm enough to be easily handled, about 2 hours.

Lightly dust a smooth work surface and your hands with flour. Using your hands, flatten the dough into a thick rectangle and then straighten each edge by knocking it against the work surface to form a loaf measuring about 2½ × 12 × 1 inch. It is important to ensure that there are no gaps or holes in the dough. Wrap the loaf in plastic and freeze for about 2 hours, or refrigerate until very firm, at least 6 hours.

Preheat the oven to 250 degrees.

Line 2 baking sheets with parchment paper.

Using a sharp knife, cut the loaf into slices about ¼-inch thick. Place the slices about 1 inch apart on the baking sheets. For the freshest cookies, slice off and bake only what is needed that day.

Bake the shortbread until firm and lightly colored, about 1 hour, turning the shortbread over halfway through the baking time. Remove the shortbread from the oven and allow it to cool.

Butter Cookies

Yields 4 dozen cookies

THE French might think of these as *biscuits au beurre,* the English might say shortbread, and in the United States it would probably be Lorna Doones. Simply put, they are butter cookies. The flavor is distinctly in the family of shortbread, rich and very buttery, without any added ingredients that might mask the purity of good butter.

3¾ sticks (14 ounces) unsalted butter, chilled
    and cut into pieces
1 cup granulated sugar
3¾ cups unbleached, all-purpose flour, plus
    additional for dusting
2 extra-large egg yolks
1 teaspoon pure vanilla extract

FILL the bowl of an electric mixer with warm water, and let stand for 2 to 3 minutes. Empty the warm water from the mixing bowl and wipe it dry with a kitchen towel. Using the paddle attachment, starting on low speed, cream the butter; as it starts to soften, increase the speed to medium. Cream the butter until smooth, about 1 to 2 minutes, scraping the sides of the bowl down as needed. Add the sugar, and continue to mix until well blended, about 2 minutes. Reduce the speed to low, add the flour, and mix just until the mixture forms a soft dough.

In a small mixing bowl, whisk together the egg yolks and the vanilla extract. Then add to the creamed butter, mixing on medium speed for about 1 minute, and scraping the sides of the bowl down as needed.

Remove the dough from the electric mixer, wrap in plastic, and refrigerate until firm, about 1 hour.

Line 2 baking sheets with parchment paper.

Divide the dough into 4 equal pieces and work with one at a time, keeping the others, wrapped, in the refrigerator. Lightly dust a work surface with flour. Turn one piece of dough out on the work surface. Lightly dust your hands, or a rolling pin, with flour, and flatten or roll the dough into a rectangle about ⅜-inch thick.

Using a cookie cutter, cut out the cookies and place them about 1 inch apart on the parchment-lined baking sheets. Repeat with the remaining pieces of dough. Gather the scraps together into a loose ball. Refrigerate until firm, about 1 hour, and reroll.

Preheat the oven to 325 degrees.

Bake the cookies until they are firm to the touch and lightly golden brown, about 12 to 15 minutes. For the freshest cookies, bake only what is needed that day.

Vanilla Ice Cream with Macadamia Nut Brittle

Yields 1½ quarts

VERY few people don't like macadamia nuts, so this is a safe bet for entertaining or large family gatherings. We usually serve this garnished with a piece of Macadamia Nut Shortbread (see page 295), as the combination is luxurious and rich in textural contrasts. The smooth ice cream, the tender shortbread, and the hard crunchy brittle all have very distinct textures.

The brittle must be made first, so it is properly chilled before being folded into the ice cream. The sugar coating of the nuts keeps them from becoming soggy in the ice cream.

Macadamia Nut Brittle

1 cup macadamia nuts, unsalted
1 tablespoon vegetable oil
1 cup granulated sugar
1 tablespoon (½ ounce) unsalted butter

Vanilla Ice Cream

2 cups whole milk
2 cups heavy cream
2 vanilla beans
8 extra-large egg yolks
½ cup granulated sugar

TO prepare the Macadamia Nut Brittle: Preheat the oven to 325 degrees.

Spread the macadamia nuts on a baking sheet and toast in the oven until lightly browned, about 8 minutes. Shake the pan about halfway through to ensure that the nuts toast evenly. Take care not to overly color the nuts, as this will produce a bitter flavor.

Using a sharp knife, chop the macadamia nuts very coarsely and set aside.

Lightly grease a baking sheet with the vegetable oil and set aside.

In a large saucepan, over medium-high heat, combine the sugar and ¼ cup of water. Bring the mixture to a boil without stirring. When the water boils, it will throw sugar onto the sides of the pan. At this point wash down the sides of the pan with a pastry brush dipped in water.

When the sugar starts to color, after about 3 to 4 minutes, begin gently stirring the mixture with a wooden spoon while swirling the pan to ensure even coloring. Continue to cook the mixture until it turns a translucent caramel color, just before it begins to smoke. If the mixture becomes opaque and slightly grainy, continue to cook, gently stirring while swirling the pan, until the sugar completely melts and the mixture becomes clear. If the mixture seizes completely and becomes solid and white, it must be discarded.

As soon as the sugar is lightly caramel colored, remove the pan from the heat and add the reserved macadamia nuts. Return the pan to medium heat and cook, stirring constantly with a wooden spoon, until the caramel darkens slightly, about 2 to 3 minutes. Add the butter. Stir to combine (the caramel may begin to bubble and smoke), and remove the pan from the heat.

Pour the caramel nut mixture onto the oiled baking sheet and spread it out evenly, using a wooden spoon. Allow to cool at room temperature for about 30 minutes.

Chop the brittle coarsely and reserve. For storage longer than overnight, the brittle should be frozen. If left at room temperature for too long it will sweat and become sticky.

To prepare the vanilla ice cream: In a medium saucepan, over medium-high heat, bring the milk and cream to a boil. Using a small paring knife, split the vanilla beans lengthwise. Use the back of the knife to scrape out the pulp and the seeds of the vanilla beans. Add the scrapings from the vanilla beans and the pods as well to the saucepan. Remove the pan from the heat and let steep, covered, for about 30 minutes. Return the mixture to medium-high heat and bring back to a boil.

In a large, stainless-steel mixing bowl, whisk together the egg yolks and sugar until the sugar is completely dissolved and the mixture is thickened, about 2 to 3 minutes.

Pour about half the hot milk-and-cream mixture into the mixing bowl, whisking constantly to prevent the eggs from curdling. Pour it back into the saucepan and return the pan to medium heat, stirring constantly with a wooden spoon, until the mixture thickens slightly and coats the back of the spoon, about 1 minute. It is better to be safe and make a slightly thin mixture rather than to curdle the eggs by cooking the mixture for too long.

Using a fine-mesh, stainless-steel strainer, strain the mixture into a clean, large mixing bowl, discarding the vanilla bean. Allow to cool for about 15 minutes, then chill in the refrigerator until cold, at least 2 hours.

Remove the mixture from the refrigerator. Pour the cold cream mixture into the container of an ice cream freezer. Freeze according to the manufacturer's instructions.

When the ice cream is completely churned, remove it to a chilled stainless-steel mixing bowl. Using a rubber spatula, fold in the Macadamia Nut Brittle, and mix thoroughly. The ice cream can be served immediately, or if a firmer texture is desired, it can be covered and frozen for 1 to 2 hours longer.

Scotch Caramel Ice Cream

Yields 1 to 1½ quarts

THERE is a natural affinity between the flavors of caramelized sugar and scotch because they share a similar subtle smokey quality. The caramel derives the flavor from the browning of the sugar, and the scotch from the charred wooden barrels in which it is aged.

Scotch Caramel Ice Cream is slightly softer and creamier than most ice creams because of its high levels of sugar and alcohol. Alcohol has a low freezing temperature, so it never solidifies completely in a home freezer, and the high proportion of sugar makes it smoother still.

It is important not to add too much scotch, or the ice cream will not freeze completely.

2 cups whole milk
2 cups heavy cream
1¼ cups plus 2 tablespoons granulated sugar
¾ cup scotch whiskey, plus additional as desired
1 vanilla bean
8 extra-large egg yolks

IN a large saucepan, over medium heat, bring the milk and cream to a boil. Remove from the heat and reserve.

In a large saucepan, over medium-high heat, combine the sugar and scotch, and bring the mixture to a boil without stirring. Using a small paring knife, split the vanilla bean lengthwise. Use the back of the knife to scrape out the pulp and the seeds of the vanilla bean, and add the pod and the scrapings to the sugar-and-scotch mixture.

When the mixture boils, it will throw sugar onto the sides of the pan. At this point wash down the sides of the pan with a pastry brush dipped in water.

When the sugar starts to color, after about 4 to 5 minutes, begin gently stirring the mixture with a wooden spoon while swirling the pan to ensure even coloring. If the mixture becomes opaque and slightly grainy, continue to cook, gently stirring while swirling the pan, until the sugar completely melts. Continue to cook the mixture until it turns a dark caramel color, and just begins to smoke.

Remove the pan from the heat, and slowly pour in the cream mixture in small amounts. Use caution, as the caramel will spatter a bit, and part of it may seize and harden.

Return the pan to medium-high heat and cook the mixture, stirring, until the sugar melts again, and the cream and caramel mixtures are completely combined, about 1 minute.

In a large mixing bowl, whisk the egg yolks briefly, just to break them up. Now whisking the egg yolks continuously, add about one-quarter of the hot caramel-cream mixture, and whisk to combine. Return this mixture to the remaining hot caramel-cream mixture, then return to medium heat.

Continue to cook, stirring constantly with a wooden spoon, until the mixture thickens slightly, about 1 minute. It is better to be safe and make a slightly thin mixture rather than curdle the eggs by cooking the mixture for too long.

Using a fine-mesh, stainless-steel strainer, strain into a clean, large mixing bowl, discarding the vanilla bean. Allow the mixture to cool for about 15 minutes, and then correct the scotch flavoring to taste with a few tablespoons of scotch as necessary. Chill in the refrigerator until cold, at least 2 hours.

Remove the mixture from the refrigerator. Pour the cold cream mixture into the container of an ice cream freezer. Freeze according to the manufacturer's instructions.

When the ice cream is completely churned, remove it to a chilled stainless-steel mixing bowl. The ice cream can be served immediately, or if a firmer texture is desired, it can be covered and frozen for 1 to 2 hours longer.

Coffee Ice Cream

A coffee flavor at the end of a meal can be doubly pleasing: it can satisfy the desire for both coffee and dessert. Our coffee ice cream has an intense coffee flavor, much more so than traditional coffee ice cream, because we use no eggs and less cream. It may not be quite as creamy, but it is more refreshing.

Crush the coffee beans with a rolling pin or with the back of a pan. Do not use a grinder or food processor because the resulting grind will be too small, and it causes the ice cream to take on an unpleasant gray color. Decaffeinated beans produce a smoother ice cream than regular beans.

4½ cups whole milk

1½ cups heavy cream

½ cup plus 1 tablespoon granulated sugar

1½ tablespoons corn syrup

½ cup decaffeinated coffee beans, espresso roast, crushed

1½ teaspoons coffee extract, or instant espresso

In a medium saucepan, over medium heat, bring the milk, cream, sugar, corn syrup, and coffee beans to a boil. Boil gently, stirring continuously using a rubber spatula, reducing until the mixture has thickened very slightly, about 20 to 25 minutes. It is necessary to taste this cream mixture as it thickens to achieve a mixture with sufficient body to provide an enveloping richness, as opposed to a watery milkiness in your mouth.

Using a fine-mesh, stainless-steel strainer, strain the mixture into a large mixing bowl. Discard the coffee beans. Add the coffee extract or instant espresso and mix just to combine. Allow to cool at least 15 minutes, then refrigerate until cold, at least 2 hours.

Remove the mixture from the refrigerator. Pour the cold cream mixture into the container of an ice cream freezer. Freeze according to the manufacturer's instructions.

When the ice cream is completely churned, remove it to a chilled stainless-steel mixing bowl. The ice cream can be served immediately, or if a firmer texture is desired, it can be covered and frozen for 1 to 2 hours longer.

Index

tartare, tuna, 50
tartar sauce, roasted garlic, 208
tart shells, *see* pastry dough
toast, scallion pumpernickel,
    steamed mussels with,
    48–49
tomato(es):
    currant, torn pasta with
      lobster, fava beans, and,
      101–2
    and grilled corn sauce, 212–13
    marinade, 62–63
    and parsley salad, grilled
      porcini mushrooms with,
      64–65
    and red pepper sauce, 210–11
    slow-roasted, 241
    soup, 88–89
tuna:
    salad, grilled rare, 74–75
    tartare, 50
    with white bean sauce, grilled,
      149–50

U
upside-down cake, pineapple,
    281–83

V
vanilla ice cream and macadamia nut
    brittle, 298–99
veal:
    Bolognese with pappardelle,
      126–27
    stock, brown, 190–92
vegetable(s), 227–56
    fall, gnocchette with beans,
      bacon, and, 123–24
    gazpacho, 84–85
    root, caramelized, 240
    stock, 196
    Tuscan minestrone, 90–91
    see also specific vegetables
vinaigrette, 50, 58, 74, 202
    apple cider, 54
    balsamic, 224
    fava bean, 44–45
    horseradish, 70–71
    lemon, 59
    lemon oil, 220
    lemon oil, with red and yellow
      peppers, 220–21
    mustard, 225
    red onion, 154
    sherry wine, 224

W
walnuts:
    chicken salad with Belgian endive,
      apples, and, 57
    haricots verts salad with
      prosciutto, mustard vinaigrette,
      and, 68–69
    penne with Gorgonzola, spinach,
      and, 128
whipped cream, unsweetened, 287
white bean sauce, grilled tuna with,
    149–50
wine:
    port, sauce, duck confit and
      cannellini-bean ravioli with,
      110–11
    port, sauce, roasted loin of pork
      with braised red cabbage and,
      174–75
    red, grilled prime rib steak with,
      180–81
    red, sauce, onion soubise with,
      244
    sherry vinaigrette, 224

Y
yam puree, 238

NANCY SILVERTON and MARK PEEL own and operate Campanile restaurant and the La Brea Bakery, both in Los Angeles.

Nancy Silverton was born and raised in Los Angeles. She attended the Cordon Bleu in London and was subsequently an assistant pastry chef at Michael's restaurant in Santa Monica, where she met her future husband, Mark Peel, the restaurant's sous chef.

Mark is also a native Californian. While still in college, he secured a job peeling vegetables at Wolfgang Puck's Ma Maison restaurant, from which he was sent to work at two three-star French restaurants, La Tour d'Argents and Moulin de Mougins. Besides his stint at Michael's, Mark worked for a year at the celebrated Chez Panisse in Berkeley, and for three years he was the head chef at Spago (Nancy was head pastry chef there) under Wolfgang Puck.

In 1985, Nancy and Mark moved to Manhattan to spend six months revamping the restaurant Maxwell's Plum. La Brea Bakery was opened in January 1989; Campanile was opened in June 1989.

In 1989, Nancy and Mark were named *Food & Wine* magazine Best New Chefs. Mark is a three-time James Beard Award nominee as Best American Chef, California; Nancy was named James Beard Best Pastry Chef of the Year in 1990. In 1995, she and Mark shared the Restaurateur of the Year and Restaurant of the Year awards from the Southern California Restaurant Writers, and in 1997 Campanile was named a DiRoNA Distinguished Restaurant of North America.

Nancy is the author of *Desserts* and *Nancy Silverton's Breads from the La Brea Bakery*. She and Mark first collaborated on *Mark Peel and Nancy Silverton at Home: Two Chefs Cook for Family and Friends*.

Nancy and Mark have three children: Vanessa, Benjamin, and Oliver.

IAN SMITH is a writer and letterpress printer living in Los Angeles.

STEVEN ROTHFELD created the images for *Nancy Silverton's Breads from the La Brea Bakery* and has contributed to many other books, including *French Dreams, Italian Dreams, Irish Dreams, Patricia Wells's Trattoria*, and *The New Italy the Beautiful Cookbook*. His photographs have appeared in *European Travel & Life, Departures, Travel & Leisure, Bon Appetit, Gourmet*, and *Food & Wine*. He travels throughout the world but loves to return to his home in the Napa Valley.

Printed in the United States
by Baker & Taylor Publisher Services